William Shakespeare's

William Shakespeare's *Hamlet* (c. 1600) is possibly his most famous play, in which the motives of revenge and love are entangled with the moral dilemmas of integrity and corruption.

Taking the form of a sourcebook, this guide to Shakespeare's remarkable play offers:

- extensive introductory comment on the contexts, critical history and many interpretations of the text, from first performance to the present
- annotated extracts from key contextual documents, reviews, critical works and the text itself
- cross-references between documents and sections of the guide, in order to suggest links between texts, contexts and criticism
- suggestions for further reading.

Part of the *Routledge Guides to Literature* series, this volume is essential reading for all those beginning detailed study of *Hamlet* and seeking not only a guide to the play, but also a way through the wealth of contextual and critical material that surrounds Shakespeare's text.

Sean McEvoy teaches English at Varndean College, Brighton, and has also taught at the University of Sussex and at Royal Holloway, University of London. He is the author of *Shakespeare: The Basics* (2000).

Routledge Guides to Literature*

Editorial Advisory Board: Richard Bradford (University of Ulster at Coleraine), Jan Jedrzejewski (University of Ulster at Coleraine), Duncan Wu (St. Catherine's College, University of Oxford)

Routledge Guides to Literature offer clear introductions to the most widely studied authors and literary texts.

Each book engages with texts, contexts and criticism, highlighting the range of critical views and contextual factors that need to be taken into consideration in advanced studies of literary works. The series encourages informed but independent readings of texts by ranging as widely as possible across the contextual and critical issues relevant to the works examined and highlighting areas of debate as well as those of critical consensus. Alongside general guides to texts and authors, the series includes 'sourcebooks', which allow access to reprinted contextual and critical materials as well as annotated extracts of primary text.

Available in this series

Geoffrey Chaucer by Gillian Rudd
Ben Jonson by James Loxley
William Shakespeare's The Merchant of Venice: A Sourcebook edited by
  S. P. Cerasano
William Shakespeare's King Lear: A Sourcebook edited by Grace Ioppolo
William Shakespeare's Othello: A Sourcebook edited by Andrew Hadfield
John Milton by Richard Bradford
John Milton's Paradise Lost: A Sourcebook edited by Margaret Kean
Alexander Pope by Paul Baines
Mary Wollstonecraft's A Vindication of the Rights of Woman: A Sourcebook
  edited by Adriana Craciun
Jane Austen by Robert P. Irvine
Jane Austen's Emma: A Sourcebook edited by Paula Byrne
Jane Austen's Pride and Prejudice: A Sourcebook edited by Robert Morrison
Mary Shelley's Frankenstein: A Sourcebook edited by Timothy Morton
The Poems of John Keats: A Sourcebook edited by John Strachan
Charles Dickens's David Copperfield: A Sourcebook edited by Richard J. Dunn
Charles Dickens's Bleak House: A Sourcebook edited by Janice M. Allan
Charles Dickens's Oliver Twist: A Sourcebook edited by Juliet John
Herman Melville's Moby-Dick: A Sourcebook edited by Michael J. Davey
Harriet Beecher Stowe's Uncle Tom's Cabin: A Sourcebook edited by Debra J.
  Rosenthal
Walt Whitman's Song of Myself: A Sourcebook and Critical Edition edited by
  Ezra Greenspan
Robert Browning by Stefan Hawlin
Henrik Ibsen's Hedda Gabler: A Sourcebook edited by Christopher Innes
Thomas Hardy by Geoffrey Harvey
Thomas Hardy's Tess of the d'Urbervilles edited by Scott McEathron

* Some books in this series were originally published in the Routledge Literary Sourcebooks series, edited by Duncan Wu, or the Complete Critical Guide to English Literature series, edited by Richard Bradford and Jan Jedrzejewski.

William Shakespeare's
Hamlet
A Sourcebook

Edited by Sean McEvoy

Routledge
Taylor & Francis Group

LONDON AND NEW YORK

First published 2006
by Routledge
2 Park Square, Milton Park, Abingdon, Oxon OX14 4RN

Simultaneously published in the USA and Canada
by Routledge
270 Madison Avenue, New York, NY 10016

Routledge is an imprint of the Taylor & Francis Group, an informa business

© 2006 Sean McEvoy

Typeset in Sabon and Gill Sans by RefineCatch Limited, Bungay, Suffolk
Printed and bound in Great Britain by TJ International Ltd, Padstow, Cornwall

British Library Cataloguing in Publication Data
A catalogue record for this book is available from the British Library.

Library of Congress Cataloging in Publication Data
William Shakespeare's Hamlet : a sourcebook / edited by Sean McEvoy.
    p. cm. – (Routledge guides to literature)
    Includes bibliographical references and index.
1. Shakespeare, William, 1564–1616. Hamlet – Handbooks, manuals, etc.   2. Hamlet
(Legendary character) – Handbooks, manuals, etc.   I. McEvoy, Sean, 1959– . II. Title.
III. Series.
    PR2807.W4564 2006
    822.3′3–dc22   2005028065

ISBN10: 0–415–31432–1   ISBN13: 9–87–0–415–31432–9 (hbk)
ISBN10: 0–415–31433–X   ISBN13: 9–87–0–415–31433–6 (pbk)

Contents

3: Key Passages

Introduction   113

Key Passages   120

4: Further Reading

Annotation and Footnotes

Annotation is a key feature of this series. Both the original notes from reprinted texts and new annotations by the editor appear at the bottom of the relevant page. The reprinted notes are prefaced by the author's name in square brackets, e.g. [Robinson's note].

Acknowledgements

Great thanks are due once again to that most excellent of editors, Liz Thompson, and also to Polly Dodson and Kate Parker at Routledge. One of the readers of the first manuscript was invaluable for her criticism and suggestions.

In planning the book I have drawn with thanks on Professor Kiernan Ryan's bibliography for the Royal Holloway Shakespeare MA course on *Hamlet*, which I taught in 2002–3 and 2005–6. Dr. Carol Atherton was also very helpful with a particular reference.

I would also like to thank the President and fellows of New Hall, Cambridge, whose grant of an Education Fellowship at the college in July 2002 facilitated much work on this sourcebook. I am also grateful to Alan Jenkins, Principal of Varndean College, Brighton, for granting me leave of absence to take up the fellowship, and to Dr. Leo Mellor for his support and encouragement throughout.

Finally, special thanks are due to Julia, παῖδα φιλ[ούμενην]/ Μούνην τηλύγετην πολλοῖσιν ἐπὶ κτεάτεσσιν, for her delightful interruptions; and, of course, most of all, to Nicky.

The following publishers have kindly given permission to reprint materials.

John Kerrigan, *Revenge Tragedy*, Clarendon Press (1996) by permission of Oxford University Press.

Lisa Jardine, *Reading Shakespeare Historically*, Routledge (1996) by permission of the publisher.

Kiernan Ryan, *Shakespeare* (third edition), Palgrave (2001) by permission of the publisher.

Stephen GREENBLATT, *HAMLET IN PURGATORY*, Princeton University Press (2001) by permission of Princeton University Press.

Ronald Bryden on Peter Hall's production of *Hamlet* at the Royal Shakespeare Theatre, Stratford-upon-Avon (27 August 1965), in *The Unfinished Hero and Other Essays*, Faber and Faber (1969) by permission of the publisher.

Robert Hapgood, ed., *Shakespeare in Production: 'Hamlet'*, Cambridge University Press (1999) by permission of the publisher.

Excerpts from Anthony Davies and Stanley Wells, *Shakespeare and the Moving Image*, Cambridge University Press (1994) by permission of the publisher.

Julie Sanders, 'The End of History and the Last Man', in Mark Thornton Burnett and Ramona Ways, eds, *Shakespeare, Film and Fin de Siècle*, Palgrave (2000) by permission of the publisher, Julie Sanders and Mark Thornton Burnett.

Neely, Carol Thomas, ' "Documents in Madness": Reading Madness and Gender in Shakespeare's Tragedies and Early Modern Culture', *Shakespeare Quarterly* 42:3 (1991), 316–19, 322–6, © Folger Shakespeare Library, by permission of The Johns Hopkins University Press.

Valerie Traub, 'Jewels, Statues and Corpses: Containment of Female erotic Power in Shakespeare's Plays' in *Desire and Anxiety: Circulations of Sexuality in Shakespearean Drama*, Routledge (1992) by kind permission of the publisher and author.

Thomson Learning for William Shakespeare, *Hamlet*, Arden 2, ed. Harold Jenkins (London: Thomson Learning, 1982).

Excerpts from *The Education of a Christian Prince* by Desiderius Erasmus, translated by Lester K. Born, © Columbia University Press (1963) by permission of the publisher.

Excerpts from S. T. Coleridge, 'Bristol Lecture' (1813), reprinted in *Critical Responses to 'Hamlet', 1600–1790*, ed., David Farley-Hills, AMS Press (1997) by permission of the publisher.

From THE INTERPRETATION OF DREAMS by SIGMUND FREUD. Translated from the German and edited by James Strachey. Published in the United States by Basic Books, Inc., 1956 by arrangement with George Allen & Unwin, Ltd. and the Hogarth Press, Ltd. Reprinted by permission of Basic Books, a member of Perseus Books, L.L.C.

Sigmund Freud © Copyrights, The Institute of Psychoanalysis and The Hogarth Press for permission to quote from THE STANDARD EDITION OF THE COMPLETE PSYCHOLOGICAL WORKS OF SIGMUND FREUD translated and edited by James Strachey. Reprinted by permission of The Random House Group Limited.

Exerpts from A. C. Bradley, *Shakesperian Tragedy*, Penguin Books (1904) by kind permission of Royal Holloway, University of London.

Excerpts from T. S. Eliot, 'Hamlet', *Selected Essays*, Faber and Faber (1951) by permission of the publisher.

John Dover Wilson, *What Happens in 'Hamlet'*, Cambridge University Press (1935) by permission of the publisher.

Terence Hawkes, 'Telmah', in *That Shakespeherian Rag: Essays on a Critical Process*, Methuen (1986) by kind permission of the author.

Graham Holderness, 'Are Shakespeare's tragic heroes "fatally flawed"? Discuss', *Critical Survey* 1 (1989) by permission of Berghahn Books.

Alan Sinfield, *Faultlines: Cultural Materialism and the Politics of Dissident Reading*, © The Regents of the University of California (1992) by permission of the publisher.

Alan Sinfield, *Faultlines: Cultural Materialism and the Politics of Dissident Reading*, Clarendon Press (1992) by permission of Oxford University Press.

FROM HAMLET, BY ANTHONY B. DAWSON, MANCHESTER UNIVERSITY PRESS (1997).

'Watching Hamlet Watching: Lacan, Shakespeare and the mirror/stage', by Philip Armstrong, in *Alternative Shakespeares volume 2*, ed. Terence Hawkes, Routledge (1996) by permission of the publisher.

Every effort has been made to trace and contact copyright holders. The publishers would be pleased to hear from any copyright holders not acknowledged here, so that this acknowledgements page may be amended at the earliest opportunity.

Introduction

In Charles Dickens's *Great Expectations* (1860–1) a 'gifted townsman' in the role of Hamlet has certain problems with his audience at a sensitive moment in the performance:

> Whenever that undecided Prince had to ask a question or state a doubt, the public helped him out with it. As for example; on the question whether 'twas noble in the mind to suffer, some roared yes, and some no, and some inclining to both opinions said 'toss up for it' . . .[1]

Shakespeare's *Hamlet* has enjoyed genuine popularity and, indeed, iconic status since it was written in (probably) 1600–1. Very many people in English-speaking countries do seem to know at least *one* line of the text. The play has been in practically constant production somewhere in the world since the late seventeenth century, and has acquired a vast encrustation of conflicting critical opinion and theatrical interpretation. *Hamlet* has been appropriated for many different ends, from an exploration of psychoanalysis to an examination of the role of the intellectual in a totalitarian state. But like the prince himself, the essence of the play – if it has one – is notoriously difficult to pin down. The play's lines, a director has claimed, can be performed in 'a hundred different ways, all at least compatible with the basic semantic references of the script'.[2] There is not even one stable text of the play from Shakespeare's own time, but three competing versions (see Key Passages, **pp. 113–15**). Shakespeare wrote nothing quite like it before, nor perhaps after, and it has the feeling of an experimental text. It is a tragedy which is packed with comedy. It is a tense and pacy thriller which can run four hours in performance. It is a play which constantly re-examines itself, and which questions the very nature of theatre and performance.

This book, which sets out to provide a set of sources for students to come to their own opinions about the play, has of necessity had to be partial and selective in the material which it presents. Critical interpretations vary enormously, but I

1   Charles Dickens, *Great Expectations* (Harmondsworth: Penguin Books, 1965), p. 275.
2   Jonathan Miller, 'Plays and Players', in *Non-Verbal Communication*, ed. R. A. Hinde (Cambridge: Cambridge University Press, 1972), p. 362.

would argue that three perspectives emerge as particularly important. These three concerns shape this sourcebook.

The first key perspective is that *Hamlet* is a political play. Three kings are murdered. Spies are set by the state on a royal prince. There is an attempted *coup*, backed by a popular uprising. There are important and secret diplomatic dealings between Denmark, Norway and England. The play ends with a foreign army seizing power. These events seem to me to be particularly significant. Whether the overthrow of an anointed king was ever justified, even if he were a tyrant, was a major question in contemporary politics. Just such a thing happened in Britain forty years after the play first appeared on stage.

The second key approach is through psychoanalysis and gender studies. Since the late eighteenth century there has been a tendency to see the play as an examination of the consciousness of troubled man whose closest relationships, especially with women, are in crisis. Hamlet has lost his father, and feels that his mother, at the very least, cannot really have loved her husband. Hamlet's affair with Ophelia comes to a difficult end. Notable twentieth century critics, and some feminists in particular, have explored this consciousness in terms of psychoanalysis.

Third, I have also chosen to focus on the play as a blueprint for a wide variety of performances at different moments in history. It is a supremely, and self-consciously, *theatrical* play. Actors and directors both in the theatre and in the cinema have interpreted it in very many exciting and illuminating ways. In doing so they have both illuminated the play itself and given an insight into their own times.

This sourcebook is divided into four parts, the first of which deals with the play's contexts. Here you will find information on relevant aspects of the theatre, politics and society in 1600. These ideas are illustrated and developed in the selection of contemporary documents which follows. A chronology puts the play in the context of Shakespeare's other work and of contemporary events.

The 'Interpretations' section begins with a brief history of critical opinion of the play from the seventeenth century to the present day, followed by extracts from a selection of notable criticism. As elsewhere in the book, each extract is prefaced by a headnote which explains more about the critic, and about the extract's place in the longer work from which it is taken. The focus in the 'Modern Criticism' sub-section tends to be on political and psychoanalytical responses to the play, but other views are also represented. Footnotes explain references or difficult terms and ideas. The section closes with reviews of some theatrical and cinematic realizations of the text, prefaced by a brief account of the play's performance history.

In the introduction to the 'Key Passages' section I deal first with the problem of play's 'unstable' text, and the implications for criticism of that instability. Each of the subsequent extracts in 'Key Passages' is prefaced by remarks which usually relate discussion of that passage back to the critical opinions in the previous section. Footnotes gloss the more difficult and obscure phrases, but also offer illustrations of how particular moments were played in a range of stage productions and films. The aim of this section is to encourage a closer reading of the text in the light of the variety of both contextual and critical material presented elsewhere. Cross-referencing to this material is intended to help here.

Finally, the 'Further Reading' section directs you to some of the enormous bibliography of criticism and stage history on *Hamlet*, as well as to significant websites, videos and DVDs.

The critic Terence Hawkes is amazed at the authority ascribed to this play in our culture:

> At one time [*Hamlet*] must obviously have been an interesting play written by a promising Elizabethan playwright. However, equally obviously, that is no longer the case. Over the years, *Hamlet* has taken on a huge and complex symbolizing function and, as part of the institution called 'English literature', it has become far more than a mere play by a mere playwright. Issuing from one of the key components of that institution, not Shakespeare, but the creature 'Shakespeare', it has been transformed into the utterance of an oracle, the lucubration of a sage, the masterpiece of a poet-philosopher replete with transcendent wisdom about the way things are, always have been, and presumably always will be.[3]

Such is the status and scope of *Hamlet*, that anyone attempting to pluck out the heart of its mystery must risk appearing either parochial or partisan, or both. I hope this book appears to be neither, but that it will encourage its readers to explore, analyse and appreciate this marvellous play, both on the page and in the theatre.

---

3   Terence Hawkes, *Meaning by Shakespeare* (London: Routledge, 1992), p. 4.

1

Contexts

Contextual Overview

'*Hamlet*', the critic James Shapiro writes, was 'born at the crossroads of the death of chivalry and the birth of globalisation'.[1] It seems most likely that the play was written in London in 1600–1 when William Shakespeare, a successful playwright and actor in a leading company, the Lord Chamberlain's Men, was in his mid-thirties (see Chronology, p. 17). Shakespeare's company had recently (1599) established itself in a rebuilt theatre, the Globe, on a new site on the south bank of the River Thames in Southwark. Purpose-built commercial public theatres had only existed in London since the 1570s, and they only flourished in the face of the hostility of London's Puritan local government because of the aristocratic patronage of men such as Lord Hunsdon, Queen Elizabeth's Lord Chamberlain. This tension between the declining aristocratic tradition, emergent capitalism and post-Reformation religious and intellectual turmoil characterizes Shakespeare's London. The same tension emerges in the power, energy and complexity of his plays.

In this section I provide contextual information about the sites of this conflict between the mediaeval and the modern which are important in *Hamlet*: the conflict between aristocratic honour-codes and the rule of law; competing ideas about the nature of monarchy; the cultural function of a commercial theatre; the status of women; and new conceptions of mental illness. The extracts which follow develop and illustrate some of these issues further.

Revenge and Tyrannicide

Hamlet was not an entirely original play, but in some ways typical of a popular contemporary genre: revenge tragedy. It seems likely that there was at least one earlier version of the play (the so-called 'Ur-*Hamlet*'), of which no text survives, but which is mentioned by the writer Thomas Nashe as early as 1589. The genre seems to have become popular with Thomas Kyd's *The Spanish Tragedy* (1587) and continued to be performed after Shakespeare's death in 1616, as the success of plays such as John Webster's *The Duchess of Malfi* (1623)

1   James Shapiro, *1599: A Year in the Life of William Shakespeare* (London: Faber and Faber, 2005), p. 309.

demonstrates. The protagonist of these dramas is typically a noble character driven to deceit and cunning in order to avenge some terrible wrong done to him. The setting is never in England: since revenge tragedy presents corrupt rulers, it was more politic (and less likely to draw the censor's attention) if these scandalous narratives were set in allegedly more hot-tempered locations. Popular as a genre, revenge tragedy ignores the 'unities', the 'rules' enshrined in high-status Greek and Roman drama. The action of a revenge tragedy unfolds over more than a day (contrary to the 'unity of time') and combines together several plotlines (contrary to the 'unity of action'). In particular, noble characters often behave in ways quite inappropriate for their social station, and can mix with characters from the lower orders. Comedy intertwines with tragedy, not only in certain characters and dialogue, but also when moments of high seriousness in these plays can seem to teeter on the edge of black comedy. The final act often features some masque or entertainment which conceals a murderous plot, and which concludes with the deaths of the main characters. Revenge tragedy thus offended against the classical notion of 'decorum' (the idea that language, action and character should all be appropriate to each another), and seemed to eighteenth-century critics to show a want of taste and refinement (see Early Critical Reception, **p. 42**). Other notable examples include George Chapman, *Bussy D'Ambois* (1604), John Marston, *Antonio's Revenge* (1600), Thomas Middleton's *Women Beware Women* (1623), Cyril Tourneur's *The Atheist's Tragedy* (1610) and John Webster's *The White Devil* (1612). *The Revenger's Tragedy* (1606), by either Middleton or Tourneur, must be counted as a hilarious parody of the genre.

Part of the inspiration for the genre also came from the tragedies of the Roman writer Seneca (c. 4BC–AD65), whose bloody versions of Greek tragedy were popular in schools and colleges. They were also presented in English translations on the stage. Jasper Heywood's *Thyestes* (1560), for example, begins with the ghost of murdered Tantalus returning to earth after infernal punishment. The appearance of the vengeful ghost of Hamlet's father would thus have been a familiar theatrical convention to many of the original audience.

Revenge as a concept had a particular resonance in the early modern period in England. The right to exact a private punishment without legal process was a privilege traditionally claimed by the aristocracy. Feuding among powerful families had been all too costly for England in the dynastic civil wars of the mid-fifteenth century, the so-called 'Wars of the Roses' which Shakespeare had dramatized in *Henry VI* and *Richard III*. The eventual victor in 1485, Henry VII, strove to outlaw the aristocratic prerogative of personal vengeance, centralizing the power to punish in the hands of the state. This process was complete in Shakespeare's time under his grand-daughter Elizabeth I. The laws of England were now in conflict with an aristocratic honour code. The stage avenger was often a figure whose mission set him beyond the margins of correct social conduct, but that mission also dramatized a political dilemma which was produced by the state claiming a monopoly on the right to dispense justice. What was an aggrieved party to do when it was the state, in the form of the monarch, who had committed the crime? Claudius is Hamlet's king, but also his father's murderer. Or should the avenger leave all to divine providence, as the Bible says

('Vengeance is mine; I will repay, saith the Lord'[2])? As the critics Graham Holderness and Alan Sinfield have shown, revenge drama brought to the surface radical questions about contemporary politics and morality (see Modern Criticism, **pp. 65–6** and **70–5**).

In the 1590s there was considerable ambivalence about the ultimate rights of the monarch. On the one hand it was claimed that as God's representative on earth, even a cruel or unjust monarch was not answerable to his or her subjects. The king or queen had 'two bodies': as a mortal the monarch may err, but their 'body politic' was immortal and represented the state. As such the ruler could be seen to have a mystical and unchallengeable authority. When under threat from the rebellious Laertes, Claudius claims that 'there's such divinity doth hedge a king / That treason can but peep at what it would' (4.5.123–4[3]; see Key Passages, **p. 155**). Some of the arguments for this 'divine right' of the monarch, as it came to be known, are set out in *A Homily Against Disobedience and Wilful Rebellion*, (see Contemporary Documents, **pp. 21–3**), a sermon read by ministers to Queen Elizabeth's subjects in all English and Welsh churches. On the other hand was an influential body of jurists who saw the monarch as merely the head of a different 'body politic', consisting of clergy, lords and commons, and subject to the law of England, not above it.[4]

A more radical political principle came from two powerful sources. The culture and society of ancient Rome, and in particular that of the Roman Republic, enjoyed enormous prestige among the intelligentsia of the time, whose education had been primarily in Latin authors of republican sentiment. The Roman Republic had been founded by upright men who drove brutal kings into exile. Just before writing *Hamlet* Shakespeare had dramatized (in *Julius Caesar*, 1599), the dilemma of those noble descendants of tyrannicides who chose to use violence to prevent Rome becoming a monarchy again. Hamlet's friend Horatio recalls portents of the death of Caesar after first seeing the ghost (1.1.116–23), and the king's chief minister, Polonius, once played the role of the murdered dictator on stage (3.2.102–5). Just as the republican conspirators in 44BC were striving in vain against the arrival of absolute rule in ancient Rome, so the proponents of the declining Renaissance humanist tradition at the turn of the sixteenth century sought to argue against the growing influence of divine-right theorists. From the late fifteenth century onwards the humanist movement had been an intellectual project inspired by the values of classical literature. Writers such as the Dutch scholar Desiderius Erasmus (c. 1467–1536; see Contemporary Documents, **pp. 23–5**) devoted their attention to human nature, and to the improvement of mankind's condition on earth, rather than take the mediaeval view that humanity was a passive victim of divine will. The 'rediscovery' of classical learning and values in the late fifteenth, sixteenth and seventeenth centuries was, in fact, a principal source of the 'rebirth' of European civilization generally known as the 'Renaissance' (though the era is also referred to as the 'early modern' period to avoid any value judgements implicit in the word). Some humanists deployed

---

2   Romans, 12:19.
3   i.e. Act 4, Scene 5, lines 123–4 in the text of *Hamlet* used for this sourcebook.
4   See Charles R. Forker's 'Introduction' to Shakespeare's *King Richard II* (London: Thomson, 2002), pp. 16–23.

mediaeval and classical arguments that a king who did not treat his subjects justly and who acted in criminal ways could forfeit the right to rule, and even to live, because no one was above the law. The Roman and humanist influence was clear. In this tradition the Scottish writer George Buchanan argued in 1579 that the people would be in the right if they sought 'vengeance on an arrogant and worthless tyrant'.[5]

Religious belief also played a political role here. The 'Reformation' of the Christian Church in western Europe in the sixteenth century had polarized the continent between those who remained loyal to the Roman Catholic Church and those whose allegiance was to the 'reformed', Protestant religion. Protestantism taught that each individual soul had a relationship with God unmediated by any authority, religious or secular. Scripture, not the traditions or teaching of the Church, was the foundation of Protestant faith. The Church of England, with the monarch as its Supreme Governor, had been the state Protestant Church since 1534. Many in England remained Catholic, covertly or otherwise, but in London radical Protestants known as puritans held positions of authority in business and on the city council. Those many puritans who followed the teachings of the Swiss theologian Jean Calvin (1509–64) put the authority of the monarch second to their own safety. They saw themselves as an 'elect', favoured by God and marked out personally for salvation by Him. Unlike Catholics, who relied on 'good works' and the sacraments of the Church to reach salvation, Protestants saw their own secure faith as a mark that God would save them. Their relationship with God thus came before their loyalty to any earthly ruler. The University of Wittenburg, where Hamlet has been studying (1.2.119), was noted for its doctrinaire Protestantism, as well as being popular with Danish students. Yet Hamlet's father's ghost, who claims to have come from purgatory, is a distinctly Catholic figure (see Modern Criticism **pp. 87–90** and Key Passages **p. 128**). Protestants denied the existence of purgatory, a place not directly mentioned in the bible. As for English Catholics, the Pope had agreed that an apostate monarch, like Elizabeth I, could be assassinated with impunity.[6]

Buchanan's book was banned in England, as were the works of the Italian political theorist Niccolò Machiavelli (1469–1527). What mattered to Machiavelli above all was stability and peace: he had no faith in Providence and knew that in contemporary politics the virtuous would lose. Deceit, and even murder, are acceptable to those in power so long as their crimes remain hidden and the ruler publicly keeps up a façade of moral behaviour and godliness. Revenge tragedy often features just such an amoral 'machiavel'. In *Hamlet* Claudius, who secretly tries to have Hamlet murdered far away in England (4.3.61–70), is trying to protect his country and himself from a destructive internal threat whom he knows enjoys popular support (4.7.16–24).

Machiavelli's refusal to subscribe to abstract ideas as principles is part of a

---

5   George Buchanan, *De Jure Regni Apud Scotos* (1579), trans. Charles Arrowood, *The Powers of the Crown in Scotland* (Austin: University of Austin Press, 1949), p. 122. Quoted on p. 10 of Margaret Healey's *Writers and their Work: 'Richard II'* (Plymouth: Northcote House, 1998), chapter one of which is an excellent brief introduction to the political debate about rebellion at the time *Hamlet* was written.
6   See Richard Wilson, *Secret Shakespeare* (Manchester: Manchester University Press, 2004), p. 107.

wider, sceptical current in early modern thought. Some writers doubted divine Providence and the idea that history has a shape or purpose; they also doubted whether individual humans had a unitary personality, or even an 'essence' at all, but rather suggested that our identity is the product of social 'custom'. Michel de Montaigne (1533–92), the French writer whom it seems Shakespeare read in the translations of his friend John Florio (1603 and 1613), considered that 'who-soever shall heedfully survey and consider himselfe, shall find ... volubility and discordance to be in himself'. Furthermore, 'we ... change as that beast that takes the colour of the place wherein it is laid ... all is but changing, motion and inconstancy.'[7] Hamlet's scepticism, 'volubility' and 'discordance' – at least until his return from England – can perhaps be seen as a representation of this strain of thought.

In 1601 London was not a city with a stable, secure social structure, but a society in turmoil. It was rapidly forgetting, or trying to forget, its Catholic, humanist past (perhaps as represented in the play by Old Hamlet; see Modern Criticism **pp. 87–90**). At the same time rampant market capitalism transformed the city. In the feudal past stable personal identities and social relations had been determined by social caste, and cemented by bonds of loyalty and hierarchy. England had been a rural society dominated by a hereditary warrior aristocracy. London was now increasingly a commercial and manufacturing city characterized by social mobility between classes, by self-fashioning individuals and by con-tractual personal relations: loyalty was not permanent, but conditional. Political absolutism emerged to challenge the confident new individualism of puritan thought. The critic Jonathan Dollimore sees the incoherent character of the stage avenger in revenge tragedy as both a product of violent social divisions and a device to draw those divisions to our attention. He is:

> malcontented – often because bereaved or dispossessed – satirical, and vengeful; at once agent and victim of social corruption, condemning yet simultaneously contaminated by it; made up of inconsistencies and contradictions, which because they cannot be understood in terms of individuality alone, constantly pressure attention outward toward the social conditions of existence.[8]

The Theatre and Politics

Hamlet's decision to put the ghost's word to the test by re-enacting on stage the murder of his father, according to the ghost's account (2.2.584–601; see Key Passages, **pp. 135–6**), puts the political function of the theatre literally at the centre of the play. If a play can cause its audience to reflect on their misdeeds and then to acknowledge their guilt, the theatre is a very powerful art form. If *The Murder of Gonzago* can disconcert and scare the super-cool Claudius (3.2.260; see Key Passages, **p. 143**), what is *Hamlet* doing to its audience?

The effectiveness of the theatre was acknowledged by many at the time.

---

7 Michel de Montaigne, *Essays*, trans. John Florio, 3 vols (London: Dent, 1965), II.2, II 8–9.
8 Jonathan Dollimore, *Radical Tragedy* (Brighton: Harvester Press, 1984), p. 50.

Modern editors of the play refer to a contemporary account of a Norfolk woman who, having watched Shakespeare's company represent a husband's murder on stage, was struck with remorse and confessed to killing her own spouse. The power of the stage was not doubted by the theatre's puritan opponents, either. Some radical Protestants regarded all forms of pictorial representation as idolatrous, and shared the fear of government officials that the theatre would teach its audience to copy the criminal activity, sexual immorality and political sedition which they saw represented on the stage. Others sought to use its influence directly, to support their own political projects. In the year of *Hamlet*'s probable first performance (1601), Shakespeare's company was asked to stage a performance of (probably) *Richard II* by the faction of the military adventurer Robert Devereux, Earl of Essex. This play tells how an ineffectual and corrupt monarch is overthrown by a dynamic and politically astute military strongman. The following morning Essex attempted an armed *coup*, but failed to seize control of Queen Elizabeth's court. Essex had been one of the elderly Queen's favourites, and his second-in-command, the Earl of Southampton, had been Shakespeare's patron earlier in the writer's career. The rebellion may well be 'the late innovation' referred to in *Hamlet* at 2.2.331. Critics once compared Hamlet with Essex;[9] but the opportunist leader of a coup in the play is Fortinbras, who unexpectedly seizes the throne at the end of the play (5.2.394–5; see Key Passages, **p. 162**).

However, the political significance of the theatre in contemporary London may have been much more subtle and more pervasive than this simple 'copy-cat' model would suggest. The conditions of urban capitalist life in Europe's fastest-growing city meant that the outward appearance of birth or rank carried as much authority as the real things. Jean Christophe Agnew describes it as 'a newly discovered, Protean social world, one in which the conventional signposts of social and individual identity had become mobile and manipulable reference points'.[10] Power depended on the ability to *act* the role convincingly, as the regicide Claudius demonstrates when, confronted by the murderous Fortinbras, he coolly claims that God will protected His anointed (4.5.123–4; see Key Passages, **p. 151**). Spectacle and display, both celebratory and punitive, were part of the theatricality of royal power. Stephen Greenblatt wrote in 1985 that the Queen's power was 'constituted in the theatrical celebrations of royal glory and theatrical violence visited upon enemies of that glory'. Furthermore, 'a poetics of Elizabethan power ... will prove inseparable, in crucial respects, from a poetics of the theatre'.[11] Hamlet and Claudius are both striving for power through performance as characters in a play which questions the nature of the relationship between the theatre and 'real' life. Hamlet's feigned madness, his 'antic disposition' (1.5.180),

---

9 'Hamlet is a tragedy of irresolution, and irresolution was Essex's dominant weakness. His, too, was a learned and sensitive mind; he, too, in his dealings with women had often shown a touch of cruelty. Each hero attempted to shoulder a task that just exceeded his individual powers; each hesitated upon the verge of action, and, when he felt his nerve was failing him, relapsed into deep neurotic gloom.' Peter Quenell, *Shakespeare: The Poet and his Background* (London: Weidenfeld and Nicholson, 1963), p. 267.

10 Jean Christophe Agnew, *Worlds Apart: the Market and the Theater in Anglo-American Thought, 1550–1750* (Cambridge: Cambridge University Press, 1986), p. 9.

11 Stephen Greenblatt, 'Invisible Bullets: Renaissance authority and its subversion, *Henry IV* and *Henry V*', in *Political Shakespeare*, eds Jonathan Dollimore and Alan Sinfield (Manchester: Manchester University Press, 1985), p. 44.

and Claudius's adoption of the persona of legitimate monarch are both public performances for a specific political purpose. But perhaps the commercial theatre undermined royal authority by showing its constructed nature at the same time as it showed the source of its power.

It is, of course, unclear whether Claudius is affected by *The Murder of Gonzago* (see Key Passages, **p.** 143), and the people of London did not respond as its patrons hoped they would to the unexpected staging of *Richard II*: Essex was defeated and executed. It can also be argued that the theatre was regarded as a frivolous, socially degraded forum with no connection to real political events. Compared to contemporary Spain, the London theatre was mildly censored, it has been argued; it was regarded as poetry, not politics, and no serious threat to the powerful. In the case of Shakespeare in particular, there is rarely a clear political call to arms in the text, argues Paul Yachnin: 'The stage's representation of power was normally not allowed to coalesce into the kind of *univocal* meaning that might be seen as an attempt to intervene in the real world.'[12] There was no single, clear political message which could be put into action outside the theatre. Hamlet finds in Claudius's reactions to the play what he wants to find. The audience in the auditorium may be less convinced. *Hamlet* could, then, alternatively be seen as a critique of contemporary claims about the power of the stage.

Marriage

Ophelia and Gertrude can superficially be seen as representatives of the two archetypes of woman in early modern drama: the virgin and the whore. This conception of women in the play is significantly complicated by an understanding of their role in property transfer and inheritance.

Ophelia's submissiveness to her father's every wish would have been regarded as wholly commendable in a society in which adult offspring still knelt for their parents' blessing when departing from them, and upper class girls would not expect to have any say in the matter of their marriage. Certainly, as Polonius says (2.2.141–2), Ophelia's marriage to Hamlet would be impossible: princes married for the sake of political alliance, not love. If she were to lose her virginity to Hamlet, however, she would render herself unmarriageable and condemn herself to a long life of spinsterhood. In a society in which most property transfer had traditionally been from the father to the legitimate first-born son, pre-marital virginity among the upper classes was supposed to ensure the husband's paternity of the first son. Laertes warns his sister of the danger she is in in language which eroticizes her at the same time as insisting on her chastity (1.3.29–44). An early modern audience would probably not have the sentimental attitude to the affair between Hamlet and Ophelia that is evident in some modern productions.

One of the first descriptions of Gertrude in the text portrays her in terms of her position in inheritance law: she is 'th' imperial jointress to this warlike state'

12 Paul Yachnin, *Stage-Wrights: Shakespeare, Jonson, Middleton and the Making of Theatrical Value* (Philadelphia: University of Philadelphia Press, 1997), p. 23.

(1.2.9). The word 'jointress' appears for the first recorded time here, and its precise meaning is unclear. The general sense is that in marrying Old Hamlet's widow, Claudius has in some sense strengthened his own claim to the throne. Widows in contemporary English law normally retained a third of their husband's estate, and Gertrude as the king's widow has a political presence in Denmark. The marriage also has implications for Hamlet: were his mother to have a child by Claudius, that offspring would become the heir to the throne. Claudius's reassurance that Hamlet is his heir (1.2.109) therefore does not make the prince feel any more secure. Hamlet calls the marriage between his mother and uncle incestuous (1.2.157; see Key Passages, **p. 128**), as does the ghost (1.5.42, 83; see Key Passages, **pp. 130, 131**). Certainly the bible forbade such unions; it was just such a marriage that King Henry VIII argued was sinful when he set out to divorce Catherine of Aragon. However, as Lisa Jardine points out, Church courts only prosecuted such 'unlawful' marriages if a complaint was brought by someone.[13] To a contemporary audience, the apparent acceptance by the court of Claudius's marriage – an acquiescence for which the king offers his thanks (1.2.16) – would signal Hamlet's political and personal isolation in Elsinore.

Madness and Melancholy

'Madness,' writes the British critic Duncan Salkeld, 'is ... not confined to a single definitive concept in Renaissance literature but is instead evoked by a loose assembly of words which indicate a differentiated shade or kind of madness.'[14] The question whether Hamlet is 'really' mad in the central acts of the play is not only a fruitless one, in that we are talking about a fictional character, not a real mind, but also a vain one because then, as now, there was no agreement about exactly how 'madness' can be defined, as even Polonius would seem to suggest (2.2.92–4). Nevertheless, the way madness in general was explained was in transition in 1601. The mediaeval conception of madness as divine or demonic possession was being replaced by the idea that insanity was a medical condition, as part of what the critic Carol Thomas Neely has called the early modern 'reconceptualization of the human' (see Modern Criticism, **p. 67**).

The mediaeval and humanist idea of 'folly' suggested that madness could be a kind of divine possession. It was thought that wisdom and insight can be found in the ravings of the foolish and insane. Since social decorum is ignored, the language of the mad, in all its ambiguities, can reveal personal, moral and political truths which would otherwise remain unsaid or repressed, as Polonius says (2.2.208–11). Hamlet's satirical and abusive remarks to Polonius (2.2.174–218) and Claudius (3.2.93–7; 4.3.17–56) may be seen to be either illustrating or exploiting the notion of the madman as licensed critic. Ophelia's utterances in Act 4 can also be seen as a commentary on her true, suppressed and repressed feelings

13 Lisa Jardine, *Reading Shakespeare Historically* (London: Routledge, 1996), p. 39.
14 Duncan Salkeld, *Madness and Drama in the Age of Shakespeare* (Manchester: Manchester University Press, 1993), p. 27.

and desires. As she says: 'Lord, we know what we are, but know not what we may be' (4.5.43–4; see Key Passages, **p. 153**).

A further conception of madness was found in classical writers: the idea of a poetic 'frenzy' or artistic inspiration as a kind of insanity. Shakespeare refers to this 'madness' being like that of the lover in *A Midsummer Night's Dream* (1596): 'The lunatic, the lover and the poet' are all composed of 'imagination' (5.1.7–8).[15] Polonius thinks Hamlet's madness is the result of his thwarted love for his daughter Ophelia (2.2.146–51). This classical *'furor'* is a secular version of the more sinister Christian doctrine of madness as demonic possession. Hamlet fears that the ghost may be a demon come to tempt him to mortal sin; indeed, his melancholy may be evidence of diabolical influence on him (2.2.594–9; see Key Passages, **p. 135**).

But medical textbooks of the time saw what we refer to as mental illness primarily in physiological terms. Different kinds of madness were caused by a serious imbalance of the body's 'humours': four fluids, each of which affected the personality in a different way. A person with an excess of blood was 'sanguine', cheerful; an excess of choler, angry; an excess of phlegm, lethargic. Those with an excess of the fourth humour, melancholy, were gloomy and broody. It has been suggested by several critics, including John Dover Wilson (in *What Happens in 'Hamlet'*), that Shakespeare drew on the work of an English medical writer, Timothy Bright's *A Treatise on Melancholy* (1586), in his depiction of the Prince. Bright wrote that:

> The perturbations of melancholy are for the most part sad and fearful
> ... as distrust, doubt, diffidence or despair, sometimes furious, and
> sometimes merry in appearance, through a kind of Sardonian [sardonic],
> and false laughter, as the humour is disposed that procureth these
> divisions.[16]

Hamlet's behaviour during his 'antic disposition' might seem to fit these symptoms. Watching comedy was regarded as a possible cure. The Protestant Bright also considered that melancholia could have a spiritual cause: those who looked into their soul and failed to find secure faith in their own salvation, but rather that God had abandoned them, could be subject to this condition. Hamlet is, after all, a man who, it seems, has doubts about his religious beliefs and his fate in the after life (3.1.66–82; see Key Passages, **pp. 137–8**). Women, especially virgins, were prone to 'hysteria', a condition thought to be the product of a diseased or 'wandering' womb (see Modern Criticism, **p. 69**).

The concepts central to people's understanding of themselves and their society in 1601 are clearly not those which are central today. An awareness of early modern political, religious and psychological ideas is obviously necessary to an informed reading of the play. The passages which follow are intended to help to

---

15 All references to other Shakespeare plays are from G. Blakemore Evans (ed.) *The Riverside Shakespeare*, second edition (Boston: Houghton Mifflin, 1997).
16 Timothy Bright, *A Treatise on Melancholy* (London: 1586); this quotation is in Kate Flint, 'Madness and melancholy in *Hamlet*' in *Longman Critical Essays; 'Hamlet'*, eds Linda Cookson and Bryan Loughrey (Harlow: Longman, 1988).

provide that contextually informed grasp of *Hamlet*. Indeed, the power of much contemporary criticism comes from reading the play both in its moment in history *and* from a self-consciously contemporary perspective. Good examples can be found in the Modern Criticism section, and in particular the extracts from Traub, Thomas Neely, Sinfield, Jardine and Greenblatt (see Modern Criticism, **pp. 62–5, 66–70, 70–5, 78–81, 87–90**).

Chronology

Bullet points are used to denote references to Shakespeare's life and posterity, and asterisks to denote historical and literary events.

1564
*   William Shakespeare born in Stratford-upon-Avon, eldest son of Mary (née Arden) and John Shakespeare, a local businessman.

1576
*   James Burbage builds The Theatre in Shoreditch, London's first purpose-built theatre.

1582
*   Shakespeare marries Ann Hathaway.

1583
*   Susanna, daughter to Ann and William, born.
*   Rebellion in Ireland.

1585
*   Hamnet and Judith, twins, born; Shakespeare probably leaves Stratford.
*   Start of war with Spain.

1587
*   Mary Queen of Scots beheaded for supposed complicity in a plot against Elizabeth; Philip Henslowe builds the Rose Theatre on Bankside; Kyd's *The Spanish Tragedy*.

1588
*   Shakespeare perhaps now working in the London theatre.
*   Spanish Armada defeated.

1589
*   First play: *King Henry VI Part One*.

1590

*   James VI of Scotland marries Anne of Denmark.

1592

•   *Richard III, The Comedy of Errors.*
*   Successful English raid on Spanish treasure fleet; plague in London. Christopher Marlowe's *Dr. Faustus* and *Edward II.*

1593

*   Marlowe murdered; plague continues.

1594

•   *The Taming of the Shrew, Titus Andronicus.*
*   Two plots on the Queen's life; rebellion in Ireland; Lord Chamberlain's Men founded; likely date of a version of the Hamlet story performed at Newington Butts.

1595

•   *A Midsummer Night's Dream, Romeo and Juliet, Richard II.*
*   Swan Theatre built.

1596

•   *The Merchant of Venice, Henry IV Part One.* Coat of arms granted to Shakespeare's father, John. Death of Hamnet Shakespeare.
*   Essex destroys Spanish fleet in Cadiz harbour. Food shortages and riots.

1598

•   *Henry IV Part Two, Much Ado About Nothing.*

1599

•   *Henry V, Julius Caesar, As You Like It.*
*   Essex fails to put down Irish rebellion; Globe Theatre built.

1600–1

•   Probable first performances of *Hamlet* and *Twelfth Night*. Possible performance of *Hamlet* at Oxford.

1601

•   *Troilus and Cressida.* Death of John Shakespeare.
*   Essex's rebellion and execution. A member of Shakespeare's company questioned by the authorities because the rebels had asked for a performance of *Richard II* on the eve of the revolt.

1603

•   Publication, probably unauthorized, of the First Quarto of *Hamlet*; Shakespeare's last recorded stage performance in Ben Jonson's *Sejanus.*
*   Death of Queen Elizabeth; accession of James I; Lord Chamberlain's Men become The King's Men.

1604
- Publication of Second Quarto of *Hamlet*. *Othello, Measure for Measure*.
* Peace with Spain.

1605
- *King Lear*. Shakespeare makes land purchases in Stratford.
* Gunpowder Plot.

1606
- *Macbeth, Antony and Cleopatra*.
* Jonson's *Volpone*; *The Revenger's Tragedy*.

1607
- Susanna Shakespeare marries John Hall. *Coriolanus*. *Hamlet* performed on a merchant ship, *The Dragon*, off Sierra Leone.

1611
- *The Tempest*. Shakespeare probably now mostly living in Stratford.
* Parliament dismissed by King James. Authorized translation of the Bible.

1613
* Globe Theatre burns down.

1616
- Susanna Shakespeare marries Thomas Quiney; William Shakespeare dies.

1623
- Publication of First Folio.

1626
- Recorded performance of *Hamlet* by English players in Dresden.

1637
- *Hamlet* still being performed at court.

1642
* London theatres closed by Parliament at the start of the Civil War.

1660
* London theatres reopen at the restoration of the monarchy.

1665
- Early critical comment from the Earl of Shaftesbury: the play was 'that piece of [Shakespeare's] which appears to have most affected English hearts, and has perhaps been oftenest acted of any which have come upon our stage.'

Contemporary Documents

From **a summary of the story of 'Amleth' in Saxo Grammaticus'**
Historicae Danicae (1514, by the sourcebook editor), based on the 1894
translation by Oliver Elton reprinted in *Narrative and Dramatic Sources of
Shakespeare*, ed. Geoffrey Bullough, 8 vols (London: Routledge and Kegan
Paul, 1973), vol. 7, pp. 60–79

What follows is a modern summary of the earliest source of the Hamlet story.
The legend itself goes back at least to the ninth century. Echoes of its phrasing
suggest that Shakespeare may have read this original Latin account, but it
seems likely that he also used an earlier, now lost *Hamlet* play of the late 1580s
(?), which in turn used a moralizing French retelling of Saxo as its source
(Belleforest's *Histoire Tragiques*, which first appeared with the Amleth story in
1570; an English translation did not appear until 1608 and itself drew on the
Shakespeare play). The Bullough volume cited above contains a full collection of
other minor possible sources for the play.

Horwendil and his brother Feng were appointed defenders of Jutland by King
Rorik of Denmark. Horwendil, already a famous warrior, fought and slew Koll,
the King of Norway, in single combat. Subsequently he married Rorik's daughter
Gerutha, who bore him a son, Amleth. 'Such great good fortune stung Feng with
jealousy', and he murdered Horwendil, proclaiming publicly but falsely that he
had carried out the killing to save Gerutha from a brutal and unkind husband.

'Amleth beheld all this, but feared lest too shrewd a behaviour might make his
uncle suspect him. So he chose to feign dullness, and pretend an utter lack of wits.'
He allowed himself to become lethargic, dirty and slovenly and spoke apparent
nonsense to all. Some suspected that he was feigning madness. It was arranged
that he should come across a 'fair woman' in 'some secluded place'. 'All men's
natural temper being too blindly amorous to be artfully dissembled', if Amleth
was seen to attempt to seduce the woman he would be proved sane after all. With
the help of a foster-brother, however, Amleth succeeded in finding a place where
could make love unseen to the young woman, whom he knew from early childhood. She was happy to pretend that he had never seduced her, though Hamlet

claimed to have done so. But his answer about where the deed had happened was so bizarre that no one believed him.

A friend of Feng next offered to overhear Amleth in private conversation with his mother, 'for if the son had any wits at all he would not . . . fear to trust himself to the fidelity of him who bore him'. The eavesdropper hid himself under 'straw', but Amleth checked for spies, found the intruder, and stabbed him. He then cut the body up and flung the parts in the sewer for pigs to eat. Returning to his mother, he berated her for her lust and betrayal, and revealed his desire to avenge himself on Feng. He also insisted on her silence about what he had revealed. 'With such reproaches he rent the heart of his mother and redeemed her to walk in the ways of virtue.'

When Feng asked for his friend, Amleth said that he had gone into the sewer to be eaten by pigs, but no one believed him. Feng could not kill Amleth outright for fear of Rorik's displeasure, but also because of Gerutha's feelings for her son. He decided to send him to the King of Britain with two retainers, 'bearing a letter graven on wood', which enjoined the King to execute 'the youth who was sent over to him'. Amleth searched the retainers' possessions while they slept. He found the letter, erased the original text and substituted a letter by Feng ordering the retainers' death – and 'added an entreaty that the King of Britain would grant his daughter in marriage to a youth of great judgment whom he was sending to him'.

A year later, having impressed the King with his perception and wisdom, Amleth returned to Jutland with the King's daughter. He also bore some gold, given as compensation for Amleth's feigned grievance at the hanging of his two companions. He found Feng's noblemen feasting to mark his presumed death. When all were very drunk and drowsy Amleth trapped the lords under a wall hanging made by his mother. He then burnt the hall down, killing them all. Feng had meanwhile retired to his own chamber. Before waking him, he substituted a sword which had been riveted into its scabbard for his uncle's own weapon. Amleth then woke him, telling him of his lords' fate and of his own thirst for revenge. 'Feng, on hearing this, leapt from his couch, but was cut down while, deprived of his own sword, he strove in vain to draw the strange one.'

Amleth justified his actions to the people and was elected king. Later he won the love of Hermutrude, Queen of Scotland, through his cunning. When Amleth was eventually killed in battle by Wikleth, Hermutrude, despite her promises never to remarry after his death, 'yielded herself unasked to be the conqueror's spoil and bride'.

From anonymous: *A Homily Against Disobedience and Wilful Rebellion,* first published 1574; this extract is from The First Part [II.21.73–83; 112–42; 150–6; 177–87], as printed by John Bill, London, 1623; spelling and punctuation modernized

The Queen, as Head of the Church of England, ordained that certain 'Homilies' were to be read from the pulpit to all congregations on specific days of the year. This particular text was added to the collection in 1574, and sets out very clearly the contemporary notion that a subject's duty was to obey a monarch no matter what crime the monarch might have committed. It is an 'official view' of the English state, not shared by all subjects (see Contextual Overview, pp. 9–10).

As in reading of the holy scriptures, we shall find in very many and almost infinite places, as well of the Old Testament, as of the new, that kings and princes,[1] as well the evil as the good, do reign by God's ordinance, and that subjects are bounden to obey them; that God doth give princes wisdom, great power, and authority; that God defendeth them against their enemies, and destroyeth their enemies horribly; that the anger and displeasure of the prince, is as the roaring of a lion, and the very messenger of death; and that the subject that provoketh him to displeasure, sinneth against his own soul.

It is most evident that kings, queens, and other princes . . . are ordained of God, are to be obeyed and honoured of their subjects; that such subjects, as are disobedient or rebellious against their princes, disobey God, and procure their own damnation; that the government of princes is a great blessing of God, given for the common wealth, specially of the good and godly; for the comfort and cherishing of whom God giveth and setteth up princes; and on the contrary part, to the fear and for the punishment of the evil and wicked. Finally, [it is most evident that] that if servants ought to obey their masters, not only being gentle, but such as be froward,[2] as well and much more ought subjects to be obedient, not only to their good and courteous, but also to their sharp and rigorous[3] princes.

It cometh therefore neither of chance and fortune (as they term it) nor of the ambition of mortal men and women climbing up of their own accord to dominion, that there be kings, queens, princes, and other governors over men being their subjects; but all kings, queens, and other governors are specially appointed by the ordinance of God. And as God himself, being of an infinite majesty, power, and wisdom, ruleth and governeth all things in heaven and earth, as the universal monarch and only king and emperor over all, as being only able to take and bear the charge of all, so hath he constituted, ordained, and set earthly Princes over particular kingdoms and dominions in earth, both for the avoiding of all confusion, which else would be in the world, if it should be without governors, and for the great quiet and benefit of earthly men their subjects [. . .] The nearer and nearer that an earthly prince doth come in his regiment, the greater blessing of God's mercy is he unto that country and people over whom he reigneth; and the further and further that an earthly prince doth swerve from the example of the heavenly government, the greater plague is he of God's wrath, and punishment by God's justice, unto that country and people, over whom God for their sins hath placed such a prince and governor [. . .]

What shall subjects do then? Shall they obey valiant, stout, wise and good

---

1   'Prince' is used in the normal early modern sense of 'monarch' here.
2   Disposed to evil.
3   Cruel and severe.

princes, and contemn, disobey and rebel against children being their princes, or against undiscreet and evil governors? God forbid. For, first, what a perilous thing were it to commit unto the subjects the judgement which prince is wise and godly, and his government good, and which is otherwise: as though the foot must judge of the head; an enterprise very heinous, and must needs breed rebellion. For who else be they that are most inclined to rebellion, but such haughty spirits? From whom springeth such foul ruin of realms? Is not rebellion the greatest of all mischiefs? And who are most ready to the greatest mischiefs, but the worst men?

From **Desiderius Erasmus, *The Education of a Christian Prince***
(1516), translated by Lester K. Born (New York: Octagon Books Columbia University Records of Civilization, 1963), pp. 160–1; 172–4

The justification of the subject's duty never to disobey even a wicked monarch was only one political doctrine at the turn of the sixteenth century. The Dutch theologian and wit Erasmus (c.1469–1536) was a central figure in the European humanist tradition. His new editions and translations of the Bible and of classical authors transformed European literary culture. Erasmus's scholarship challenged the authenticity of traditional texts, especially parts of the 'Vulgate', the Latin Bible. He was a frequent visitor to England, where his works advocating simple piety, following Christ's teachings, were well known. In *The Education of a Christian Prince* Erasmus asserts the right of the governed to overthrow a monarch who rules in his or her own interest, not that of the people, and indeed to limit the very institution of monarchy. In this he follows the Stoic philosophy of Roman republicans (as represented in *Hamlet* at 3.2.63–74 and 5.2.215–20; see Contextual Overview, **p. 9**, and Modern Criticism, **p. 71**). But Erasmus also contends that a Christian monarch, as distinct from a pagan ruler, can only deserve obedience if he rules as a Christian, obeying all Christ's precepts. *Hamlet* does not only dramatize, albeit with considerable ambiguity, the view that it is God's will that a murderous king should be overthrown (see, for example, 3.4.175–7, 5.2.67–70), but also it presents a Danish people who are impatient with a lack of voice in political matters, and who even, reportedly, challenge the rights of the nobility to rule (4.5.102–6; see Key Passages, **pp. 154–5**).

Only those who govern the state not for themselves but for the good of the state itself, deserve the title 'prince'. His titles mean nothing in the case of one who rules to suit himself and measures everything to his own convenience: he is no prince, but a tyrant. There is no more honorable title than 'prince', and there is no term more detested and accursed than 'tyrant'. There is the same difference between a prince and a tyrant as there is between a conscientious father and a cruel master. The former is ready and willing to give even his life for his children; the latter thinks of nothing else than his own gain, or indulges his caprices to his own taste, with no thought to the welfare of his subjects. Do not be satisfied just because you are called 'king' or 'prince'. Those scourges of the earth,

Phalaris and Dionysius,[1] had those titles. Pass your own judgment on yourself. Seneca[2] was right, the distinction between tyrant and king is one of fact, not of terminology.

To summarize: In his *Politics* Aristotle[3] differentiates between a prince and a tyrant on the basis that the one is interested in his own pursuits and the other is concerned for the state. No matter what the prince is deliberating about, he always keeps this one thing in mind: 'Is this to the advantage of all my subjects?' A tyrant only considers whether a thing will contribute to his cause. A prince is vitally concerned with the needs of his subjects, even while engaged in personal matters. On the other hand, if a tyrant ever chances to do something good for his subjects, he turns that to his own personal gain [. . .]

Since God is the very opposite of a tyrant, so it must follow unfailingly that there is nothing more loathsome to Him than a baneful king. Since no wild beast is more deadly than a tyrant, it consistently follows that there is nothing more odious to all mankind than a wicked prince. But who would want to live hated and accursed by gods and men alike? [. . .]

In ancient times, those who ruled their empires well were decreed divine honours. Toward tyrants the ancients had the same law which we now apply to wolves and bears – the 'reward' comes from the people who have had the enemy in their very midst. In very early times, the kings were selected through the choice of the people because of their outstanding qualities, which were called 'heroic' as being all but divine and superhuman. Princes should remember their beginnings, and realize that they are not really princes if they lack that quality which first made princes. Although there are many types of state, it is the consensus of nearly all wise-thinking men that the best form is monarchy. This is according to the example of God that the sum of all things be placed in one individual but in such a way that, following God's example, he surpasses all others in his wisdom and goodness and, wanting nothing, may desire only to help his state. But if conditions were otherwise, that would be the worst form of state. Whosoever would fight it then would be the best man. If a prince be found who is complete in all good qualities, then pure and absolute monarchy is the thing. (If that could only be! I fear it is too great a thing even to hope for.) If an average prince (as the affairs of men go now) is found, it will be better to have a limited monarchy checked and lessened by aristocracy and democracy. Then there is no chance for tyranny to creep in, but just as the elements balance each other, so will the state hold together under similar control. If a prince has the interests of the state at heart, his power is not checked on this account, so it will be adjudged, but rather helped. If his attitude is otherwise, however, it is expedient that the state break and turn aside the violence of a single man.

---

1   Phalaris and Dionysius were ancient Sicilian tyrants and were renowned for their cruelty.
2   Lucius Annaeus Seneca (c. 4BC–AD65), Roman philosopher and politician.
3   Greek philosopher (384–322BC).

From **Francis Bacon, The Essays: 'Of Revenge'** (first published in the third edition, 1625); ed. John Pitcher (Harmondsworth: Penguin Books, 1985), pp. 72–3

Francis Bacon (1561–1626) was one of the most important statesmen and philosophers of Shakespeare's lifetime. Having originally been the client of the Earl of Essex (see Contextual Overview, **p. 12**), he became his prosecutor at his trial in 1601. Under James I he rose to be Chancellor of England in 1618. Bacon did not rely on the authority of ancient writers; he was a rationalist who applied reason to his own observations of the world. Here he questions the mediaeval notion of a duty to take personal revenge, contrasting it to the modern civil state's monopoly over the enforcement of justice: Hamlet's dilemma (see Contextual Overview, **p. 8**). He condemns private revenge, it seems, but admits at the end of the essay that rulers who avenged assassination do seem to have often prospered.

Revenge is a kind of wild justice, which the more man's nature runs to, the more ought law to weed it out. For as for the first wrong, it doth but offend the law; but the revenge of that wrong putteth the law out of office.[1] Certainly, in taking revenge, a man is but even with his enemy, but in passing it over, he is superior; for it is a prince's part to pardon. And Solomon, I am sure, saith, *It is the glory of a man to pass by an offence.*[2] That which is past is gone, and irrevocable, and wise men have enough to do with things present and to come: therefore they do but trifle with themselves, that labour in past matters. There is no man doth a wrong for the wrong's sake, but thereby to purchase himself profit or pleasure or honour or the like. Therefore why should I be angry with a man for loving himself better than me? And if any man should do wrong merely out of ill nature, why, yet it is but like the thorn or briar, which prick and scratch, because they can do no other. The most tolerable sort of revenge is for those wrongs which there is no law or remedy: but then let a man take heed the revenge be such as there is no law to punish; else a man's enemy is still beforehand, and it is two for one.[3] Some, when they take revenge, are desirous the party should know whence it cometh. This is the more generous, for the delight seemeth to be not so much in doing the hurt as in making the party repent. But base and crafty cowards are like the arrow that flieth in the dark. Cosmus, Duke of Florence,[4] had a desperate saying against perfidious or neglecting friends, as if those wrongs were unpardonable: *You shall read* (saith he) *that we are commanded to forgive our enemies; but you never read that we are commanded to forgive our friends.* But yet the spirit of Job was in a better tune: *Shall we* (saith he) *take good at God's hands, and not be content*

---

1 Puts the law out of a job.
2 Solomon was an ancient and proverbially wise King of Israel; see the Bible, *Proverbs* 19.11.
3 If you commit an illegal act in vengeance for a legal slight, your enemy still has an advantage over you, two wrongs of yours (one legal, one illegal) for his one.
4 Cosimo de Medici, who died in 1574.

to take evil also?[5] And so of friends in a proportion.[6] This is certain, that a man that studieth revenge keeps his own wounds green, which otherwise would heal and do well. Public revenges are for the most part fortunate: as that for the death of Caesar; for the death of Pertinax, for the death of Henry the Third of France, and many more.[7] But in private revenges it is not so. Nay rather, vindictive persons live the life of witches, who, as they are mischievous, so end they infortunate.

---

5   Job was a long-suffering Old Testament sage; see Job 2.10.
6   'To a proportionate extent (i.e. God may treat us as he will: friends have less power to do us good, and less right to do us harm)', Francis Bacon, *The Essays: 'Of Revenge'*, ed. John Pitcher (Harmondsworth: Penguin Books), p. 73.
7   The rulers who took revenge for these three deaths (the Romans Augustus Caesar and Septimus Severus, and the French King Henry IV respectively) all prospered and proved good monarchs.

2

Interpretations

Critical History

This section provides a historical overview of the development of *Hamlet* criticism. The range of commentary on the play is vast, but the extracts which follow are all of some significance. There is an emphasis on important and influential contemporary work.

Pre-Romantic Criticism: Can We Admire the Prince?

Unlike many of Shakespeare's plays, *Hamlet* seems to have stayed in the theatrical repertory in London from 1601 until the Civil War closed the playhouses in 1642. However, at the restoration of the monarchy in 1660 one of the two licensed acting companies, The King's Men, declined the rights to perform the play, and they passed to The Duke's Men, and their leading actor Thomas Betterton.

Criticism of the play in this period was criticism of the play in performance. Even if individual editions of the play did continue to be produced and sold to readers (five between 1676 and 1703),[1] critical writing about Shakespeare's plays as 'literature' in the modern sense was in its infancy. Betterton's Hamlet was a heroic avenger, vivacious and energetic. Cuts and emendations to the text smoothed over the more cruel, irrational and savage aspects of Hamlet's behaviour for good reason. The king, Charles II, had been a prince who avenged a murdered father, and royal vengeance was a very suitable subject for what was now an audience dominated by the upper class. Betterton's *Hamlet* was very popular; it made more money at the door than any other of The Duke's Men's plays during this period.[2] He continued to play the role until 1709, when he was well into his seventies.

The taste of the intelligentsia had changed, however. The diarist John Evelyn declared in 1660 that the play 'began to disgust this refined age'.[3] The churchman Jeremy Collier, writing in 1698, found, for example, the depiction of Ophelia

1 Gary Taylor, *Reinventing Shakespeare: A Cultural History from the Restoration to the Present* (London: The Hogarth Press, 1990), p. 46.
2 *Shakespeare in Production: 'Hamlet'*, ed. Robert Hapgood (Cambridge: Cambridge University Press, 1999), p. 11.
3 Cited in Taylor (see note 1), p. 40.

'lewd' and 'unreasonable'.[4] However, all were not in agreement. The playwright and pamphleteer James Drake (see Early Critical Reception, **pp. 41–2**) sought to defend the play against Collier as an example of divine justice at work, and the Earl of Shaftesbury, writing in 1710 (see Early Critical Reception, **pp. 42–3**), also defended the moral qualities of the play, while admitting its failings. All the same, *Hamlet* did not meet the requirements of the dominant theatrical taste in the first half of the eighteenth century. French neo-classical drama, which self-consciously followed the 'unities', the conventions of ancient and Italian renaissance drama (see Contextual Overview, **p. 8**), was regarded as superior and refined in comparison to the English theatre of Shakespeare's day. In an age that prided itself on its rationality, *Hamlet*'s plot seemed implausible. The first sustained critical dissertation on the play, attributed to Thomas Hanmer (*Some Remarks on the Tragedy of 'Hamlet'*, 1736), pointed out that Hamlet's feigning madness,

> so far from Securing himself from any Violence which he fear'd from the Usurper, which was his design in so doing, . . . seems to have been most likely Way of getting himself confin'd, and consequently, debarr'd from an Opportunity of Revenging his Father's Death . . .[5]

Moral education was an important function of neo-classical drama, and required that a protagonist be uncontroversially virtuous. Hanmer found Hamlet's conduct cruel and unworthy of a hero, especially in his desire to kill Claudius at a time when his damnation was most likely (3.3.74–96; see Key Passages, **p. 145**). 'There is something very Bloody in it, so inhuman, so unworthy of a Hero, that I wish our poet had omitted it,' he wrote.[6] It was also felt that a play's language should be polished and give no offence. These qualities were not evident in *Hamlet*. Lewis Theobald, writing in 1726, says of the obscene pun in Hamlet's line to Ophelia about 'country matters' (3.2.115) that 'if ever the Poet deserved Whipping for low and indecent Ribaldry, it was for this passage'.[7] In 1748 the French philosopher Voltaire summed up the play for neo-classical taste as 'a vulgar and barbarous drama, which would not be tolerated by the vilest populace of France, or Italy'. And yet he also admitted that there are nevertheless 'some sublime passages, worthy of the greatest genius'.[8] Samuel Johnson, perhaps the play's most judicious eighteenth-century editor, broadly agreed, though with some significant reservations (see Early Critical Reception, **pp. 43–4**). The editor George Steevens, writing in 1778, reasserted this critical view to admonish the prince's popularity with popular audiences who did not seem to share the neo-classical aesthetic. As Philip Edwards points out in his introduction to the Cambridge Edition of *Hamlet*, Steevens thought it was more necessary 'to point out the immoral tendency of his character . . . because Hamlet seems to have hitherto been regarded as a hero not undeserving the pity of the audience'.[9]

David Garrick, whose productions of Shakespeare came to dominate the late

4   Cited in Taylor (see note 1), p. 40.
5   Cited in Arthur F. Kinney (ed.), *'Hamlet': New Critical Essays* (London: Routledge, 2002), p. 20.
6   Cited in Kinney (see note 5), p. 21.
7   Cited in Kinney (see note 5), p. 20.
8   'Dissertation sur la Tragédie', in *Semiramis*; cited in Kinney (see note 5), p. 26.
9   'Introduction', in *Hamlet*, ed. Philip Edwards (Cambridge: Cambridge University Press, 1985), p. 33.

eighteenth century and were important in establishing Shakespeare's place at the centre of English national culture, performed a *Hamlet* in 1763 which seemed to reconcile both camps. He cut even more than Betterton. Garrick eliminated the scene in which Hamlet declines to kill the praying Claudius so that his damnation is more likely (3.3), as well as any mention of Hamlet's responsibility for the deaths of Rosencrantz and Guildenstern (5.2.38–62). The crude taunting of Ophelia while she and Hamlet await *The Murder of Gonzago* (3.2.110–133) was also omitted, as well as Hamlet's conversation with the gravediggers (5.1.65–210; see Key Passages, **pp. 160–2**). This dialogue was thought to be tasteless, and beneath a prince's dignity. According to Voltaire: 'Hamlet responds to their nasty vulgarities in silliness no less disgusting.'[10] Garrick's Hamlet was universally regarded as 'princely', 'natural' and was praised for its fashionable 'sensibility' – showing the appropriate sentiments and reactions to whatever happened to him. The line condemning Claudius as a 'treacherous, lecherous, kindless villain', for example (2.2.577; see Key Passages, **p. 135**), was marked by a shift from thunderous indignation on 'treacherous, lecherous' to a sudden anguished tear on the word 'kindless'.[11]

Romantic Criticism: Why We Should Identify With the Prince

Garrick's 'sensible' *Hamlet* foreshadowed an emerging view of the protagonist as a sensitive, suffering intellectual incapable of carrying out the ghost's wishes. The emergent Romantic movement sought to turn away from scientific rationalism and detailed observation of the *external* world to give 'natural' human emotion more priority. In particular, they valued spontaneity of feeling and imaginative freedom. The Romantic critics constructed a new kind of hero in Hamlet. Shakespeare's plays, wrote the poet Samuel Taylor Coleridge, were 'dramatic romances . . . [which] appealed to the imagination rather than to the senses . . . and the workings of the passions in their most retired recesses'.[12] Furthermore, paralysis in the face of a challenging political crisis seemed to cause many intellectuals to identify with the prince in the years following the French Revolution of 1789. How should romantic sympathizers respond to the violent but daring abolition of monarchy, Church and aristocracy in France? As Gary Taylor writes: 'The quoting of *Hamlet* by English critics in the decades after 1789 . . . expresses their obsession with political inaction and artistic failure.'[13] When Coleridge said that 'I have a smack of Hamlet myself',[14] he meant that he saw his own personality in the prince's character. The radical journalist and critic William Hazlitt wrote that 'it is *we* [the audience] that are Hamlet'.[15]

For the German critic August von Schlegel, writing in 1811, the depth of

10 Cited in Kinney (see note 5), p. 26.
11 Hapgood (see note 2), p. 15.
12 *Coleridge's Essays and Lectures on Shakespeare* (London: Dent, no date), p. 6; quoted in Michael Hattaway, '*Hamlet': an Introduction to the Variety of Criticism* (London: Macmillan, 1987), p. 36.
13 Taylor (see note 1), p. 110.
14 Cited in Taylor (see note 1), p. 102.
15 William Hazlitt, *Characters of Shakespeare's Plays* (1817; London: Dent, 1906), p. 79.

Hamlet's intellectualization of every problem he faced prevented him from coming to a decision about what he should do in reality;[16] but for the English poet Coleridge (see Early Critical Reception, pp. 44–5), the imagination was more 'real' to Hamlet than what his senses told him, a trait which also prevented him from taking action. For Coleridge and those who thought like him, the imagination was a realm which can be more beautiful than the physical world, and thus this feature of the prince's characterization gave the play its 'sublime' quality (by which he meant its awe-inspiring ability to produce powerful emotion). Coleridge and Schlegel wrote about Hamlet to give, as they saw it, an insight into general human nature. Hazlitt, on the other hand, saw Hamlet as a portrait of a young, energetic and spirited philosophical idealist who, 'because he cannot have his revenge perfect, according to the most refined idea his wish can form, he declines it altogether' (see Early Critical Reception, p. 46). He also recognized that Hamlet's conduct was a product of his being out of sympathy with the particular historical circumstances in which he found himself.

In the theatre Hazlitt admired the Hamlet of Edmund Kean (performed 1814–32). Kean's dynamic and emotional, if not conventionally heroic prince had a 'force and animation', an 'extreme boldness', which could have 'an electrical effect upon the house'.[17] Yet Hazlitt came to a view shared by Coleridge and Charles Lamb (who famously turned Shakespeare's plays into stories for children) that *no one* could do justice to the part on the stage.[18] Romantic writers tended to think that the imagination was a realm where beauty and truth dwelt more convincingly than in reality: thus the ideal performance was in the mind. A consequence of this is that from the early nineteenth until the late twentieth century, Shakespeare criticism became focused on the text and not on performance, as it had been in the eighteenth century. Furthermore, if the 'truth' of the play was better apprehended in the study than the theatre, it is not surprising that in the nineteenth century the writing of literary critics began to influence how the play should be presented on stage. A good example of this trend is the American actor Edwin Booth's *Hamlet* (performed 1860–91; see The Work in Performance, pp. 95–8), which drew heavily on the ideas of the romantic critics in its portrayal of the prince as the owner of a gentle and sensitive soul tortured by a demand for action which it cannot satisfy.

Modernist Criticism: Below the Surface

The romantic emphasis on the individual consciousness was perpetuated in later nineteenth-century Shakespeare criticism, which focused on the individual

16 See *The Romantics on Shakespeare*, ed. Jonathan Bate (Harmondsworth: Penguin Books, 1992), pp. 307–10.
17 William Hazlitt in *The Morning Chronicle* reviewing Kean at the Theatre Royal, Drury Lane, London, 14 March 1814; reprinted in *Shakespeare in the Theatre: An Anthology of Criticism*, ed. Stanley Wells (Oxford: Oxford University Press, 1997), p. 43; see also The Work in Performance, p. 91.
18 'We do not like to see our author's plays acted, and least of all, HAMLET. There is no play that suffers so much in being transferred to the stage. Hamlet himself seems hardly capable of being acted . . . Mr Kean's Hamlet is much too splenetic and rash' (Hazlitt, *Characters of Shakespeare's Plays*, pp. 86–7).

characters of the plays. In the twentieth century this developed into detailed psychological studies both of the characters and of the playwright himself.[19] Perhaps the most influential work of character criticism is A. C. Bradley's *Shakespearean Tragedy* (1904), still in print after a century.[20] The medical language evident in his writing reveals that he saw the critic's job as one of psychological analysis, treating the character as if he or she were a real person with a life beyond the words on the page or the actors' performance: '[Hamlet's] speculative habit would be *one* indirect cause of the morbid state which hindered action: and it would also reappear in a degenerate form as one of the *symptoms* of this morbid state' (see Modern Criticism, p. 51). Bradley diagnosed a condition of melancholia at the root of Hamlet's problems. Shakespeare's 'genius' thus lay in his insight into the human mind.[21] When the founder of psychoanalysis, Sigmund Freud, sought in 1900 to justify and explain his 'Oedipus complex' he turned to *Hamlet* (see Modern Criticism, pp. 48–9). According to Freud's theory, mental health in an adult male depended on the ability to resolve the infantile jealousy which the infant boy had felt for his father's physical relationship with his mother. Hamlet has failed to do this: he cannot kill Claudius because he identifies with him, for Claudius has done the very things he would wish to do himself – that is, kill his father, Old Hamlet, and have sex with Hamlet's mother. As Freud notes: 'The play is built up on Hamlet's hesitations over fulfilling the task of revenge that is assigned to him; but its text offers no reasons or motives for these hesitations' (see Modern Criticism, p. 48). Thus the critic finds the truth hidden deep within the play, in this case by applying a sophisticated general theory about the nature of the human mind. Such an approach can be seen to be a product of the modern technological age, where the workings of much that we depend on in our day-to-day lives are invisible and incomprehensible to us, and are only able to be mended or serviced by experts. This tended to be the literary critic's approach to the play in the twentieth century: the expert with specialist knowledge of psychoanalysis, or philosophy, or history or human society will reveal the play's superficially hidden workings for the reader or audience.

Freud's reading transformed the way the play was understood. Since 1927 the 'closet scene' (3.4; see Key Passages, pp. 146–50) between Hamlet and his mother was often set in her bedroom, even though there is no textual or historical warrant for this.[22] Eight years earlier the English critic and poet T. S. Eliot had taken Freud's argument further, and avoided the Bradleyan pitfall of treating Hamlet as a real person: Eliot thought that to attempt to psychoanalyse Hamlet was to delve into the murky subconscious of Shakespeare himself (see Modern Criticism, p. 54). Eliot felt that the play is an artistic failure because Hamlet's

19 For an account of how twentieth-century critics characterized Shakespeare himself from his writings see Michael Taylor, *Shakespeare Criticism in the Twentieth Century* (Oxford: Oxford University Press, 2001), pp. 70–81.
20 A. C. Bradley, *Shakespearean Tragedy* (Harmondsworth: Penguin Books, 1991).
21 For a disturbing account of how the play was used as a medical text to diagnose mental illness in young women see Elaine Showalter, 'Representing Ophelia: Woman, Madness and the Responsibilities of Feminist Criticism', in *Shakespeare and the Question of Theory*, ed. Patricia Parker and Geoffrey Hartman (New York and London: Methuen, 1985).
22 See Stanley Wells, *Looking for Sex in Shakespeare* (Cambridge: Cambridge University Press, 2004), p. 24; pp. 98–9.

emotions are too profound for what he sees to have been the cause of his distress, his mother's over-hasty marriage to his uncle. According to Eliot, Shakespeare is trying to express his own deep emotion through Hamlet, and he does so. But it does not convince artistically because the grounds for that emotion are inadequate. An 'explanation' of Hamlet's conduct will always elude us, like the reason for the smile on the face of Da Vinci's famous *Mona Lisa* (see Modern Criticism, **p. 53**).

However, it was not only psychoanalytic critics who sought to explain the play by invoking deeper, mysterious transhistorical forces at work. The German philosopher Friedrich Nietzsche, in his *Birth of Tragedy* (1872), thought Hamlet resembled the archetype of the violent and visionary 'Dionysiac' man, the man who sees through the façade of order and reason of western culture. For Nietzsche, such men

> have looked into the true nature of things; they have *understood* and are now loth to act. They realise that no action of theirs can work any change in the eternal condition of things, and they regard the imputation as ludicrous or debasing that they should set right the time which is now out of joint.[23]

Bradley had a particular interest in German philosophy, having written his doctoral thesis on the German philosopher G. F. Hegel. But Bradley saw tragedy in a more conventionally Christian framework, as an embodiment of a profound and abstract process in human development, outside mere history. In order for evil (Claudius) to be defeated, it is necessary for that goodness which is flawed (Hamlet) to perish. Our inexpressible sense of the rightness of this, despite its sadness, is what constitutes tragedy (see Modern Criticism, **pp. 50–1**). This way of thinking about the play permeated much twentieth-century criticism. G. Wilson Knight thought that an audience's vision of the play could only be 'baffling and indecisive', but there are 'universal issues' at stake in the play's final conflict.[24] For Knight, 'life' in the abstract was engaged in a complex struggle with 'death-forces' throughout the play. The idea that the play beautifully touches some inexpressible but vital truth beyond words also became popular. The critic and novelist C. S. Lewis wrote in 1942 that: 'The sense, unextinguished by over a century of [critical] failures, that we have something here of inestimable importance, is surely the best evidence that the real and lasting mystery of our human situation has been greatly depicted.'[25]

---

23 Friedrich Nietzsche, *The Birth of Tragedy*, trans. F. Golffing (New York: Anchor Books, 1956), § 7 p. 51; quoted in Philip Edwards (ed.), *Hamlet* (Cambridge: Cambridge University Press, 1985), pp. 34–5.
24 G. Wilson Knight, *The Imperial Theme* [1931] (London: Methuen, 1965), p. 124.
25 C. S. Lewis, '*Hamlet*: The Prince or the Poem?', British Academy Shakespeare Lecture, 1942 in *Shakespeare's Tragedies: An Anthology of Modern Criticism*, ed. Laurence Lerner (Harmondsworth: Penguin, 1968), p. 77; see also Modern Criticism, **pp. 86–7**.

Late Twentieth-Century Criticism (1): Psychoanalysis

The arrival of 'critical theory' transformed English studies in the last three decades of the twentieth century. Critical theory uses the insights of philosophers, historians, anthropologists and psychologists from the European continental tradition to explore the 'field of thinking and theorizing about literature itself – from its formal and linguistic structures to its relations with power politics, gender and history'.[26] This new approach to criticism was popular with a new generation of university students and teachers which featured more women, and more men from less privileged backgrounds. This was a generation whose radical political outlook made them eager to use what Terence Hawkes has called the 'new methods of analysis . . . whose conclusions reveal the limitations of the Anglo–American outlook we inherit'.[27] Terry Eagleton cheekily remarked that: 'Though conclusive evidence is hard to come by, it is difficult to read Shakespeare without feeling that he was almost certainly familiar with the writings of Hegel, Marx, Nietzsche, Freud, Wittgenstein and Derrida.'[28] Shakespeare's plays became the site of an acrimonious critical battle. When they read Shakespeare, the new critics wanted to engage with questions of power (New Historicism), class (Marxism) or gender politics (Feminist and Queer criticism); or to explore the fundamental instability of language (Deconstruction) and of individual consciousness (Psychoanalysis). Their traditionalist opponents, who stood accused of holding limited, even reactionary, views about the nature of literary studies, defended their corner in return. While the older approach is still evident in criticism today, the insights critical theory has brought to Shakespeare studies are now much more accepted, even if the political confidence and ambition of such writing has receded in the face of recent history.

Since critical theory sets out to challenge established cultural power, it is not surprising that the different types of feminist criticism are a vital element. Feminist critics are broadly concerned with the study of women writers and the analysis of women in literature, and seek to address the question of male dominance in our culture. Feminist critics have challenged misogyny wherever they have found it.

T. S. Eliot's idea that Gertrude is not worth Hamlet's anguish (see **p. 54**) is an example of the kind of patriarchal assumptions found in traditional criticism. In this case feminists with an interest in psychoanalysis have responded ingeniously. Jacqueline Rose, for example, has argued that Eliot's problem with the play reveals the troublingly 'excessive' nature of female sexuality in both male-dominated society and in psychoanalytic theory, in that it cannot be rationally categorized. Both our society and psychoanalytical theory idealize or demonize femininity, and yet the 'feminine' is actually the (consequently) unstable category on which stable meaning and identity in our culture depend: stable meaning and

---

26 Patricia Parker, 'Introduction' in *Shakespeare and the Question of Theory*, eds Patricia Barker and Geoffrey Hartman (London and New York: Routledge, 1985), p. xi.
27 'General Editor's Preface' in *Alternative Shakespeares*, ed. John Drakakis (London and New York: Routledge, 1985), p. vii.
28 Terry Eagleton, *William Shakespeare* (Oxford: Basil Blackwell, 1986), pp. ix–x.

identity, according to Rose, define themselves in opposition to that category.[29] But perhaps it is the play itself that is misogynistic: Janet Adelman argues that Gertrude's sexuality in the play 'is literally the sign of her betrayal and her husband's death': as a sexual woman, no longer the possession of his forgotten father, she makes it difficult for Hamlet to assume a fully masculine identity in the image of his father: 'The idealised father's absence releases the threat of maternal sexuality, in effect subjecting the son to annihilating power.'[30] For both Rose and Adelman, psychoanalytical criticism can show that Hamlet's anguish is the product of the play's revelation of the essential but destabilizing function of female sexuality in a patriarchal society.

But modern psychoanalytical criticism is not exclusively feminist. Critics influenced by the French psychoanalyst Jacques Lacan take an interest in the play's examination of performance itself – of being watched and watching. One of the first things Hamlet says is that he has hidden feelings which no actor could represent (1.2.76–86; see Key Passages, **p. 125**). Later, Hamlet will seek to convince himself that the ghost has told him the truth by careful observation of Claudius's response to the on-stage re-enactment of the murder of Old Hamlet (2.2.584–601; see Key Passages, **p. 135**). For Lacan (to oversimplify), the troubled and insecure formation of individual identity stems from a stage in our infancy when we struggle to define ourselves both by the image we think that others have of us and by our own sense of who we are. The sense that we have in life of our desires never being totally fulfilled, or of language never being quite able to express our real intentions and feelings, springs from the unresolved conflict between these two (as Hamlet says: 'I have that within that passes show' [1.2.85]). Critics following Lacan seize on the fact that *Hamlet* is suffused with a sense of loss and meaninglessness, and features a protagonist who is all too concerned with comparing himself to Hercules (1.2.153; see Key Passages, **p. 128**), the First Player (2.2.554–66; see Key Passages, **p. 134**), to Laertes (4.7.101–4), to Fortinbras (4.4.46–65), and who even contrives to have put on stage a mirror image of his father's death (2.2.590–2; see Key Passages, **p. 135**). Philip Armstrong (see Modern Criticism, **pp. 75–8**) uses a Lacanian reading of the play to show the text's continuing significance for a contemporary anxiety: is it possible to give an intelligible account of our own identity, and of our own lives?[31]

Late Twentieth-Century Criticism (2): History and Politics

Most contemporary critics reject the view that the play's tragedy is an expression of mystical forces (see Critical History, **p. 34**). In philosophical terms, they take a 'materialist' approach to the play. They take the view that we can only talk

29 Jacqueline Rose, '*Hamlet*: The Mona Lisa of Literature', in *Shakespeare and Gender: A History*, ed. Deborah E. Barker and Ivo Kamps (London and New York: Verso, 1995).
30 Janet Adelman, *Suffocating Mothers: Fantasies of Maternal Origin in Shakespeare's Plays, 'Hamlet' to 'The Tempest'* (London: Routledge, 1992), p. 35; p. 18.
31 On this issue see also Linda Charnes, 'We were never early modern', in *Philosophical Shakespeares*, ed. John J. Joughin (London: Routledge, 2000), pp. 51–67.

meaningfully about *Hamlet*, or any text, by discussing that text in the real contexts in which it was written, has been performed, and is now performed and read. This approach is distinct from the 'idealist' approach as exemplified by Bradley or Knight, which considers the play as an expression of purely abstract ideas or forces outside of history: good and evil, or the 'lasting mystery of the human situation', for example. Materialist critics are more interested in the depiction of actual social and ideological forces at work in real time, perhaps expressed in the consciousness of individual characters, rather than in those characters themselves, whom they tend to see as functions of those forces.

The focus of these critics on the place of the play in the world, rather than on the individual's consciousness of the world in the play, can be seen in the British critic Arnold Kettle's critique of Freud's views. For Kettle, writing in 1964, although Freud's views

> can throw light on the nature of Hamlet's experience and reactions . . . they tend to draw attention away from the real dramatic significance of that experience, that it makes him see the world differently in ways which have little to do with the experience itself.[32]

Kettle sees Hamlet as 'along with Marlowe's Faustus . . . the first modern intellectual in our literature', who holds 'the view of the world of the most advanced humanists [see Contextual Overview, **pp. 9–10**] of his time. It rejects as intolerable the ways of behaviour which formed the accepted standard of the contemporary ruling class.'[33] *Hamlet*, written at a time when the feudal mediaeval society was being transformed into the beginnings of modernity (see Contextual Overview, **p. 11**), dramatizes the response of an 'advanced' contemporary intellectual to the specific political circumstances of his day. In the same vein Graham Holderness (see Modern Criticism, **pp. 65–6**), argues that Hamlet is a tragic figure precisely because he is caught between the spent values of his father's heroic feudalism and Claudius's 'modern', ruthlessly pragmatic conception of how a ruler should behave. Kiernan Ryan (see Modern Criticism, **pp. 85–7**) sees Hamlet's humanist disgust as still relevant to the world we live in today, and suggests that the power of the play lies in its ability 'to expose the alterable causes of injustice, violence and despair, and expand our awareness of alternative fates hovering in the wings of what happens'.

The careful attention paid by materialist critics to the historical moment which produced the text can be seen exemplified in Alan Sinfield's chapter (see Modern Criticism, **pp. 70–5**) in his book *Faultlines*. Sinfield shows how the play dramatizes conflicting ideas about determinism in 1600: ancient stoicism versus Protestant predestinarianism; Protestant ideas are consequently undermined. Stephen Greenblatt has written of how the ghost, as a temporary refugee from pre-reformation Catholic purgatory in Protestant London, suggests how the power of Shakespeare's play may have something to do with the theatre taking the place of the abolished Catholic institutions which made communal sense of

---

32 Arnold Kettle, 'From *Hamlet* to *Lear*' in *Shakespeare in a Changing World*, ed. Arnold Kettle (London: Lawrence & Wishart, 1964), p. 150.
33 Kettle (see note 32), p. 156, p. 147.

life, and, in this case, death and grief (see Modern Criticism, **pp. 87–90**). But this is not treating the plays as mere pieces of historical evidence. This sort of historicist criticism seeks to explain the functions of political power in the text of the play itself, in the society that created it, and also in the formation and expression of critical views about the play in the contemporary situation of the critic. The play, and writing about the play, are equally the product of conflicting historical forces: there is no one 'objective' position outside history or writing where an impartial truth can be concluded. Terence Hawkes' provocative and radical essay 'Telmah' (see Modern Criticism, **pp. 56–62**) proposes a controversial 'negative' of the play, where its formal unity and even clear narrative progress are questioned, and where Claudius emerges as central, and the play constantly doubles back on itself and offers no unquestioned events or assumptions. But Hawkes is not merely trying, as an authority, to impose another interpretation on the play; all 'interpretations' are in some sense authoritarian attempts to limit the play's many meanings and close down our responses to it. He calls for a criticism which plays with the text in an improvisatory way.

Such was the play's cultural status for much of the twentieth century[34] that its appropriation for a particular cause has made it the site of political conflict, especially in the 1970s and 1980s. Some feminist critics have sought to acquit the play from the charge that it asks its audience to admire a protagonist who hates women.[35] Rebecca Smith, for example, has argued that close attention to Gertrude's role in the play shows her to be a nurturing and caring maternal presence rather than a shallow sensualist.[36] Juliet Dusinberre has argued that the play shows that 'Ophelia has no chance to develop an independent conscience of her own, so stifled is she by the authority of the male world'.[37] Ophelia always does what she is told by men, even when it against her will (see 1.3.85–6; 104; 136; 2.2.124; 4.5.43–4; and Key Passages, **p. 153**). Critics also sought to align the play with left-wing causes. Annabel Patterson has argued that study of the play in the context of social unrest in England in 1601 can lead us to 'its protagonist's alienated, fragmentary and guilty adoption of a popular voice [,] . . . [to a] symptom of troubled intellectualism that might, in other circumstances, have led him towards organised resistance to Claudius'.[38] Uncharacteristically for a Shakespearean prince, Hamlet imagines himself as a plasterer (2.2.375), a peasant (2.2.544), an actor (2.2.545–64), and a clerk (5.2.32–7); 'privilege do[es] not necessarily make one superior to the common man . . . He partly perceives the paradox of an elitist education, that only those who profit from it have the faculties to question its social justice.'[39] In the spirit of Kettle's

---

34 Until it seems to have been superseded by *King Lear*; see R. A. Foakes, 'Hamlet' versus 'Lear': *Cultural Politics and Shakespeare's Art* (Cambridge: Cambridge University Press, 1993).
35 Made, for example, by Lisa Jardine in *Still Harping on Daughters* (Hemel Hempstead: Harvester Wheatsheaf, 1983), pp. 72–3.
36 Rebecca Smith, 'A Heart Cleft in Twain: The Dilemma of Shakespeare's Gertrude', in *The Woman's Part: Feminist Criticism of Shakespeare*, ed. Carolyn Ruth Swift Lenz, Gayle Greene and Carol Thomas Neely (Urbana, Chicago and London: University of Illinois Press, 1980).
37 Juliet Dusinberre, *Shakespeare and the Nature of Women* (Basingstoke and London: Macmillan, second edition, 1996; first published 1975), p. 94.
38 Annabel Patterson, *Shakespeare and the Popular Voice* (Oxford and Cambridge MA: Basil Blackwell, 1989), p. 31.
39 Patterson (see note 38), p. 99.

analysis, Terry Eagleton regards Hamlet as a character who refuses to acknowledge himself as the possessor of any kind of fixed identity, 'whether as chivalric lover, obedient revenger or future king'; he even denies that any word or term can express his inner being (1.2.76–86; see Key Passages, **p. 125**). He is a 'radically transitional figure, strung out between a traditional social order to which he is marginal, and a future epoch of achieved bourgeois individualism that will surpass it'.[40] Hamlet's refusal to accept the identity demanded of him either by his feudal father or by his uncle's machiavellian society of amoral competitive individualists (see Contextual Overview, **p. 11**) makes him, for Eagleton, a modern and indeed radical figure:

> What it is to be a subject,[41] in short, is a political problem for Hamlet, as it has once more become a political problem for us . . . If we too are as yet unable to give a name to a different form of subjectivity, it is for the opposite reason – that we, unlike Hamlet, are the end-products of a history of bourgeois individualism beyond which we can only gropingly feel our way.[42]

If in the late twentieth century Shakespeare criticism sought to locate the plays in specific historical moments of both production and reception, it was natural that a great deal of attention should once more be drawn to the play in performance. The script of *Hamlet* is, of course, an as-yet unrealized blueprint for productions on stage and, latterly, on film, video and DVD. Those individual realizations on stage and screen can be studied as complex and concrete events and their design, direction and performance related to the social and historical moment of their creation (see, for example, Anthony B. Dawson's or Julie Sanders' accounts of Laurence Olivier's and Kenneth Branagh's films; The Work in Performance, **pp. 103–5** and **pp. 107–10**). Film, whose enormous authority in our culture has tended to undermine the status of the printed text as the prime instance of this play, can become, of its nature, a new fixed and perhaps idealized authoritative version: 'Because film and video allow us repeated versions of a single performance, they encourage us to assimilate that performance to the condition of a literary text – a stable artefact rather than a contingent, ephemeral experience.'[43]

If film versions come to dominate how the play is seen, this trend to monumentalism runs counter to the dominant trend in contemporary criticism. Nineteenth- and early twentieth-century editors of the play sought to resolve the 'problem' of there being multiple versions of the play from Shakespeare's time (see Key Passages, **pp. 113–15**), by attempting to produce a single 'ideal' version which they thought suited Shakespeare's inferred 'intentions'. Their edition would demonstrate the product of the unified consciousness of the universal genius, just as the 'ideal' performance was, for the Romantics, in the imagination

---

40 Eagleton (see note 28), p. 71; p. 72.
41 The term 'subject' in critical theory means an apparently individual consciousness which thinks of itself as unified and autonomous, but is in fact constructed by language ('subject' in the grammatical sense) and by social and political forces ('subject' in the political sense).
42 Eagleton (see note 28), p. 75.
43 James C. Bulman, 'Introduction: Shakespeare and Performance Theory' in *Shakespeare, Theory and Performance*, ed. James C. Bulman (London and New York: Routledge, 1996), p. 2.

and not on the stage. However, the most recent British editor of the play, Ann Thompson, makes no attempt to assimilate the three texts of the play but prints them one after another in the same volume.[44] Just as *Hamlet* exists as multiple and different performances on stage, it also exists as multiple editions of the script. Ironically, as Anthony B. Dawson points out, the self-referential action of *Hamlet* itself constantly undermines any claim the play may have to be a single, stable entity.[45]

That the play in performance, or as we read it, should speak for itself and through us as individuals seems to be the conclusion of some contemporary critics. John Kerrigan's account of the play (see Modern Criticism, **pp. 81–5**) stresses the importance of theatricality in the play: only performance can meaningfully bring back the longed-for past; vengeance is inadequate because it merely recapitulates the past vainly in the present. One act of violence replaces another, but the past cannot be restored. Hamlet is so interested in the players (2.2.318–542; 3.2.1–45) because their profession is, in a sense, to restore the past, and their acts of remembrance, unlike revenge, have no apparent dire consequences. The play demonstrates the power of acting, not actions, in making sense of our world. It's the performance of *The Murder of Gonzago* which bestows certainty on Hamlet (3.2.280–1) and perhaps produces guilt in Claudius (3.3.36–72; see Key Passages, **pp. 144–5**). Catherine Belsey compares the experience of the play to mediaeval and early-modern representations of the 'Dance of Death', where the frightening but enticing images of the dead lead the living, both king and beggar, in the dance. Her notion embodies both the play's political 'levelling' and also its playful engagement with that which cannot be described and yet which gives shape and meaning to life: death. She advises us not to try to impose a single critical reading which 'explains' the text, but to let it speak of what cannot be said in the way that it so marvellously does:

> As the history of criticism shows, we can pick up the challenge of *Hamlet* by supplying the thematic content it withholds, telling the *play's* secret, mastering the text to prevent it mastering us ... A possible alternative, however, is to relinquish the desire for closure and to follow the dance-steps of the signifier, permitting the text to take the lead. By this means, we allow the play, like the mortality it depicts, to retain its mystery, its a-thetic[46] knowledge, its triumphant undecidability – and its corresponding desire to seduce.[47]

Like Hawkes, Belsey wishes to remake criticism in a non-authoritarian, text-centred way. If this is the optimistic future of criticism, it seems likely that *Hamlet* will remain a core text for this kind of reading.

44 *Hamlet*, ed. Ann Thompson (London: Thomson, 2006).
45 Anthony B. Dawson, *Shakespeare in Performance: 'Hamlet'* (Manchester: Manchester University Press, 1995), pp. 1–3.
46 By the 'a-thetic' Belsey means that: '[*Hamlet*] withholds as much as it delivers, plays with its readers, luring us down a path of speculation, towards a prohibited knowledge, towards a knowledge of what cannot be known.' Catherine Belsey, *Shakespeare and the Loss of Eden* (Basingstoke and London: Macmillan,1999), p. 169.
47 Belsey (see note 46), p. 172.

Early Critical Reception

Throughout this section, references to *Hamlet* in square brackets are my insertions.

From **James Drake, *The Ancient and Modern Stages Surveyed*** (1699), reprinted in *Critical Responses to 'Hamlet', 1600–1790*, ed. David Farley-Hills (New York: AMS Press, 1997), pp. 23–5; I have modernized the spelling and punctuation

> James Drake (1667–1707) was a political pamphleteer and playwright. Here he is writing to defend *Hamlet* against the attacks of Jeremy Collier, a churchman who attacked the 'profanity' and immorality of the stage at a time when the court had been closely associated with a theatre that was noted for bawdy comedy. Here Drake argues that the play is a morally edifying tale that shows the workings of divine Providence: God will punish the wicked, no matter how great their status in the world.

Whatever defects the critics may find in this fable, the moral of it is excellent. Here was a murder privately committed, strangely discovered, and wonderfully punished. Nothing in antiquity can rival this plot for the admirable distribution of poetic justice. The criminals are not only brought to execution, but they are taken in their own toils.[1] Their own stratagems recoil upon them, and they are involved themselves in that mischief and ruin which they had projected for Hamlet. Polonius by playing the spy meets a fate which was neither expected by nor intended for him. Guildenstern and Rosencrantz, the king's decoys, are counter-plotted, and sent to meet that fate to which they were trepanning the prince.[2] The tyrant[3] himself falls by his own plot, and by the hand of the son of that brother whom he had murdered. Laertes suffers by his own treachery, and dies by a weapon of his own preparing. Thus everyone's crime naturally produces his

---

1 Caught in their own traps.
2 Preparing (?) ('Trepanning' means to drill into the skull of.)
3 Claudius.

punishment, and everyone (the tyrant excepted) commences a wretch almost as soon a villain.[4] The moral of all this is very obvious. It shows us that the greatness of the offender does not qualify the offence, and that no human power or policy are a sufficient guard against the impartial hand and eye of Providence,[5] which defeats their wicked purposes and turns their dangerous machinations upon their own heads. This moral Hamlet itself insinuates to us when he tells Horatio that he owed the discovery of the design against his life in England to a rash indiscreet curiosity, and thence makes this inference [5.2.8–11].

From **Anthony Cooper, Earl of Shaftesbury, Soliloquy, or Advice to an Author** (1710), reprinted in Critical Responses to 'Hamlet', 1600–1790, ed. David Farley-Hills (New York: AMS Press, 1997), p. 32; I have modernized the spelling and punctuation

Shaftesbury (1671–1713) was best known as a philosopher of morality and aesthetics. Like Drake, Shaftesbury claims Hamlet to be a moral play. It is interesting, however, that while he accepts the criticisms of those neo-classical writers who, following the models of ancient literature, castigated Shakespeare for a lack of elegance and decorum in his language, plot and characters (see Critical History, **pp. 29–30**; Contextual Overview, **p. 8**), Shaftesbury nevertheless finds a more genuine tragic feeling in the play than in the plays of his own day. In this he looks forward to critics like Bradley (see Modern Criticism, **pp. 49–53**), who read the ending as producing the 'pity and fear' which the Greek philosopher Aristotle required of the ending of a tragedy.

Notwithstanding his [Shakespeare's] natural rudeness,[1] his unpolished style, his antiquated phrase and wit, his want of method and coherence,[2] and his deficiency in almost all the graces and ornaments of this kind of writing, yet by the justness of his moral, the aptness of his many descriptions, and the plain and natural turn of several of his characters he pleases his audience, and often gains their ear without a single bribe from luxury[3] or vice. That piece of his [Hamlet] which appears most to have affected English hearts, and has perhaps been oftenest acted upon our stage, is almost one continued moral: a series of deep reflections, drawn from one mouth, upon the subject of one single accident and calamity, naturally fitted to move horror and compassion. It may be properly said of this play, if I mistake not, that it only has one character or principal part. It contains no adoration or flattery of the sex;[4] no ranting at the Gods; no blustering heroism; nor any thing of that curious mixture of the fierce and tender which makes the

---

4   Becomes unhappy almost as soon as they become wicked.
5   Christian divine justice, which will ensure that the wicked are punished both in this life and after death.

---

1   Lack of education.
2   Shakespeare does not obey the classical 'unities'; see Contextual Overview, **p. 8**.
3   Sensational or salacious action or language.
4   Women.

hinge of modern tragedy,[5] and nicely varies it between the points of love and honour.[6]

From **Samuel Johnson, Notes to the Edition of Shakespeare's Plays** (1765), reprinted in *Samuel Johnson on Shakespeare*, ed. H. R. Woudhuysen (Harmondsworth: Penguin Books, 1989), pp. 243–4

Samuel Johnson (1709–84) was one of the great eighteenth-century editors of Shakespeare. He brought a rational, logical approach to both editing and criticism, while still observing the mid-eighteenth-century concern with 'sentiment'. Here he takes a rather practical line on the play's structure and plotting, and finds the latter to be lacking not so much because of its refusal to subscribe to neo-classical rules (see Contextual Overview, **p. 8**), but rather because of the implausibility of some of the characters' behaviour, and the inability of the play's ending to provide its audience with that feeling of providential justice which earlier critics admired. Nevertheless, Johnson finds the emotions which the stage action produces of particular interest.

If the dramas of Shakespeare were to be characterized, each by the particular excellence which distinguishes it from the rest, we must allow the tragedy of *Hamlet* the praise of variety. The incidents are so numerous that the argument of the play[1] would make a long tale. The scenes are interchangeably diversified with merriment and solemnity; with merriment that includes judicious and instructive observations and solemnity not strained by poetical violence above the natural sentiments of man. New characters appear from time to time in continual succession, exhibiting various forms of life and particular modes of conversation. The pretended madness of Hamlet causes much mirth, the mournful distraction of Ophelia fills the heart with tenderness and every personage produces the effect intended [4.5.21–73; 153–197; see Key Passages, **pp. 152–3, 156**], from the apparition that in the first act chills the blood with horror [1.1.43–54;129–46; 1.4.37–86; 1.5.1–91, see Key Passages, **pp. 128–32**], to the fop [Osric; 5.1.81–180] in the last that exposes affectation to just contempt.

The conduct is perhaps not wholly secure against objections. The action is indeed for the most part in continual progression, but there are some scenes which neither forward nor retard it. Of the feigned madness of Hamlet there appears no adequate cause, for he does nothing which he might not have done with the reputation of sanity. He plays the madman most when he treats Ophelia with so much rudeness, which seems to be useless and wanton cruelty [3.1.103–151; 3.2.108–119; 240–246, see Key Passages, **p. 142**].

Hamlet is through the whole play rather an instrument than an agent. After he has by the stratagem of the play convicted the King, he makes no attempt to

---

5 Is the key feature of Restoration tragedy (1660–c. 1710).
6 Presents the conflicting claims of both love and honour even-handedly.

---

1 Account of the plot.

punish him and his death is at last effected by an incident which Hamlet has no part in producing.

The catastrophe[2] is not very happily produced; the exchange of weapons is rather an expedient of necessity than a stroke of art. A scheme might easily have been formed to kill Hamlet with the dagger and Laertes with the bowl.

The poet is accused of having shown little regard to poetical justice and may be charged with equal neglect of poetical probability. The apparition left the regions of the dead to little purpose; the revenge which he demanded is not obtained but by the death of him that was required to take it; and the gratification which would arise from the destruction of an usurper and a murderer is abated by the untimely death of Ophelia, the young, the beautiful, the harmless and the pious.

From **Samuel Taylor Coleridge, 'Bristol Lecture'** (1813), reprinted in *Critical Responses to 'Hamlet', 1600–1790*, ed. David Farley-Hills (New York: AMS Press, 1997), pp. 61–3; I have modernized the punctuation

Samuel Taylor Coleridge (1772–1834) was a major Romantic poet and critic. He finds the source of the prince's inaction in a psychological condition. For Coleridge, Hamlet is a man for whom the imagination, in all its ambiguity, seems somehow more real than the external world.

The seeming inconsistencies in the conduct and character of Hamlet have long exercised the conjectural ingenuity of critics; and, as we are always loth to suppose that the cause of defective apprehension is in ourselves, the mystery has too commonly been explained by the very easy process of setting it down as a fact inexplicable, and by resolving the phenomenon into a misgrowth or *lusus*[1] of the capricious and irregular genius of Shakespeare. The shallow and stupid arrogance of these vulgar and indolent decisions I would fain do my best to expose. I believe the character of Hamlet may be traced to Shakespeare's deep and accurate science in mental philosophy. Indeed, that this character must have some connection with the common fundamental laws of our nature may be assumed from the fact, that Hamlet has been the darling of every country in which the literature of England has been fostered. In order to understand him, it is essential that we should reflect on the constitution of our own minds. Man is distinguished from the brute animals in proportion as thought prevails over sense:[2] but in the healthy process of the mind, a balance is constantly maintained between the impressions from outward objects and the inward operations of the intellect; for if there be an overbalance in the contemplative faculty, man thereby becomes the creature of mere meditation, and loses his natural power of action. Now one of Shakespeare's modes of creating characters is, to conceive any one intellectual

---

2 Play's conclusion.

1 A playful puzzle.
2 The senses.

or moral faculty in morbid excess, and then to place himself, Shakespeare, thus mutilated or diseased, under given circumstances. In Hamlet he seems to have wished to exemplify the moral necessity of a due balance between our attention to the objects of our senses, and our meditation on the workings of our minds – an *equilibrium* between the real and the imaginary worlds. In Hamlet this balance is disturbed: his thoughts, and the images of his fancy, are far more vivid than his actual perceptions, and his very perceptions, instantly passing through the *medium* of his contemplations, acquire, as they pass, a form and colour not naturally their own. Hence we see a great, an almost enormous intellectual activity, and a proportionate aversion to real action consequent upon it, with all its symptoms and accompanying qualities. This character Shakespeare places in circumstances, under which it is obliged to act on the spur of the moment: Hamlet is brave and careless of death; but he vacillates from[3] sensibility, and procrastinates from thought, and loses the power of action in the energy of resolve.[4] Thus it is that this tragedy presents a direct contrast to that of *Macbeth*; the one proceeds with the utmost slowness, the other with a crowded and breathless rapidity.

The effect of this overbalance of the imaginative power is beautifully illustrated in the everlasting brooding and superfluous activities of Hamlet's mind, which, unseated from its healthy relation, is constantly occupied with the world within, and abstracted from the world without, giving substance to shadows, and throwing a mist over all common place actualities. It is the nature of thought to be indefinite; definiteness belongs to external imagery alone. Hence it is that the sense of sublimity[5] arises, not from the sight of an outward object, but from the beholder's reflection upon it; not from the sensuous impression, but from the imaginative reflex.[6] Few have seen a celebrated waterfall without feeling something akin to disappointment: it is only subsequently that the image comes back full into the mind, and brings with it a train of grand or beautiful associations. Hamlet feels this; his senses are in a state of trance, and he looks upon external things as hieroglyphics. His soliloquy 'O, that this too too solid flesh would melt, etc.' [1.2.129–59; see Key Passages, **pp.** 126–7] springs from that craving after the indefinite – for that which is not – which most easily besets men of genius; and the self- delusion common to this temper of mind is finely exemplified in the character which Hamlet gives of himself:

> — it cannot be
> But I am pigeon-liver'd, and lack gall
> To make oppression bitter [2.2.573–4].

he mistakes the seeing his chains for the breaking them, delays action till action is of no use, and dies the victim of mere circumstance and accident.

---

3   Out of.
4   Exertions of making his mind up.
5   An awe-inspiring ability to produce powerful emotion; see Critical History, **p. 32**.
6   [Farley-Hills's note.] 'These ideas are derived from *Kant's Critique of Aesthetic Judgement*.

From **William Hazlitt,** *Characters of Shakespeare's Plays* (1817),
reprinted in *The Romantics on Shakespeare,* ed. Jonathan Bate
(Harmondsworth: Penguin Books, 1992), pp. 325–6

William Hazlitt (1778–1830) was an anti-establishment political journalist and
literary critic. If Coleridge saw Hamlet as the admirable victim of his imagination, the more radical contemporary Hazlitt saw the prince as a man over-given
to philosophical inquiry. Unless an action will produce the ideal state which he
regards as solely intellectually justifiable, he will not act. Hazlitt's criticism foreshadows modern critics (for example Ryan – see Modern Criticism, **pp. 185–7**)
in considering Hamlet not as a psychological case study into a generalized
human condition, but as a man reacting to a very specific situation for which
particular conditions of living and thinking apply.

The character of Hamlet stands quite by itself. It is not a character marked by
strength of will or even of passion, but by refinement of thought and sentiment.
Hamlet is as little of the hero as a man can well be: but he is a quick and princely
novice, full of high enthusiasm and quick sensibility – the sport of circumstances,
questioning with fortune and refining on his own feelings, and forced from
the natural bias of his disposition by the strangeness of his situation. He seems
incapable of deliberate action, and is only hurried into extremities on the spur
of the occasion, when he has no time to reflect, as in the scene where he kills
Polonius [3.4.22–6], and again, where he alters the letters which Rosencrantz and
Guildenstern are taking with them to England, purporting his death [5.2.29–53].
At other times, when he is most bound to act, he remains puzzled, undecided, and
sceptical, dallies with his purposes, till the occasion is lost, and finds out some
pretence to lapse into indolence and thoughtfulness again. For this reason he
refuses to kill the King when he is at his prayers, and by a refinement in malice,
which is in truth only an excuse for his own want of resolution, defers his revenge
to a more fatal opportunity, when he shall be engaged in some act 'that has no
relish of salvation in it' [3.3.92; see Key Passages, **p. 145**].

   He is the prince of philosophical speculators; and because he cannot have his
revenge perfect, according to the most refined idea his wish can form, he declines
it altogether. So he scruples to trust the suggestions of the ghost [2.2.594–600;
see Key Passages, **p. 135**], contrives the scene of the play to have surer proof of his
uncle's guilt, and then rests satisfied with this confirmation of his suspicions, and
the success of his experiment, instead of acting upon it. Yet he is sensible of his
own weakness, taxes himself with it, and tries to reason himself out of it . . .

   The moral perfection of this character has been called in question, we think, by
those who did not understand it. It is more interesting than according to rules;
amiable, though not faultless. The ethical delineations of 'that noble and liberal
casuist'[1] (as Shakespeare has well been called) do not exhibit the drab-coloured
quakerism of morality. [. . .] The neglect of punctilious exactness in his behaviour

---

1   A solver of problems of conscience with clever or false reasoning. The phrase is a quotation from
    Charles Lamb's *Specimens of English Dramatic Poets* (1808).

either partakes of the 'license of the time,' or else belongs to the very excess of refinement in his character, which makes the common rules of life, as well as his own purposes, sit loose upon him. He may be said to be amenable only to the tribunal of his own thoughts, and is too much taken up with the airy world of contemplation to lay as much stress on the practical consequences of things. His habitual principles of action are unhinged and out of joint[2] with the time.

2   Hamlet's phrase at 1.5.196.

Modern Criticism

From **Sigmund Freud, *The Interpretation of Dreams,*** ed. James
Strachey (first published 1900), in *The Complete Psychoanalytical Works of
Sigmund Freud*, trans. James Strachey (London: The Hogarth Press, 1953),
vol. 4, pp. 264–5

Sigmund Freud (1856–1939) was the founder of psychoanalysis. From his
reading of literature, among other sources, Freud developed his idea of the
'Oedipus Complex'. In Sophocles' Greek tragedy *Oedipus The King* (c. 430BC),
the hero, who had grown up apart from his parents, unwittingly kills his father
and marries his mother. Freud postulated that the future psychological health of
an adult man depended on his being able to overcome, and to repress fully in his
subconscious, two powerful infant desires: to have sex with his mother, and to
kill his father. Hamlet's inability to carry out the ghost's commands, for which
the text offers no clear reason, are thus explained: Hamlet's melancholy is a
neurosis caused by his unresolved incestuous feelings towards his mother; furthermore, he cannot kill Claudius because Claudius has taken on the role which
the prince still wants – that of murderer of Old Hamlet. Freud's interpretation
of Hamlet is evident in the film versions of Laurence Olivier (1948) and Franco
Zeffirelli (1990) (see The Work in Performance, **pp. 103–5** and **pp. 105–7**).

Another of the great creations of tragic poetry, Shakespeare's *Hamlet*, has its
roots in the same soil as *Oedipus Rex*. But the changed treatment of the same
material reveals the whole difference in the mental life of these two widely separated epochs of civilization: the secular advance of repression in the emotional life
of mankind. In the *Oedipus* the child's wishful phantasy that underlies it is
brought into the open and realized as it would be in a dream. In *Hamlet* it remains
repressed; and—just as in the case of a neurosis—we only learn of its existence
from its inhibiting consequences. Strangely enough, the overwhelming effect produced by the more modern tragedy has turned out to be compatible with the fact
that people have remained completely in the dark as to the hero's character. The
play is built up on Hamlet's hesitations over fulfilling the task of revenge that is
assigned to him; but its text offers no reasons or motives for these hesitations and

an immense variety of attempts at interpreting them have failed to produce a result. According to the view which was originated by Goethe and is still the prevailing one to-day, Hamlet represents the type of man whose power of direct action is paralysed by an excessive development of intellect.[1] (He is 'sicklied o'er with the pale cast of thought' [3.1.85].) According to another view, the dramatist has tried to portray a pathologically irresolute character which might be classed as neurasthenic. The plot of the drama shows us, however, that Hamlet is far from being represented as a person incapable of taking any action. We see him doing so on two occasions: first in a sudden outburst of temper, when he runs his sword through the eavesdropper behind the arras, and secondly in a premeditated and even crafty fashion, when, with all the callousness of a Renaissance prince, he sends the two courtiers to the death that had been planned for himself. What is it, then, that inhibits him in fulfilling the task set him by his father's ghost? The answer, once again, is that it is the peculiar nature of the task. Hamlet is able to do anything—except take vengeance on the man who did away with his father and took that father's place with the mother, the man who shows him the repressed wishes of his own childhood realized. Thus the loathing which should drive him on to revenge is replaced in him by self-reproaches, by scruples of conscience, which remind him that he himself is literally no better than the sinner whom he is to punish. Here I have translated into conscious terms what was bound to remain unconscious in Hamlet's mind; and if anyone is inclined to call him a hysteric, I can only accept the fact as one that is implied by my interpretation. The distaste for sexuality expressed by Hamlet in his conversation with Ophelia fits in very well with this [3.1.89–150] [. . .]

From **A. C. Bradley, *Shakespearean Tragedy*** (1904) (Harmondsworth: Penguin Books, 1991), pp. 49–51; pp. 116–8; pp. 125–6

A. C. Bradley (1851–1935) was originally a philosopher who studied the work of the German idealist G. W. F. Hegel (1770–1831), and the Hegelian idea that human history is continuing conflict between unseen cosmic forces of good and evil is evident in the first extract below, from Lecture I, where Bradley sets out his views on the essence of Shakespearean tragedy. Later critics attacked Bradley's tendency to write about the text of the plays as if they were evidence for insights into the psychologies of characters who had a real existence. The extracts from Lecture III show Bradley explaining the true source and nature of the mental condition that prevents the prince from taking action. Bradley finds it natural that Hamlet should loath all women after his mother's hasty remarriage, and the same implicit misogyny can also be found in another important twentieth-century response to the play, that of T. S. Eliot (see Modern Criticism, **pp. 53–5**).

1   Johann Wolfgang von Goethe, *Wilhelm Meister's Apprenticeship* (1795–6), ed. and trans. Eric A. Blackhall (Princeton NJ: Princeton University Press, 1995), pp. 127–9; 144–6.

[From Lecture I] [There] are aspects of the tragic world at least as clearly marked as those which, taken alone, suggest the idea of fate. And the idea which they in their turn, when taken alone, may suggest, is that of an order which does not indeed award 'poetic justice', but which reacts through the necessity of its own 'moral' nature both against attacks made upon it and against failure to conform to it. Tragedy, on this view, is the exhibition of that convulsive reaction; and the fact that the spectacle does not leave us rebellious or desperate is due to a more or less distinct perception that the tragic suffering and death arise from collision, not with a fate or blank power, but with a moral power, a power akin to all that we admire and revere in the characters themselves. This perception produces something like a feeling of acquiescence in the catastrophe, though it neither leads us to pass judgement on the characters nor diminishes the pity, the fear, and the sense of waste, which their struggle, suffering and fall evoke. And, finally, this view seems quite able to do justice to those aspects of the tragic fact which give rise to the idea of fate. They would appear as various expressions of the fact that the moral order acts not capriciously or like a human being, but from the necessity of its nature, or, if we prefer the phrase, by general laws – a necessity or law which of course knows no exception and is as 'ruthless' as fate.

It is impossible to deny to this view a large measure of truth. And yet without some amendment it can hardly satisfy. For it does not include the whole of the facts, and therefore does not wholly correspond with the impressions they produce. Let it be granted that the system or order which shows itself omnipotent against individuals is, in the sense explained, moral. Still – at any rate for the eye of sight – the evil against which it asserts itself, and the persons whom this evil inhabits, are not really something outside the order, so that they can attack it or fail to conform to it; they are within it and a part of it. [. . .]

Nor does the idea of a moral order asserting itself against attack or want of conformity answer in full to our feelings regarding the tragic character. We do not think of Hamlet merely as failing to meet its demand [. . .] What we feel corresponds quite as much to the idea that they are *its* parts, expressions, products; that in their defect or evil *it* is untrue to its soul of goodness, and falls into conflict and collision with itself; that, in making them suffer and waste themselves, *it* suffers and wastes itself; and that when, to save its life and regain peace from this intestinal struggle, it casts them out, it has lost a part of its own substance – a part more dangerous and unquiet, but far more valuable and nearer to its heart, than that which remains – a Fortinbras, [for example] [. . .] There is no tragedy in its expulsion of evil: the tragedy is that this involves the waste of good. Thus we are left at last with an idea showing two sides or aspects which we can neither separate nor reconcile. The whole or order against which the individual part shows itself powerless seems to be animated by a passion for perfection: we cannot otherwise explain its behaviour towards evil. Yet it appears to engender this evil within itself, and in its effort to overcome and expel it is agonised with pain, and driven to mutilate its own substance and to lose not only evil but priceless good. That this idea, though very different from the idea of a blank fate, is no solution of the riddle of life is obvious; but why should we expect it to be such a solution? [. . .] He was writing tragedy, and tragedy would not be tragedy if it were not a painful mystery. Nor can he be said even to point distinctly, like some writers of tragedy, in any direction where a solution might lie. We find a few references to gods or God, to the influence of the stars, to another life: some of them certainly, all of them perhaps, merely dramatic – appropriate to the person from whose lips they fall. A ghost comes from Purgatory to impart a secret out of the reach of its hearer who presently meditates on the question whether the sleep of death is dreamless. Accidents once or twice remind us strangely of the words, 'There's a divinity that shapes our ends' [5.2.10]. More important are other impressions. Sometimes from the very furnace of affliction a conviction seems borne to us that somehow, if we could see it, this agony counts as nothing against the heroism and love which appear in it and thrill our hearts. Sometimes we are driven to cry out that these mighty or heavenly spirits who perish are too great for the little space in which they move, and that they vanish not into nothingness but into freedom. Sometimes from these sources and from others comes a presentiment, formless but haunting and even profound, that all the fury of conflict, with its waste and woe, is less than half the truth, even an illusion, 'such stuff as dreams are made on'.[1] But these faint and scattered intimations that the tragic world, being but a fragment of a whole beyond our vision, must needs be a contradiction and no ultimate truth, avail nothing to interpret the mystery. We remain confronted with the inexplicable fact, or the no less inexplicable appearance, of a world travailing for perfection, but bringing to birth, together with glorious good, an evil which it is able to overcome only by self-torture and self-waste. And this fact or appearance is tragedy. [. . .]

[From Lecture III] [U]nder conditions of a peculiar kind, Hamlet's reflectiveness certainly might prove dangerous to him, and his genius might even (to exaggerate a little) become his doom. Suppose that violent shock to his moral being of which I spoke [his mother's remarriage]; and suppose that under this shock, any possible action being denied to him, he began to sink into melancholy; then, no doubt, his imaginative and generalizing habit of mind might extend the effects of this shock through his whole being and mental world. And if, the state of melancholy being thus deepened and fixed, a sudden demand for difficult and decisive action in a matter connected with the melancholy arose, this state might well have for one of its symptoms an endless and futile mental dissection of the required deed. And, finally, the futility of this process, and the shame of his delay, would further weaken him and enslave him to his melancholy still more. Thus the speculative habit would be *one* indirect cause of the morbid state which hindered action; and it would also reappear in a degenerate form as one of the *symptoms* of this morbid state.

Now this is what actually happens in the play. Turn to the first words Hamlet utters when he is alone; turn, that is to say, to the place where the author is likely to indicate his meaning most plainly [1.2.129–37; see Key Passages, **p. 127**]. What do you hear? [. . .]

Here are a sickness of life, and even a longing for death, so intense that nothing stands between Hamlet and suicide except religious awe. And what has caused them? The rest of the soliloquy so thrusts the answer upon us that it might seem

---

1   *The Tempest*, 4.1.157.

impossible to miss it. It was not his father's death; that doubtless brought deep grief, but mere grief for some one loved and lost does not make a noble spirit loathe the world as a place full only of things rank and gross. It was not the vague suspicion that we know Hamlet felt. Still less was it the loss of the crown; for though the subserviency of the electors might well disgust him,[2] there is not a reference to the subject in the soliloquy, nor any sign elsewhere that it greatly occupied his mind. It was the moral shock of the sudden ghastly disclosure of his mother's true nature, falling on him when his heart was aching with love, and his body doubtless was weakened by sorrow. And it is essential, however disagreeable, to realize the nature of this shock. It matters little here whether Hamlet's age was twenty or thirty: in either case his mother was a matron of mature years. All his life he had believed in her, we may be sure, as such a son would. He had seen her not merely devoted to his father, but hanging on him like a newly-wedded bride, hanging on him.

> As if increase of appetite had grown
> By what it fed on. [1.2.144–5]

He had seen her following his body 'like Niobe; all tears' [1.2.149]. And then within a month – 'O God! [. . .] a beast would have mourned longer' [1.2.150–1] – she married again, and married Hamlet's uncle, a man utterly contemptible and loathsome in his eyes; married him in what to Hamlet was incestuous wedlock;[3] married him not for any reason of state, nor even out of old family affection, but in such a way that her son was forced to see in her action not only an astounding shallowness of feeling but an eruption of coarse sensuality, 'rank and gross' [1.2.136],[4] speeding post-haste to its horrible delight. Is it possible to conceive an experience more desolating to a man such as we have seen Hamlet to be; and is its result anything but perfectly natural? It brings bewildered horror, then loathing, then despair of human nature. His whole mind is poisoned. He can never see Ophelia in the same light again: she is a woman, and his mother is a woman: if she mentions the word 'brief' to him, the answer drops from his lips like venom, 'as woman's love' [3.2.148]. The last words of the soliloquy, which is *wholly* concerned with this subject, are,

> But break, my heart, for I must hold my tongue! [1.2.159]

He can do nothing. He must lock in his heart, not any suspicion of his uncle that moves obscurely there, but that horror and loathing; and if his heart ever found relief, it was when those feelings, mingled with the love that never died out in him,

---

2 Danish kings were elected by the nobility, though this fact is not referred to in the play.

3 [Bradley's note.] This aspect of the matter leaves *us* comparatively unaffected, but Shakespeare evidently means it to be of importance. The Ghost speaks of it twice, and Hamlet thrice (once in his last furious words to the King). If, as we must suppose, the marriage was universally admitted to be incestuous, the corrupt acquiescence of the court and the electors to the crown would naturally have a strong effect on Hamlet's mind.

4 [Bradley's note.] It is most significant that the metaphor of this soliloquy reappears in Hamlet's adjuration to his mother: 'Repent what's past; avoid what is to come; / And do not spread the compost on the weeds / To make them ranker' (3.4.152–4; see Key Passages, p. 150).

poured themselves forth in a flood as he stood in his mother's chamber beside his father's marriage-bed.[5] [. . .]

I have dwelt thus at length on Hamlet's melancholy because, from the psychological point of view, it is the centre of the tragedy, and to omit it from consideration or to underrate its intensity is to make Shakespeare's story unintelligible. But the psychological point of view is not equivalent to the tragic; and, having once given its due weight to the fact of Hamlet's melancholy, we may freely admit, or rather may be anxious to insist, that this pathological condition would excite but little, if any, tragic interest if it were not the condition of a nature distinguished by that speculative genius on which the Schlegel–Coleridge type of theory lays stress.[6]

From **T. S. Eliot, 'Hamlet'** (1919), in *Selected Essays* (London: Faber and Faber, 1951), pp. 145–6

The poet and critic T. S. Eliot (1888–1965) found the play unsatisfying as a work of art. He could not accept that the emotion Hamlet displays is appropriate for its apparent cause: his mother's hasty remarriage. Shakespeare fails to make Gertrude an object adequate to explain Hamlet's feelings, which is why Hamlet is incapable of any action that will satisfy him. Eliot's near-Freudian identification of a troubled and troubling subconscious working beneath the surface of Hamlet's speeches, and of the play itself, has led other critics to probe the play's puzzling qualities from a psychoanalytical point of view.

[P]robably more people have thought *Hamlet* a work of art because they found it interesting, than have found it interesting because it is a work of art. It is the 'Mona Lisa' of literature.

The grounds of *Hamlet's* failure are not immediately obvious. Mr. Robertson is undoubtedly correct in concluding that the essential emotion of the play is the feeling of a son towards a guilty mother:

'[Hamlet's] tone is that of one who has suffered tortures on the score of his mother's degradation. . . . The guilt of a mother is an almost intolerable motive for drama, but it had to be maintained and emphasized to supply a psychological solution, or rather a hint of one.'

This, however, is by no means the whole story. It is not merely the 'guilt of a mother' that cannot be handled as Shakespeare handled the suspicion of Othello, the infatuation of Antony, or the pride of Coriolanus. The subject might conceivably have expanded into a tragedy like these, intelligible, self-complete, in the sunlight. *Hamlet*, like the sonnets, is full of some stuff that the writer could not drag to light, contemplate, or manipulate into art. [. . .]

---

5   [Bradley's note.] If the reader will now look at the only speech of Hamlet's that precedes the soliloquy, and is more than one line in length – the speech beginning 'Seems, madam! nay, it *is*' – he will understand what, surely, when first we come to it, sounds very strange and almost boastful. It is not, in effect, about Hamlet himself at all; it is about his mother (I do not mean that it is intentionally and consciously so; and still less that she understood it so).

6   See Critical History, **pp. 31–2** and Early Critical Reception, **pp. 44–6**.

The only way of expressing emotion in the form of art is by finding an 'objective correlative'; in other words, a set of objects, a situation, a chain of events which shall be the formula of that *particular* emotion; such that when the external facts, which must terminate in sensory experience, are given, the emotion is immediately evoked. If you examine any of Shakespeare's more successful tragedies, you will find this exact equivalence; you will find that the state of mind of Lady Macbeth walking in her sleep has been communicated to you by a skilful accumulation of imagined sensory impressions; the words of Macbeth on hearing of his wife's death strike us as if, given the sequence of events, these words were automatically released by the last event in the series. The artistic 'inevitability' lies in this complete adequacy of the external to the emotion; and this is precisely what is deficient in *Hamlet*. Hamlet (the man) is dominated by an emotion which is inexpressible, because it is in *excess* of the facts as they appear. And the supposed identity of Hamlet with his author is genuine to this point: that Hamlet's bafflement at the absence of objective equivalent to his feelings is a prolongation of the bafflement of his creator in the face of his artistic problem. Hamlet is up against the difficulty that his disgust is occasioned by his mother, but that his mother is not an adequate equivalent for it; his disgust envelops and exceeds her. It is thus a feeling which he cannot understand; he cannot objectify it, and it therefore remains to poison life and obstruct action. None of the possible actions can satisfy it; and nothing that Shakespeare can do with the plot can express Hamlet for him. And it must be noticed that the very nature of the *données*[1] of the problem precludes objective equivalence. To have heightened the criminality of Gertrude would have been to provide the formula for a totally different emotion in Hamlet; it is just *because* her character is so negative and insignificant that she arouses in Hamlet the feeling which she is incapable of representing.

The 'madness' of Hamlet lay to Shakespeare's hand; in the earlier play[2] a simple ruse, and to the end, we may presume, understood as a ruse by the audience. For Shakespeare it is less than madness and more than feigned. The levity of Hamlet, his repetition of phrase, his puns, are not part of a deliberate plan of dissimulation, but a form of emotional relief. In the character Hamlet it is the buffoonery of an emotion which can find no outlet in action; in the dramatist it is the buffoonery of an emotion which he cannot express in art. The intense feeling, ecstatic or terrible, without an object or exceeding its object, is something which every person of sensibility has known; it is doubtless a subject of study for pathologists. It often occurs in adolescence: the ordinary person puts these feelings to sleep, or trims down his feelings to fit the business world; the artist keeps them alive by his ability to intensify the world to his emotions. [. . .] We must simply admit that here Shakespeare tackled a problem which proved too much for him. Why he attempted it at all is an insoluble puzzle; under compulsion of what experience he attempted to express the inexpressibly horrible, we cannot ever know. [. . .] We should have to understand things which Shakespeare did not understand himself.

---

1   Given circumstances.
2   The so-called 'Ur- *Hamlet*' (see Contextual Overview, p. 7).

From **John Dover Wilson,** What Happens in 'Hamlet' (Cambridge: Cambridge University Press, 1935), pp. 217–20

> John Dover Wilson (1881–1969) was a popular and influential English critic who tended to take a robust, assertively 'common sense' attitude to Shakespearean criticism. In this extract he argues, in opposition to the speculations of Freud, Bradley and Eliot (see Modern Criticism, **pp. 48–55**), that we should treat the Prince as a purely literary and dramatic creation for the stage.

We are driven, therefore, to conclude with [. . .] Bradley [. . .] and other critics that Shakespeare meant us to imagine Hamlet suffering some kind of mental disorder throughout the play. Directly, however, such critics begin trying to define the exact nature of the disorder, they go astray. Its immediate origin cannot be questioned; it is caused, as we have seen, by the burden which fate lays upon his shoulders. We are not, however, at liberty to go outside the frame of the play and seek remoter origins in his past history. It is now well known, for instance, that a break-down like Hamlet's is often due to seeds of disturbance planted in infancy and brought to evil fruition under the influence of mental strain of some kind later in life. Had Shakespeare been composing Hamlet to-day, he might conceivably have given us a hint of such an infantile complex. But he knew nothing of these matters and to write as if he did is to beat the air. We may go further. It is entirely misleading to attempt to describe Hamlet's state of mind in terms of modern psychology at all, not merely because Shakespeare did not think in these terms, but because—once again—Hamlet is a character in a play, not in history. He is part only, if the most important part, of an artistic masterpiece, of what is perhaps the most successful piece of dramatic illusion the world has ever known. And at no point of the composition is the illusion more masterly contrived than in this matter of his distraction.

In Hamlet Shakespeare sets out to create a hero labouring under mental infirmity, just as later in Macbeth he depicted a hero afflicted by moral infirmity, or in Othello a hero tortured by an excessive and morbid jealousy. Hamlet struggles against his weakness, and the struggle is in great measure the ground-work of his tragedy. But though he struggles in vain, and is in the end brought to disaster, a disaster of his own making and involving his own house and that of Polonius, we are never allowed to feel that his spirit is vanquished until "the potent poison quite o'er-crows" it [5.2.358; see Key Passages, **p. 168**]. Had he been represented as a mere madman, we should of course have felt this; he would have ceased to be a hero and, while retaining our pity, would have forfeited our sympathy, our admiration—and our censure. Ophelia exclaims,

O, what a noble mind is here o'erthrown! [3.1.152]

We know better: we realise that the mind is impaired, but we do not doubt for a moment that its nobility remains untouched; we see his sovereign reason often

Like sweet bells jangled, out of tune and harsh, [3.1.160]

yet all the while it retains its sovereignty and can recall its sweetness. There may be contradiction here; but we are not moving in the realm of logic. From the point of view of analytic psychology such a character may even seem a monster of inconsistency. This does not matter, if here it also seems to spectators in the theatre to be more convincingly life-like than any other character in literature. For most critics have agrees that Hamlet is one of the greatest and most fascinating of Shakespeare's creations; that he is a study in genius. Shakespeare, in short, accomplished that which he intended; he wrote a supreme tragedy. In poetic tragedy we contemplate beings greater than ourselves, greater than it is possible for man to be, enduring and brought to a calamitous end by sorrow or affliction or weakness of character which we should find unendurable; and we contemplate all this with unquestioning assent and with astonishment that deepens to awe. In the making of Hamlet, therefore, Shakespeare's task was not to produce a being psychologically explicable or consistent, but one who would evoke the affection, the wonder and the tears of his audience, and would yet be accepted as entirely human.

From **Terence Hawkes, 'Telmah',** in *That Shakespeherian Rag: Essays on a Critical Process* (London: Methuen, 1986), pp. 92–101; 117–8

The influence of Bradley and Dover Wilson remained strong until the arrival of critical theory in universities in the 1970s began to transform literary studies (see Critical History, **pp. 34–5**). Terence Hawkes is a left-wing critic who finds a radical, contradictory meaning in the play, existing alongside the conventional accounts of plot and character which might embody more conservative political values. Hawkes finds in the performance of *Hamlet* a work which is struggling against its usual interpretation. Rather than moving directly forwards to a single, determinate conclusion, the play, according to Hawkes, is constantly looking back, revising and replaying itself, and reaches no definite end. Hawkes calls this *Telmah*, *Hamlet* backwards. In *Telmah*, Claudius, the uncle who usurps the father role, becomes central to the whole play. In a central section of the essay which I have omitted for reasons of space, Hawkes describes the terrible shock which John Dover Wilson experienced in 1917, at the moment of the Russian Revolution. Wilson read the critic W. W. Greg's suggestion that the players' re-enactment of Old Hamlet's murder fails to produce a trace of guilty recognition in the watching King. In Wilson's mind, writes Hawkes, Greg's reading is an insurrection against the status quo of a similar kind to and as shocking as that of the striking munitions workers whom he is about to visit as a wartime government inspector. In suggesting that the ghost may have lied about the circumstances of the murder, Greg undermines and subverts Dover Wilson's own reading of this iconic play's moral structure. One of the insights of the new critical theory in the 1980s proposed that all narratives suggest a view of the world which makes certain kinds of power or inequality seem 'natural'. Hawkes's point is that all acts of interpretation have this 'ideological' function: they seek to impose a single authoritative reading on what is, by its very nature, something fluid and open to many different meanings; something about which the last word can never be said.

It begins without words. A man walks out on to the stage and takes up his position, evidently as a sentry. Another man, also evidently a sentry, follows shortly after him. Approaching the first man, the second suddenly halts, seemingly apprehensive and afraid. He quickly raises the long military spear he carries, the partisan, and brings it into an offensive position. That movement – before a word is spoken – immediately pushes the action forward: it enters a different dimension. A mystery has been posited (why are the sentries nervous, why do they make elementary mistakes of military discipline?) and a story starts to unfold.

It ends without words. Two dead bodies are taken up. A troop of soldiers, among them four captains, carries them off, ceremonially and to martial music, after which we hear a 'peal of ordnance'. These sounds, music, the cannon, also forward the action. They imply a new, ordered world of correct military discipline and principled yet firm political rule that will now replace a disordered society riven by betrayal and murder.

At the beginning, it is immediately noticeable that the military are not in complete control. Fundamental errors occur. Barnardo's challenge (and the play's first line), 'Who's there?', is uttered, as Francisco immediately points out, correcting him, by the wrong sentry. The password, 'Long live the King!' [1.1.3; see Key Passages, p. 120], could hardly be less appropriate: we know that a king has recently not lived long, and that another incumbent will soon cease to live.

At the end, similar misconceptions abound. We know, from what we have seen, that the story Horatio proposes to recount to the 'yet unknowing world' [5.2.383–91; see Key Passages, p. 169] [. . .] fails adequately to reflect what happened. It was not as simple, as like an 'ordinary' revenge play as that. His solemnity – 'All this can I/Truly deliver' – mocks at the subtleties, the innuendoes, the contradictions, the imperfectly realized motives and sources for action that have been exhibited to us. We are hardly surprised when Fortinbras attempts to sum up Hamlet's potential:

> he was likely, had he been put on,
> To have prov'd most royal [5.2.402–3; see Key Passages, p. 170]

– but his account must, surely, wring a tiny gasp of disbelief from us. Nobody, so far as we have seen (and of course Fortinbras has not seen what we have seen), was likely to have proved less royal. Fortinbras's own claim to authority is decisively undermined by this poor judgement which must strike us as fundamentally misconceived. The 'friends' to this present ground, the 'liegemen' to this latest Dane (he is of course 'wrong' even in that, being a Norwegian) may well find the future just as bleak as their mistaken predecessors.

At the beginning, the action is overshadowed by war: by the 'fair and warlike form' [1.1.50] (the Ghost) who dominates it even in his absence. There is much talk of preparation for war.

At the end, the warlike form of Fortinbras also hangs over the action in his absence: he finally obtrudes heralded by a 'warlike noise' [5.2.354; see Key Passages, p. 168]. Military rule, by a foreigner, is what lies in store for the Danish state. The war promised at the beginning has not taken place, but at the end the results are the same as if it had.

At the beginning a dead king's presence overhangs the action and the nervousness of the sentries evokes it. At the end another dead king's presence overhangs the action, and is evoked by those final cannons, whose sound has been associated with him throughout.

There is even a mirror reflection of phrases. At the beginning Barnardo comments, 'How now, Horatio? You tremble and look pale' [1.1.56]. At the end, Hamlet's words echo to a larger audience: 'You that look pale and tremble at this chance' [5.2.339; see Key Passages, p. 168].

It would be wrong to make too much of 'symmetries' of this sort, and I mention them only because, once recognized, they help, however slightly, to undermine our inherited notion of *Hamlet* as a structure that runs a satisfactorily linear, sequential course from a firmly established and well-defined beginning through a clearly placed and signalled middle to a causally related and logically determined end which, planted in the beginning, develops, or grows out of it.

Like all symmetries, the ones I have pointed to suggest, not linearity, but circularity: a cyclical and recursive movement wholly at odds with the progressive, incremental ordering that, our society, dominated perhaps by a pervasive metaphor of the production line, tends to think of as appropriate to art as to everything else.

If we add to this the judgement that the beginning of *Hamlet* also operates, in a quite perplexing sense, as an ending (the spear's movement forces us to look back to events that have already occurred: the Ghost presupposes a complexity of happenings that lead to its current ghostliness), and that the ending in effect constitutes a beginning (the cannons at the end make us look forward to the new order of Fortinbras, as much as back: Fortinbras's future rule is clearly presaged as the play ends), the complexity of the whole business begins to proliferate.

We can even ask, as amateurs in playhouse dynamics, and in respect of the experience of a live audience in the theatre, when does the play *effectively* begin? Is it when the first sentry walks out on to the stage? Or has the play already begun in our mind's eye as we enter the theatre, leave our house, get up on that morning, buy our ticket some days/weeks ago? In our society, in which *Hamlet* finds itself embedded in the ideology in a variety of roles, the play has, for complex social and historical reasons, always already begun. And on to its beginning we have always already imprinted a knowledge of its course of action, and its ending. [. . .]

The modern curtain call functions of course very firmly as part of the planned production, fully rehearsed in all its complicated entrances and exits. This in itself gives us a sense of the force of the modern director's feeling that he must *seal* finally and inescapably the 'interpretation' he has thrust on and through the play. Yet the curtain call cannot be thus simply nailed down any more than the play can be thus simply sealed up and made subject to the director's will, however hard he tries. In a way that makes it representative of the play at large, the curtain call slips from under the director's fingers to generate its own wider and wilder implications. Here the play's dead acquire a kind of life once more. Here, most significantly, any apparent movement of the play in one direction halts, and it begins to roll decisively in the opposite direction (if only towards the next performance, when its 'beginning' will emerge again from these smiling actors). In short, the sense of straight, purposive, linear motion forward through the play – the sense required by most 'interpretations' of it – evaporates at the moment of the curtain call, and we sense an opposing current.

In so far as that current connects decisively with elements or aspects of the play already noticed, and in so far as its force seeks to roll the play backwards, reinforcing its recursive mode, making it, as it were, move only unwillingly and haltingly forward, constantly, even as it does so, looking over its own shoulder, then I propose to recognize it and for the sake of convenience and argument to name it in relation to *Hamlet*. I call it *Telmah*: *Hamlet* backwards.

In search of *Telmah*, we can begin by noticing the extent to which looking backwards, re-vision, or re-interpretation, the running of events over again out of their time-sequence, ranks, in effect, as a fundamental aspect of *Hamlet*. Sub-sequence, posteriority, these are the substantive modes of the opening, generating phrases like 'has this thing appear'd *again* tonight', 'this dreaded sight *twice seen of us*', 'What we have *two nights* seen', 'Thus *twice before*, and jump at this dead hour, . . . hath he gone by our watch' [1.1.24, 28,[1] 68] and so on, which eventually provoke the great retailing of past events offered by Horatio as preface to the Ghost's second appearance [1.1.129–45].

This leads to the full story of Young Fortinbras and so by backward-looking implication brings in, from behind, Hamlet [1.1.98–110; see Key Passages, **pp. 123–4**]. [. . .]

Then, as a sort of climax of this revising, we find Claudius's great revisionary proposal, his reinterpretation of the past which leads up to his own present position [1.2.1–18]. [. . .]

Throughout, it seems to me, the audience of *Hamlet* might legitimately feel that it is being buttonholed, cajoled, persuaded by participants in the play to look back, to 'revise', to see things again in particular ways, to 'read' or inter-pret them along specific lines and to the exclusion of others. It is a procedure notoriously mocked by Hamlet himself at the expense of Polonius in a famously deconstructive moment [3.2.366–73] [. . .]

– and easily its most memorable manifestation occurs when the Ghost buttonholes the Prince with a peculiarly insistent version of the murder [1.5.59–73; see Key Passages, **p. 131**]. [. . .]

These slow-motion 'action replays' of past events become a feature of the play. It seems constantly to 'revise' itself in this way and this serves to pull back against any 'forward' progressive movement which it might otherwise appear to instigate.

On a larger scale, a series of insistent thematic rhythms seems to run counter to or – better word – syncopate with those apparently fostered by the play's sequen-tial development. The death of fathers, which Claudius stresses as a 'common theme' – one which has reason's backing in his assertion 'this must be so'

---

1   Hawkes uses the Second Quarto reading here; see Key Passages, **pp. 113–15**.

> But you must know your father lost a father,
> That father lost, lost his [1.2.89–90]

– nevertheless begins to bulk disconcertingly large. It is almost a case of paternal overkill. By the middle of the play our attention has been forcefully drawn to the death of no fewer than *five* fathers: King Fortinbras; King Hamlet; Polonius; Priam; and Gonzago, the Player King. In three of the cases an avenging son presents himself: Fortinbras; Hamlet; Laertes. The pattern seems to push Hamlet, in his role as revenger, into the foreground. But then we notice the countervailing pattern hinted at by and available within the same structure: that which focuses on the dead father's brother, who, as *uncle* to the son, controls and redirects the son's revenging energies. The clearest case involves Young Fortinbras, whose uncle Norway has succeeded to the throne, whereupon he reintegrates the displaced Young Fortinbras into the society. This rhythm is underscored when Claudius tries to perform exactly the same operation in respect of Hamlet: as uncle who has taken over the throne, he tries famously to reintegrate the displaced Hamlet into the society. And it is underscored again when, the operation having failed with Hamlet, Claudius assumes the avuncular role in respect of Laertes after Polonius's death and, again famously, redirects his revenging energy and integrates him into the society. In short, the death of all these fathers serves to establish and to sound a counter-balancing 'avuncular' chord that reverberates deep within the play's harmonic structure.

The avuncular function seen in opposition to the paternal one then becomes a palpable aspect of the range of themes *Hamlet* deploys. The opposition derives from and works consistently with traditional European conceptualizations which construct the father as a figure of stern discipline and authority, and the uncle as a contrary figure of laxity and good humour. Claudius notoriously abrogates this disposition of polarities (Hamlet's bitter description of him as 'my uncle–father' [2.2.372] reinforces the collapse of meaningful categories) and thus commits a transgression as destructive as the one collaterally perpetrated by Gertrude. [. . .]

The insistent, nagging quality of these aspects of the play acts as an apparently 'disruptive' element in *Hamlet* because it finally serves to promote Claudius. Its 'catchy' pulse wins the attention, and draws it away from the Prince. Claudius ceases to be the simple stage-villain described by the Ghost and required by the smoothing-over process of interpretation that linear progression demands. He has many more than one role, and these are intricate and manifold. He functions as brother (even the primal brother, Cain, as he himself suggests [3.3.37; see Key Passages, **p. 144**], father, in a legal and political sense to Hamlet, lover and later husband to Gertrude, murderer of King Hamlet, monarch, and political head of state. In a sense, all these roles congregate within his enormously forceful role of uncle on the basis of which his opposition to Hamlet is determined. He becomes, as the play terms him, no simple villain, but a complex, compelling figure, Hamlet's 'mighty opposite', whose mightiness constantly tugs back, recursively, against the smooth flow of a play that bears, perhaps surprisingly, only the Prince's name. It is not insignificant that, at the play's most recursive moment, in the performance of another play, the murderer (Lucianus) is clearly and coolly presented as a nephew, murdering his uncle. In this play-within-the-play, right at the centre of *Hamlet*, *Telmah* disconcertingly surfaces.

The Mousetrap marks *Hamlet*'s most recursive moment: the point at which time runs most obviously backwards, and where the play does not just glance over its shoulder, so much as turn fully round to look squarely at the most prominent action replay of them all. More than a play-within-a-play, *The Mousetrap* offers a replay of a replay: the Ghost's revisionary account of the murder, fitted out with actions. Equally, in so far as the design of *The Mousetrap* aims decisively to generate events that will forward the action of *Hamlet*, it also firmly looks towards the future. [. . .]

[. . .] There is no unitary self-presenting play. [. . .] I am not going to suggest that we can approach *Hamlet* by recognizing *Telmah*, or that *Telmah* is the real play, obscured by *Hamlet*. That would be to try to reconcile, to bring to peace, to appease a text whose vitality resides precisely in its plurality: in the fact that it contradicts itself and strenuous resists our attempts to resolve, to domesticate that contradiction. I am trying to suggest that its contradiction has value in that a pondering of some of the attempts that have been made to resolve it, to make the play speak coherently, within a set of limited bound-aries, reveals the political, economic and social forces to which all such 'inter-pretation' responds and in whose name it must inevitable, if covertly, be made. I am not suggesting an 'alternative' reading of *Hamlet*, because that would fall into the same trap. I offer my title of *Telmah* as what it is: a sense of ever-present potential challenge and contradiction *within* and *implied by* the text that we name *Hamlet*. In this sense, *Telmah* coexists with, is coterminous with *Hamlet*, in a way that must strike us, finally, as impossible. A thing, we are taught, cannot be both what it is and another thing. But that is precisely the principle challenged by *Telmah*. Our notion that it cannot coexist with *Hamlet* marks the limit, I suggest, of our Eurocentric view of 'sense', of 'order', of 'presence' if you like, and of 'point of view'. That Eurocentricity lies behind and validates a limited notion of 'interpretation' which will allow us to have *Hamlet* in various guises, and will also, as an alternative, allow clever and sophisticated interpreters to have, say, *Telmah*. But it will not allow us to have both, because that would explode our notion of the single and unified 'point of view' whose 'authority', as that term suggests, derives from its source, the author.

And yet, to conclude, we have only to step beyond the shores of Europe to encounter quite a different notion of interpretation which will allow exactly what I propose: the sense of a text as a site, or an area of conflicting and often contradictory potential interpretations, no one group of which can claim 'intrinsic' primacy or 'inherent' authority, and all of which are always ideological in nature and subject to extrinsic political and economic determinants.

The abstract model I reach for is of course that of jazz music: that black American challenge to the Eurocentric idea of the author's, or the composer's, authority. For the jazz musician, the 'text' of a melody is a means, not an end. Interpretation in that context is not parasitic but symbiotic in its relationship with its object. Its role is not limited to the service, or the revelation, or the celebration of the author's/composer's art. Quite the reverse: interpretation *constitutes* the art of the jazz musician.

From **Valerie Traub, 'Desire and Anxiety'**, *Circulations of Sexuality in Shakespearean Drama* (London and New York: Routledge, 1992, essay originally published 1988), pp. 26–33

One objection to the use of psychoanalysis in literary criticism is that it does not take into account the fact that human consciousness is not the same in different periods of history (see Critical History, p. 36–7). Valerie Traub is an American feminist critic (see Critical History, pp. 35–6) who succeeds in taking a psychoanalytical approach whilst paying close attention to the historical circumstances in which the play was written. Here she explains how the fear of female sexuality which haunted early modern men becomes, in *Hamlet*, a fear of sex itself. The language of the play reveals a subconscious desire for women to be asexual. The dead Ophelia becomes the embodiment of male needs; Hamlet transfers his own need to be free of sexual desire for treacherous femaleness onto the image of the cold, still female body of his lover.

Shakespeare's preoccupation with the uncontrollability of women's sexuality - witness the many plots concerning the need to prove female chastity, the threat of adultery, and even when female fidelity is not a major theme of the play, the many references to cuckoldry in songs, jokes and passing remarks – was not individual to him, but a shared vulnerability of men in his intensely patriarchal and patrilineal[1] culture. Socially and psychologically, early modern men's erotic vulnerability was overdetermined: their infantile dependence on women, the development of their subjectivity (see Critical History, **p. 59 n. 41**) in relation to 'femininity', and their adult dependence on women's word for paternity of children (see Contextual Overview, **p. 13**) all secure the importance of female chastity for the early modern male subject. [. . .] Male power is restored through such mechanism as cuckold jokes; by means of the vilification of women upon which cuckold jokes depend, female erotic autonomy is reduced to silence and absence. [. . .]

The masculine imposition of silence, and more particularly of stasis,[2] on women is connected, I believe, with a fear of chaos associated with heterosexual inter-course. [. . .] [I]n the act of orgasm, male experience of the female body is not so much that of an object to be penetrated and possessed, but of an enclosure into which the male subject merges, dissolves, and in the early modern pun, dies. [. . .]

It is this fear, ultimately, of the subject's demise that leads Hamlet [. . .] to long for stasis, for a reprieve from the excitations and anxieties of erotic life. In response to [his] fear that such security and calm are not forthcoming, [he] dis-place[s] [his] own desire for stasis onto the wom[a]n with whom [he is] most intimate. The result is [. . .] the fetishization of the dead, virginal Ophelia [. . .].

The metaphorical displacements of women into static objects takes various

---

1   Where inheritance is through the male line.
2   A state of inactivity.

forms according to the requirements of genre; the specific strategy of objectification is modified as Shakespeare's art uncovers, releases, and the reorganizes masculine anxieties into new modes of expression. [. . .]

[I]n *Hamlet*, Gertrude's adultery and incest – the uncontrollability, in short, of her sexuality – are, in Hamlet's mind, projected outward to encompass the potential of such contamination in all heterosexual liaisons.[3] As Gertrude's adultery turns all women into prostitutes and all men into potential cuckolds, Hamlet's entire world is contracted into 'an unweeded garden / That's grown to seed, things rank and gross in nature / Possess it merely' [1.2.135–7; see Key Passages, **p. 127**]. In this vile yet seductive garden, sexually threatening women poison vulnerable and unwitting men. Thus, through their erotic power, women are seen to adjudicate life and death – a connection nicely summed up by the 'Mousetrap' player who reads the speech inserted by Hamlet in the play performed to 'catch the conscience of the King' (2.2.601; see Key Passages, **p. 136**): 'A second time I kill my husband dead, / When second husband kisses me in bed' [3.2.179–80].

The threat posed by Gertrude's sexuality is paranoiacally projected onto Ophelia, whom Hamlet exhorts: 'Get thee to a nunnery. Why wouldst thou be a breeder of sinners? . . . I could accuse me of such things that it were better my mother had not borne me' [3.1.121–4]. As the culmination of this speech makes clear, those things of which Hamlet could accuse himself are less the pride, ambition, and knavery that he mentions, as they are his suspicion that he, like his father before him, will be cuckolded: 'Get thee to a nunnery, farewell. Or if thou wilt needs marry, marry a fool, for wise men know well enough what monsters you make of them' (3.1.138–41). As the pun on nunnery and brothel makes clear, Hamlet is not concerned with Ophelia's ability to contaminate other men; trapped as he is within the boundaries of the oedipal relation (see Modern Criticism, **pp. 48–9**), Hamlet's paranoia extends only to himself and his beloved father.[4] Women make men into monsters, the early modern euphemism for cuckolds, because they deceive:

> I have heard of your paintings, well enough. God hath given you one face, and you make yourselves another. You jig and amble, and you lisp, you nickname God's creatures and make your wantonness your ignorance. Go to, I'll no more on't, it hath made me mad. I say we will have no mo marriage. (3.1.144–9)

No more marriage because all marriage is madness and whoredom - degrading to both parties, but especially to the man who never knows who else has slept between his sheets. And not only is marriage likened to whoredom, but Hamlet himself self-identifies as a whore as he, unable to carry out the revenge thrust upon him by his father's Ghost, 'Must like a whore unpack [his] heart with

---

3   [Traub's note.] It also turns all sons into bastards. At least part of Hamlet's anxiety is about his own legitimacy.
4   [Traub's note.] [. . .] I find the most persuasive evidence of Oedipal conflict in the ambiguous syntax of the following lines spoken by Hamlet: 'How stand I then, that have a father kill'd, a mother stain'd' (4.4.56–7). [. . .].

words / And fall a-cursing like a very drab, / A stallion' [male prostitute] (2.2.581–3; see Key Passages, **p. 135**).[5]

However potent Hamlet's fear of cuckoldry, one senses something else behind his vituperation of Ophelia: an anxiety associated with sexual activity itself. The language with which Hamlet describes sexuality is riddled throughout with metaphors of contagion and disease; his mother's hidden adultery and incest are imagined as an 'ulcerous place' that 'infects unseen' (3.4.149–51; see Key Passages, **p. 150**). For Hamlet, who early asks, 'And shall I couple hell?' (1.5.93; see Key Passages, **p. 132**) – the phraseology of which suggests the possibility of coupling *with* hell – *all* sex is unnatural.

Hamlet's sexual nausea finds its antecedent in his father's Ghost, who characterizes Gertrude thus: 'But virtue, as it never will be mov'd, / Though lewdness court it in a shape of heaven / So lust, though to a radiant angel link'd, / Will sate itself in a celestial bed / And prey on garbage' (1.5.53–7; see Key Passages, **p. 131**).[6] Here the dualistic ideology that divides women into lustful whores and radiant angels collapses upon itself, revealing the fear upon which it is based: Women are imagined either as angels or whores as a psychological defence against the uncomfortable suspicion that underneath, the angel *is* a whore. The collapse of this defensive structure unleashes precisely the masculine aggression it was originally built to contain. Even the Ghost's ostensible protection of Gertrude from Hamlet's wrath is sexually sadistic: 'Taint not thy mind, nor let thy soul contrive / Against thy mother aught. Leave her to heaven, / And to those thorns that in her bosom lodge / To prick and sting her' (1.5.85–8; see Key Passages, **p. 132**). Gertrude's conscience is imagined as an aggressive phallus, pricking and stinging her female breasts, in an act that reinscribes Hamlet Sr. within Gertrude's body, and thereby reappropriates the alien serpent, Claudius, as the legitimate patriarch-within: the conscience. It is at once a repossession, replication, and reprojection of the action that simultaneously 'effeminized' King Hamlet, and deprived him of his life and wife: 'The serpent that did sting they father's life / Now wears his crown' (1.5.39–40; see Key Passages, **p.130**), crown symbolizing both his kingship and his wife's genitalia.

Identified as he is with his father, Hamlet displaces disgust for the Queen's erotic mobility onto Ophelia, and adopts his father's strategy of aggression. Although Hamlet's violence remains verbal rather than physical, Ophelia's death is as much an outcome of Hamlet's rage as it is an expression of her grief, madness, or self-destruction. Killed off before she can deceive or defile Hamlet, only in death can Ophelia-as-whore regain the other half of her dichotomized being: chaste virgin. Contaminated in life by the taint of Gertrude's adultery, Ophelia reclaims sexual desirability only as a dead, but perpetual, virgin. [. . .]

In the graveyard scene – the last scene in which her presence is required –

---

5   Traub uses the reading here from the Second Quarto; the Folio text has 'scullion'. See Key Passages, **pp. 113–15** and **135**.

6   [Traub's note.] My interpretation depends on reading both 'lust' and 'radiant angel' as referring to Gertrude. '[R]adiant angel' is equally compelling as King Hamlet's self-characterization. I suggest that the passage should be read both ways, as a fine example of Shakespeare's overdetermined use of language.

Ophelia's dead, virginal body is fetishized by Hamlet and Laertes alike. As Ophelia's funeral procession reaches her newly dug grave, Laertes exclaims, 'Lay her i' th' earth, / And from her fair and unpolluted flesh / May violets spring!' (5.1.231–3). Soon thereafter he leaps on top of her casket: 'Hold off the earth a while, / Till I have caught her once more in mine arms' (5.1.242–3). Such passion, of course, incites Hamlet to claim his place as chief mourner: 'Dost come here to whine? / To outface me with leaping in her grave?' (5.1.272–3).

Critics largely focus on the grave as a site of masculine competition, neglecting to mention that Ophelia's grave becomes the only 'bed' upon which Hamlet is able to express his sexual desire [. . .]. And yet, it is neither the right to mourn Ophelia, nor the right to give her pleasure that is actually being contested; rather, Laertes and Hamlet fight over the right to Ophelia's chastity. Fetishized to the extent that it is utterly divorced from the rest of her being, Ophelia's chastity embodies, as it were, a masculine fantasy of a female essence wonderfully devoid of that which makes women so problematic: change, movement, inconstancy, unpredictability - in short, life. The conflict between Hamlet and Laertes is over the right and rite of sexual possession; it occurs only after Ophelia's transformation into a fully possessible object. The earlier punning of the gravedigger [. . .] seems eerily premonitory as he responds to Hamlet's query regarding who is to be buried in the newly turned grave: 'One that was a woman, but, rest her soul, she's dead' (5.1.131–2; see Key Passages, **p. 161**). No longer a woman, Ophelia is no longer likely to incite sexual anxiety; she is, however, a likely object to figure in sexual fantasies of masculine prowess. In addition to masculine competition, then, the conflict between Hamlet and Laertes suggests an underlying necrophiliac fantasy, by which I mean not so much a perversion, as a logical extension of the system of sexualization in place. As an eroticized yet chaste corpse, Ophelia signifies not only the connection between sexuality and death previously explored in *Romeo and Juliet,* but also suggests that sexuality is finally safely engaged in only with the dead. Earlier, Hamlet spoke of his own death as 'a consummation / Devoutly to be wish'd' (3.1.63–4; see Key Passages, **p. 137**), narcissistically linking his own death with sexual intercourse, and imagining both as the perfection of his desire. [. . .] Here, the fear shared by Hamlet and Laertes of a dynamic, expressive female sexuality culminates in the imposition of stasis on that which threatens to bring sexual (and for Hamlet, metaphysical) chaos, and in the desire, having acquired a fully immobile object, to possess her fully.

From **Graham Holderness, 'Are Shakespeare's tragic heroes "fatally flawed"? Discuss',** in *Critical Survey* I (1989), pp. 58–9

Graham Holderness undermines the assumptions of which underlie A. C. Bradley's treatment of Shakespearean characters as individuals with 'real' psychologies (see Modern Criticism, **p. 49**). Holderness represents here the renewal of Marxist criticism in 1980s. He turns Bradley's own Hegelian conflict between cosmic forces into a conflict of material, historical forces (see Critical History, **pp. 36–7**), feudal and modern (see Contextual Overview, **p. 11**), which is dramatized in Hamlet's personal tragedy.

[. . .] *Hamlet* raises problems about the very nature of 'character' as Bradley conceived it. No critic has had any more success than the other characters in the play in their efforts to analyse Hamlet's 'character', to 'pluck out the heart of [his] mystery' [3.2.356–7]. In the course of the play Hamlet enacts so many different roles, employs so many different theatrical dialects, constitutes himself into so many different 'subject positions' [see Critical History, **p. 39, note 41**] that the very idea of an integrated character seems inappropriate when applied to this chameleon creature. To put it psychologically, Hamlet is intensely aware of himself as an 'actor' who is continually being cast by other people into roles with which he partially engages, but which he ultimately resists—the revenge hero, the lover, the 'noble mind . . . o'erthrown' [3.1.152], the 'sweet prince' [5.2.364]. To put it dramatically, *Hamlet* is a play in which theatricality becomes much more than the means by which drama can 'represent an action': it becomes an object of attention in its own right, so that we are continually being offered insights into the complex relations between representation and reality, illusion and truth, 'action' and 'acting'. In such a dramatic medium the naturalistic notion of a psychologically integrated character scarcely arises.

[. . .] [I]t is quite evident that the world which Hamlet is seen to inhabit is itself no more integrated and whole than the personality of the tragic hero. This is not merely a matter of saying that the kingdom of Denmark is corrupt. Hamlet thinks it is, but Hamlet is not necessarily a reliable judge. Hamlet also idealises the medieval world of his father, that strange chivalric realm in which kings could gamble with their territories in fighting heroic single combats [1.1.83–98; see Key Passages, **p. 123**]. The Denmark of the play is no longer ruled by such values, or by such a medieval warrior-king; when Claudius is confronted by the same kind of challenge from Norway, he settles it with a little summit negotiation [1.2.17–39; 2.2.58–82]. This may be an ignoble solution, but it is certainly a more modern one, and arguably more in the interests of the commonwealth than the heroic irresponsibility of old Hamlet. Hamlet himself seems stranded between the two worlds, unable to emulate the heroic values of his father, unable to engage with the modern world of political diplomacy. He is, in other words, confronted by the tension between those two great Renaissance oppositions, idealism and machiavellianism [see Contextual Overview, **pp. 10–11**]; and that is the true source of his tragedy.

From **Carol Thomas Neely, ' "Documents in Madness": Reading Madness and Gender in Shakespeare's Tragedies and Early Modern Culture'**, *Shakespeare Quarterly* 42 (1991), pp. 316; 317; 318–19; 322; 323; 324–6

Carol Thomas Neely is a feminist critic who reads the play here in the context of changes in the early modern understanding of madness (see Contextual Overview, **pp. 14–15**). She identifies the characteristic features of Ophelia's disturbed language in Act 4, Scene 5 (see Key Passages, **pp. 152–3, 156**), and argues that they reveal the nature of male oppression of women in the play: Ophelia has no control over her life or even her body. The language of Hamlet's 'antic disposition' (1.5.180) stands in complete contrast: it is active social criticism.

[. . .] Today, as in the early modern period, it [madness] is detected by laypersons before it is referred to doctors. Because it is "theoretically indeterminate,"[1] it must be defined and read from within some framework; its definitions and therapies are always constructed from a particular historical moment and within a particular social order, influenced by and influencing that order. [. . .]

Madness, a concept in transition in the period, begins to be read/constructed/experienced differently in the sixteenth and seventeenth centuries than it had been in the Middle Ages (where it marked the intersection of the human and the transcendent) or than it will be in subsequent eras. [. . .]

In the early modern period the discourse of madness gained prominence because it was implicated in the medical, legal, theoretical, political, and social aspects of the reconceptualization of the human. Gradually madness, and hence sanity, began to be secularized, medicalized, psychologized, and (at least in representation) gendered. In the Middle Ages, madness was seen as the point of intersection of the human, the divine and the demonic. [. . .] By theorizing and representing madness, the Renaissance gradually and with difficulty began to try to separate human madness from the supernatural (from divine and demonic possession [. . .]); from the spiritual [. . .]; from witchcraft and bewitchment [. . .]; from frauds who imitated these conditions [. . .]; and from the sheerly physical [. . .]. Splitting the supernatural from the natural, and attempting to define what remained, the period began to separate mind from body, man from woman, insanity from both sanity and other types of aberrance such as poverty, heresy, and crime. [. . .]

[. . .] In Shakespeare's plays that make this diagnosis, the speech of the mad characters constructs madness as secular, socially enacted, gender- and class-marked, and medically treatable. [. . .]

Shakespeare [. . .] dramatizes madness primarily through a peculiar language more often than through physiological symptoms, stereotyped behaviours, or iconographic conventions. This characteristic speech is both something and nothing, both coherent and incoherent. Spectators, onstage and off, read this language, trying to make "sense" of it, translating it into the discourse of sanity. Shakespeare's language of madness is characterized by fragmentation, obsession, and repetition, and most importantly by what I will call "quotation," which might instead be called "bracketing" or "italicization."[2] The mad are "besides

1 [Thomas Neely's note.] Andrew Scull, *Social Order/Mental Disorder: Anglo-American Psychiatry in Historical Perspective* (Berkeley; University of California Press, 1989), p. 8.
2 [Thomas Neely's.] I take the notion of italicized writing from Nancy K. Miller, 'Emphasis Added: Plots and Plausibilities in Women's Fiction' in *The New Feminist Criticism: Essays on Women, Literature and Theory*, ed. Elaine Showalter (New York: Pantheon, 1985), pp. 339–60. She extends Luce Irigaray's analysis of women's special relationship to the mimetic (in *This Sex Which Is Not One*) and defines italics as a modality of intensity, intonation and emphasis that characterizes women's writing (p. 343).

themselves"; their discourse is not their own. But the voices that speak through them are not [. . .] supernatural voices but human ones—cultural ones perhaps. The prose that is used for this mad speech (although it includes embedded songs and rhymes) implies disorderly shape,[3] associates madness with popular tradition, and contributes to its colloquial, "quoted" character. These quoted voices, however, have connections with (or can be interpreted to connect with) the mad characters' pre-mad gendered identity and history, their social context and psychological stresses—as well as with larger themes of the plays and of the culture. The alienated speech allows psychological plausibility, thematic resonance, cultural constructions, and social critique. Using it, Shakespeare represents distinctions between female hysteria and feigned male melancholy in *Hamlet* [. . .].

[. . .] Ophelia's alienated discourse invites a psychological, thematic and gendered interpretation. It resituates sacred material in a secular, psychological context, and she and Hamlet act out distinctions between feigned and actual madness and between rational and mad suicide, distinctions that the culture was gradually establishing.

Ophelia's madness is represented almost entirely through fragmentary, communal, and thematically coherent quoted discourse. Through it, rituals elsewhere involving the supernatural are appropriated and secularized. Ophelia recites formulas, tales, and songs that ritualize passages of transformation and loss—lost love, lost chastity, and death. These transitions are alluded to in social formulas of greeting and leave-taking: "Well, God dild you," "Good night, ladies, good night" [4.5.42, 72]; in religious formulas of grace and benediction: "God be at your table!" "God 'a' mercy on his soul. / And of all Christian souls, I pray you" [4.5.44, 196–7]; in allusions to folk legends or tales of daughters' metamorphic changes in status: tales of the "owl [who] was a baker's daughter" [4.5.42–3] and of the master's daughter stolen by the steward.

Her songs likewise enact truncated rites of passage. Love and its loss are embodied in the song of the "truelove," imagined with a cockle hat, staff, and sandals, all icons of his pilgrimage. She sings of Valentine's Day loss of virginity when a maid crosses a threshold both literal and psychological: "Then up he rose and donned his clothes / And dupped the chamber door, / Let in the maid, that out a maid / Never departed more. . . . / Young men will do't if they come to't, / By Cock, they are to blame" [4.5.52–5, 60–1]. This imagined deflowering preempts and precludes a marriage ritual. The other songs mourn a death and represent the concrete markers of a spare funeral ritual—a flaxen poll, a bier, a stone, no flowers. They enable Ophelia to mourn her father's death, enact his funeral, encounter his dead body, and find consolation for her loss: "He is gone, he is gone, / And we cast away moan" [4.5.194–5]. Into this central loss and its rituals, Ophelia's other losses or imagined losses—of lover, of virginity, of "fair judgement"—are absorbed. Her distribution of flowers to the court is an extension of her quoted discourse, an enacted ritual of dispersal, symbolizing lost love,

---

3   [Thomas Neely's note.] A. C. Bradley notes, in *Shakespearean Tragedy*, that Shakespeare invariably uses prose to represent abnormal states of mind like madness [. . .].

deflowering, and death. A secularized cultural ritual of maturation and mourning is enacted through Ophelia's alienated speech.[4]

Ophelia's madness, as the play presents it, begins to be gender-specific in ways that later stage representations of Ophelia and of female hysterics will exaggerate.[5] Her restlessness, agitation, shifts of direction, her "winks and nods and gestures" [4.5.11] suggest the spasms of "the mother"[6] and show that madness is exhibited by the body as well as in speech; gesture and speech, equally convulsive, blend together: Ophelia "beats her heart, / Spurns enviously at straws" [4.5.5–6]. The context of her disease, like that of hysteria later, is sexual frustration, social helplessness, and enforced control over women's bodies. The content of her speech reflects this context. Laertes's anguished response to Ophelia as a "document in madness"—"Thought and affliction, passion, hell itself, / She turns to favour and to prettiness" (4.5.176–7)—shows how the reading of madness's self-representation can aestheticize the condition, mitigating both its social critique and its alien aspects. In a similar fashion Gertrude narrates Ophelia's death as beautiful, natural, and eroticized, foreshadowing later representations of it and representations of female hysterics as sexually frustrated and theatrically alluring. The representation of Ophelia implicitly introduces conventions for reading madness as gender-inflected.

Gender distinctions likewise begin to take shape in the contrasts between Hamlet and Ophelia. Although Ophelia in her mad scenes can be seen to serve as a double for Hamlet during his absence from Denmark and from the play,[7] Hamlet's madness is in every way contrasted with hers, in part, no doubt, to emphasize the difference between feigned and actual madness. His discourse, although witty, savage, and characterized by non sequiturs and bizarre references, almost never has the "quoted," fragmentary, ritualized quality of Ophelia's—as we are instructed: "Nor what he spake, though it lacked form a little, / Was not like madness" [3.1.165–6]. Significantly, the one time it is "like madness"— that is, like Ophelia's speech—is after the encounter with his father's ghost, when Hamlet must abruptly reenter the human, secular world of his friends. The "wild and whirling words" [1.5.139] that he utters to effect this transition are quoted truisms and social formulas for parting which are incoherently deployed:

---

4   [Thomas Neely's note.] Joan Klein, "'Angels and Ministers of Grace': *Hamlet*, IV, v-vii," *Allegorica*, 1, 2 (1976), 156–76, reads Ophelia's madness closely and attends to the cultural lore that she draws on. But whereas she sees Ophelia's role as providential, as a minister to Hamlet, I see religious references as split off from their theological context in her mad speech. Much of the attention devoted to Ophelia's speeches has been directed toward identifying the referents of her songs, especially the "truelove," and determining to which characters the songs are addressed. My analysis suggests that it is not possible to pinpoint a single referent or audience since the discourse's referents are multiple and are both personal and cultural. See Peter J. Seng, *The Vocal Songs in the Plays of Shakespeare: A Critical History* (Cambridge, Mass.: Harvard University Press, 1967), pp. 131–56, for a summary of commentary.

5   [Thomas Neely's note.] Cf. Elaine Showalter, *The Female Malady: Women, Madness and English Culture, 1830–1980* (New York: Pantheon, 1985).

6   The early modern term for 'hysteria', caused it was thought by the womb becoming detached and diseased, a complaint to which under-employed virgins were especially susceptible.

7   [Thomas Neely's note.] Joan Klein sees Ophelia as Hamlet's surrogate and minister, and Lyons sees her as mirroring aspects of Hamlet's melancholy (pp. 11–12), but I see her as a 'dark double' who [. . .] acts out what is repressed in Hamlet.

> And so, without more circumstance at all,
> I hold it fit that we shake hands and part:
> You, as your business and desire shall point you,
> For every man hath business and desire
> Such as it is, and for my own poor part,
> Look you, I'll go pray. [1.5.133–8]

After this moment of dislocation he announces a plan to feign madness, to "put an antic disposition on" [1.5.180]; and he is able to "go in together" [1.5.194] with his friends, reuniting himself with the world of human fellowship and sanity, although he is himself marked by the remembrance of the Ghost's "commandment" [1.5.102].

The stylistic distinction between Hamlet's feigned madness and Ophelia's actual madness is emphasized by other distinctions. Henceforth in the play, Hamlet is presented as fashionably introspective and melancholy while Ophelia becomes alienated, acting out the madness Hamlet only plays at. Whereas her madness is somatized[8] and its content eroticized, Hamlet's melancholy is politicized in form and content. Caused purportedly by Claudius's usurpation of the throne and by his father's commandment, it manifests itself in social criticism, and it is viewed as politically dangerous. Ophelia must be watched, contained within the family, within the castle; Hamlet must be first contained and later expelled to England to be murdered. By acting out the madness Hamlet feigns and the suicide that he theorizes, the representation of Ophelia absorbs pathological excesses open to Hamlet and enables his reappearance as a sane, autonomous individual and a tragic hero in the last act. There he appears detached from family and from sexuality, seemingly freed from passivity and loss of control, capable of philosophical contemplation and revenge, worthy a spiritual epitaph and a soldier's funeral; his restored identity is validated—symbolically as well as literally—over Ophelia's grave: "This is I, / Hamlet the Dane" [5.1.250–1].

From **Alan Sinfield,** *Faultlines: Cultural Materialism and the Politics of Dissident Reading* (Oxford: Clarendon Press, 1992), pp. 222–30

Alan Sinfield is one of the original late twentieth-century British critics known as Cultural Materialists. This extract can be taken as typical of the careful historicization and progressive politics which are the hallmarks of that school. In *Faultlines* he argues for a central proposition of Cultural Materialism: that literary texts reveal to us the conflicts and inconsistencies in the ideologies of the age in which they are written; conflicts and contradictions which point towards progressive resolutions in the future. No matter what an author may have thought at the time, there are always meanings available to the reader

---

8   Expressed bodily.

beyond the political beliefs and intentions of the writer, especially to readers in later historical eras.

Here Sinfield is concerned with the classical philosophy of Stoicism, which was influential among intellectuals in the early modern period and represented in the extract in the writings of Seneca (c. 4BC–AD65). Stoicism taught that men could achieve equanimity through restraining pointless emotions in a deterministic world: all events and all human actions were the expression of an unchangeable fate, which the wise man accepted as part of the divine plan for the universe. He contrasts Stoicism with Calvinism, the form of Protestantism (see Contextual Overview, **p. 10**) in the ascendancy in London in 1600. The Swiss theologian Jean Calvin (1509–64) taught that each of our fates was fixed by God's incomprehensible providence from the beginning of time – and in particular whether we are to be saved or damned. Sinfield finds both of these deterministic systems of thought in conflict in the text, and concludes that the play serves to undermine Protestant ideas in its conclusion. As part of his argument, Sinfield writes of the 'change' in Hamlet's 'character' after he returns from England. But Sinfield is not saying that Hamlet has a 'character' in the sense that Bradley did (see Modern Criticism, **pp. 49–53**). Many contemporary critics, including Sinfield, do not accept that there is such a thing as a simple, single and united human consciousness which exists apart from real time and space ('a continuous subjectivity'; see Critical History, **pp. 36–40**). Instead of this, modern critics typically think that all human thought and personal identities are dependent on the language we speak and on the social systems in which we live. Both language and society are constantly changing and both, it is argued, are an expression of the power-relationships of the world in which we live. Sinfield is not saying that he has uncovered Hamlet's 'inner truth' because there is no such thing – both texts and consciousnesses are permanently unstable. However, the way that we follow the story of the play brings into the foreground this clash between two powerful thought systems, Stoicism and Calvinism, in an illuminating way.

We defy augury. There is a special providence in the fall of a sparrow. If it be now, 'tis not to come; if it be not to come, it will be now; if it be not now, yet it will come. The readiness is all. Since no man, of aught he leaves, knows aught, what is't to leave betimes? Let be.

[5.2.215–20; see Key Passages, **p. 164**]

[God is] a Governor and Preserver, and that, not by producing a kind of general motion in the machine of the globe as well as in each of its parts, but by a special Providence sustaining, cherishing, superintending, all the things which he has made, to the very minutest, even to a sparrow.

(Calvin, *Institutes* 1.16.1)

Fate guides us, and it was settled at the first hour of birth what length of time remains for each. Cause is linked with cause, and all public and private issues are directed by a long sequence of events. Therefore

everything should be endured with fortitude, since things do not, as we
suppose, simply happen—they all come.

(Seneca, *De providentia* 5.7)[1]

Seneca and Calvin both seem relevant when Hamlet says, "There is a special
providence in the fall of a sparrow." Indeed, rival views of the play have
amounted to glosses on their divergent implications for its interpretation. [. . .]
Hamlet is either a pagan in a pagan play, a good Christian in a Christian play, or a
reprobate[2] in a Christian play.

A Senecan frame of reference seems appropriate in the first four acts of *Hamlet*,
for the dialogue puts Stoic tranquility of mind firmly on the agenda. [. . .] For
Hamlet, Stoicism is an ideal he hopes to see achieved. He values Horatio because
he perceives in him "a man that Fortune's buffets and rewards / Hast ta'en with
equal thanks; . . . not a pipe for Fortune's finger / To sound what stop she please
. . . not passion's slave" [3.2.67–72]. By subduing his emotions, Horatio is said to
free himself from the effects of fortune and become the Stoics' wise and happy
man. If Hamlet could do that then revenge might not be a problem. [. . .] Hamlet's
problem seems prior to such considerations: it is the achievement of a state
of mind where he can act purposively at all, and especially upon the Ghost's
allegations. [. . .]

It is quite appropriate, therefore, that Hamlet presents himself as a failed Stoic
in his first exchange with Rosencrantz and Guildenstern. The dialogue here is in a
mode of light-hearted philosophical banter (such as might have occurred when
they were students), but the subtext is maneuvering to discover each other's purposes. Rosencrantz denies that Denmark is a prison; Hamlet replies, "Why, then
'tis none to you; for there is nothing either good or bad but thinking makes it so"
[2.2.249–50]. This characteristically Stoic notion usually has a contrary import—
that one can be happy and free if the mind chooses. So Rosencrantz should be
amused, but he is determined to turn the discussion to ambition. Hamlet's response
is more earnest: "O God, I could be bounded in a nutshell and count myself a king
of infinite space—were it not that I have bad dreams" [2.2.254–6]. [. . .] It is
Stoic reluctance to live with the mind in chains that puts suicide on the agenda.
Horatio, wanting to die with Hamlet, terms himself "more an antique Roman than
a Dane" [5.2.346; see Key Passages, **p. 168**]. To Seneca, it is indeed a "question"
whether it is nobler in the mind to suffer or to make a dignified exit; death is always
a way of escaping intolerable pressure, yet it is base to flinch [. . .]. Seneca's point
is that it is superstitious and irrational to fear death or what might follow it, but
just such anxieties preoccupy Hamlet, who again falls short of Stoic detachment.

For Seneca, the man who achieves Stoic mastery is godlike [. . .]. Such
presumption, of course, ran precisely counter to the Protestant doctrine of human
wretchedness.[3] [. . .] But Hamlet is perplexed and disillusioned at the failure of the
Stoic ideal in others and himself. Man is said to be "in apprehension how like a

---

1   [Sinfield's note.] *Calvin's Institutes* [trans. Henry Beveridge] (MacDill Fla.: Macdonald publishing,
    no date); Seneca, *Moral Essays*, trans. John A. Basore (Cambridge, Mass.: Harvard University
    Press, 1958), 1:36–39.
2   Someone predestined to damnation.
3   Contemporary Protestant theology saw fallen man as a degraded and sinful, only to be saved by
    God's grace.

god: the beauty of the world, the paragon of animals—and yet, to me, what is this quintessence of dust?" [2.2.306–9]. Hamlet would like to believe that human reason is a godlike instrument by which people may act in the world:

> Sure he that made us with such large discourse,
> Looking before and after, gave us not
> That capability and godlike reason
> To fust in us unus'd.
>
> [4.4.36–9]

At issue here is optimistic humanism—the strand in Renaissance thought that exalted human capacity to achieve, through the exercise of rational powers, a moral stature that the incautious termed godlike. [. . .] Such an aspiration is at stake when Ophelia laments "that noble and most sovereign reason / Like sweet bells jangled out of tune and harsh" [3.1.159–60]. In the play this is not Hamlet's failure alone. In some ways he contrasts with the other young men, but Laertes is no more successful in establishing and pursuing rational purposes (he kills Hamlet but wishes he had not), and Fortinbras is elected king of Denmark (presumably) not because of the schemes of his father and himself but by default and by arriving at the right time. Even Horatio has to be dissuaded from suicide. At this point, *Hamlet* seems Calvinist rather than Senecan. Calvin termed "absurd" the Stoic hero "who, divested of humanity, was affected in the same way by adversity and prosperity, grief and joy; or rather, like a stone, was not affected by anything" (*Institutes* 3.8.9). [. . .]

[. . .] There was [. . .] a [further] dispute with Protestantism. While the optimistic estimate of Man contradicts the doctrine of the "fall," Senecan pessimism about how the world goes contradicts the doctrine of providence. It is against Stoic fate or fortune that Calvin is arguing when he speaks [in the 1561 English translation of *The Institutes*] of special providence and the fall of a sparrow [. . .]

Upon his return from England, Hamlet seems to have abandoned his Stoic aspirations and become a believer in providence. Now sermon tags roll off his tongue—"There's a divinity that shapes our ends, / Rough-hew them how we will"; "even in that was heaven ordinant" (i.e., "directing, controlling": [5.2.10–11, 48]); "There is a special providence in the fall of a sparrow." This is very strong phrasing. In fact, in the first quarto Hamlet says, "theres a predestiuate prouidence in the fall of a sparrow." Even if that is no more than a faulty memorial reconstruction [see Key Passages, **p. 114**] it shows how one well-placed contemporary read the prince's thought: it is Calvinist.

Hamlet seems to have changed. To say this is to *expect* (but not necessarily to find) some continuity in his character. I argued in chapter 3 that many dramatis personae in Shakespearean plays are written, at least for some of the time, in ways that suggest that they have continuous subjectivities. This is not to suppose, in a Bradleyan or essentialist-humanist manner, that these dramatic personae are unified subjects, or independent of the multiple discursive practices of the culture. Indeed, I have been trying to locate Hamlet at the intersection point of Senecan and Calvinist discourses, and it is in their terms that I perceive a break upon his return from England. (I do not say that these are the only relevant discourses; but they were powerful enabling systems through which, in some measure, subjectivities were constructed.) It is recognizing cues that some continuity in the character of Hamlet is to be expected that makes it possible to allege a break [. . .].

At such a breaking point, readers and audiences may either declare the play incoherent or attempt to intuit an appropriate linking factor. If we do the former, we may either complain about artistic quality (as did T. S. Eliot [see Modern Criticism, **pp. 53–5**]) or triumphantly discover once more [. . .] the twin instabilities of subjectivity and textuality. Wishing to push further than either of these, I try instead to envisage a linking factor through which an audience might (having in mind Hamlet's changed mode of utterance and the play so far) plausibly renew the sense of Hamlet as a continuous subjectivity. This, again, sounds Bradleyan but is in fact only a specially determined application of the process through which any story is understood. The mistake would be to efface the work required, and to imagine that one is uncovering the inner truth of Hamlet's character. I am observing that, as well as producing a breaking point, the text does suggest at least one plausible link.

This is Hamlet's awareness, which is in the dialogue, of the extraordinary turns events have taken—the appearance of the Ghost when Claudius seemed secure, the arrival of the Players prompting the test of the king, Hamlet's inspired discovery on the boat of the plot against his life, and then his amazing delivery from the pirates. The latter is so improbable, and unnecessary to the plot, as to suggest the specially intricate quality of divine intervention wherein even a sparrow's death is purposive. It is when explaining how he found Claudius's letter and changed it that Hamlet attributes events to "a divinity that shapes our ends"; and when describing how he was able to seal the altered instructions that he says heaven was "ordinant." The sequence seems to require the providential explanation; so the prince recognizes the folly and pretension of humanistic aspiration and the controlling power of God.

For so much strenuous narration to be necessary, and with such sudden consequences for character and theme, the play must be labouring at a particularly awkward ideological moment. The strain, it appears, is getting Hamlet to the point where he can express belief in a special providence. This could produce a Christian moral [. . .]. The "carnal, bloody, and unnatural acts" and "purposes mistook / Fall'n on th'inventors' heads" (5.2.386, 389–90; see Key Passages, **p. 169**) are quite compatible with a violent and punitive deity. In Calvin's view, both believers and the wicked must expect such afflictions (for the former, "it is not properly punishment or vengeance, but correction and admonition"; for the latter, God is "confounding, scattering, and annihilating" his enemies [*Institutes* 3.4.31]). So we may envisage an Elizabethan audience not finding *Hamlet* sad and bleak (or even strangely uplifting in its sense of wasted human potential), but being satisfied by the working out of events in the providential manner described in the sermons they had heard. The same might be true of other tragedies. Yet all texts, I have said, produce meaning in excess of any ostensible ideological project. In *Hamlet* the difficulties emanate from the concept of special providence.

The problem, as in respect of Stoic theory earlier, is focused by Hamlet's state of mind. For as Bradley said, the tone and implication of the sparrow speech, however Christian its phrasing, are fatalistic. Of course, predestination means that individual actions can make no difference, but Protestant sermonizers, always afraid of antinomianism,[4] urged all the more that the believer should show his or her delight in God's will by cooperating as far and as eagerly as possible. [. . .] Hamlet believes that providence wants Claudius removed, and that he should do it. He rehearses the king's manifold crimes and asks:

> is't not perfect conscience
> To quit him with this arm? And is't not to be damn'd
> To let this canker of our nature come
> In further evil?
>
> (5.2.67–70)

However, when he says, "The readiness is all," he means not for action but for death. He is not making a reverent general statement about the rightness of God's control of the world, but dismissing Horatio's very reasonable suspicion about the duel. He plays with Osric (this scene seems purposefully desultory), competes recklessly with Laertes, makes no plan against the king. The final killing occurs in a burst of passionate inspiration, and when Hamlet himself is, in effect, slain. He seems to have fallen into the fatalistic heresy [. . .]. [. . .] Hamlet manifests the tendency of the objector: he sees no point, now, in bothering. He acknowledges divine determination, but without enthusiasm. At this point the play turns back upon itself, retrieving the Stoicism that it has seemed to dismiss [. . .] "If it be now, 'tis not to come; if it be not to come, it will be now; if it be not now, yet it will come. The readiness is all. . . . Let be" [5.2.215–20; see Key Passages, **p. 164**]. Hamlet falls back upon the fatalism that often underlies the Stoic ideal of rational self-sufficiency.

There is no speech saying that Hamlet feels thus because he feels alienated from the Protestant deity; probably that could have been said on a stage only by a manifest villain. But as members of an audience try to make sense of events in the play and Hamlet's responses to them, it may appear that the divine system revealed in the action is not as comfortable and delightful as protestants proclaimed. It makes Hamlet wonder and admire; temporarily, when he is sending Rosencrantz and Guildenstern to their deaths, it exhilarates him; but ultimately it does not command his respect. The issue in Stoicism, for Hamlet, is how the mind might free itself, for to him Denmark and the world are a prison. But protestantism offers no release from mental bondage.

From **Philip Armstrong, 'Watching *Hamlet* Watching: Lacan, Shakespeare and the Mirror/Stage'**, in *Alternative Shakespeares*, vol. 2, ed. Terence Hawkes (London: Routledge, 1996), pp. 223–6

The psychoanalytical tradition of Hamlet criticism is interestingly turned back to front by Philip Armstrong here. He argues that whereas it may be true that Lacan's ideas about the formulation of the 'subject' (see Critical History, **p. 36**) offer a genuine insight into the play's awareness of itself as theatre, the

---

4   A heretical view that Christians need not obey the moral law.

play itself seems to have provided the stimulus for Lacan's theory of the 'mirror stage' of infant development, a theory which seeks to explain the nature of our awareness of who we are, and of how we understand our place in the world.

Like the apparition confronting Hamlet at this point [1.5], the ghost of patriarchy haunts both the Renaissance stage and modern psychoanalysis. [. . .] Hamlet typifies the theatregoer confronted by the spectacle of her or his own subjection to an accusing and masculinist gaze. For Lacan, patriarchal power will be prefigured at first by the position of the 'actual' father within the family unit, but thereafter manifested in what he calls the symbolic, the operation of language, through which the subject comes into being as such and upon which she or he remains dependent. Lacan nicknames this patriarchal linguistic order the *nom-du-père*, with a pun on *non-du-père*: the name (word), or 'no' (prohibition), of the father.[1] Once it has been assimilated into the psyche, he applies to this embodiment of the Law the psychoanalytic term 'super-ego'.[2] The word introjection, then, refers specifically to this process, 'when something like a reversal takes place – what was the outside becomes the inside, what was the father becomes the super-ego'.[3] Or, in Hamlet's case, what was the father reappears . . . where?

> HAMLET   My father – methinks I see my father –
> HORATIO   Where, my lord?
> HAMLET   In my mind's eye, Horatio.
>   [1.2.184–5]

All of these models of cognition – the eye of the mind, mirror of the intellect, mind as inner arena – have been identified by Richard Rorty as emerging in the Renaissance and deriving from Greek and particularly Platonic philosophy.[4] Moreover, Rorty relates such metaphors to the capacity of the Cartesian subject[5] to 'reflect' and to 'speculate', thereby emphasizing the close affinity, in the Western philosophical tradition, between the process of conceptual thought and the function of vision; even more specifically, between the perception of the self and the function of the mirror.

It would seem that the psychological and perceptual spaces represented by both mirror and stage have been influential not just in early modern theatre, but also in the subsequent development of both philosophy and psychoanalysis. Lacan, in

---

1 [Armstrong's reference.] Jacques Lacan, *Ecrits: A Selection*, trans. Alan Sheridan (London: Tavistock, 1977), pp. 67, 199, 217; *The Seminar of Jacques Lacan*, vol. 2: *The Ego in Freud's Theory and in the Technique of Psychoanalysis 1954–5*, trans. Sylvana Thomaselli (Cambridge: Cambridge University Press, 1988), pp. 259–60.
2 [Armstrong's reference.] Ibid., p. 83.
3 [Armstrong's reference.] *The Seminar of Jacques Lacan*, vol. 1: *Freud's Papers on Technique 1953–4*, trans. John Forester (Cambridge: Cambridge University Press, 1988), p. 169.
4 [Armstrong's reference.] Richard Rorty, *Philosophy and the Mirror of Nature* (Oxford: Basil Blackwell, 1980), pp. 38–69.
5 The philosopher René Descartes (1596–1650) saw human consciousness as an insubstantial thinking substance (the soul) connected mysteriously to the physical body.

fact, entitles his initial paradigm for the child's entry into relation with its surroundings 'The Mirror Stage', '*Le stade du miroir*'. The word '*stade*', like its English translation, signifies both a developmental phase and a stadium, an arena for the repeated performance or playing out of identity: 'The *mirror stage* is a drama'.[6]

Instead of worrying about the problem of anachronism in reading modern theory alongside early modern drama, the critic might more profitably address the extent to which psychoanalytic models of identity construction remain dependent for their development and representation upon drama; more specifically, upon Shakespeare; in fact, upon *Hamlet* itself. Lacan, for example, uses this play as a primary instance of the imaginary identification between the ego and its ideal image in the mirror.[7]

In the mirror stage, the child constructs its fantasy ego according to the upright and coordinated figure in the glass. This always and only offers what Lacan calls a *méconnaissance*, a misleading recognition, because the masterful image apprehended in the mirror does not correspond to the actual degree of muscular coordination attained by the infant. The imaginary identification thereby produces a frustrated aggressivity, for the spectator desires to assimilate this image of the body as a totality, but remains at odds with it, experiencing its own body only partially and in fragments. The ego then desires the destruction of the ideal other but, dependent upon it for its own identification, remains locked in a disabling impasse [. . .]. In his seminar 'Desire and the Interpretation of Desire in *Hamlet*', Lacan takes Hamlet's relation to Laertes as a model for this imaginary fascination. He quotes the Prince's description of Laertes to Osric – 'his semblable is his mirror and who else would trace him his umbrage, nothing more' [5.2.118–20] – commenting that 'The image of the other . . . is presented here as completely absorbing the beholder'.[8] In this struggle only one outcome is possible: the destruction of both parties. In eventually fighting his ego ideal, therefore, Hamlet effects his own death. [. . .]

Characters other than Laertes also function as mirror images in this play. Most interestingly, from the point of view of the theatrical transaction between audience and actor, Hamlet identifies himself with the player who delivers the speech about Pyrrhus, especially at the moment where he describes how the avenger's sword, raised over the head of Priam,

> *seem'd i'th' air to stick;*
> *So, as a painted tyrant, Pyrrhus stood,*
> *And like a neutral to his will and matter,*
> *Did nothing.*
>
> [2.2.475–8]

Acting out as well as speaking these lines, the player vividly foreshadows the moment at which Hamlet, a few scenes later, will stand with his sword poised

6   [Armstrong's reference.] Lacan, *Ecrits* (see note 1), p. 4.
7   [Armstrong's note.] Just as Sigmund Freud and Ernest Jones took the play as a paradigm for the Oedipus Complex.
8   [Armstrong's reference.] Jacques Lacan, 'Desire and the Interpretation of Desire in *Hamlet*', trans. James Hulbert, *Yale French Studies* 55/56, pp. 11–52.

above his uncle's head, embodying once again the inert aggressivity produced by an imaginary identification with the 'painted tyrant' before him.

Hamlet makes his identification with this minidrama even clearer [in 2.2.545–51; 561–4; see Key Passages, **p. 134**].

Despite the arguments of the contemporary theatrical pamphleteers,[9] the acting out of Pyrrhus's 'dream of passion' before Hamlet's eyes suggests that an imaginary identification with the dramatic 'fiction' produces in its spectator only a disabling fantasy, a speechless fascination. It fails to prompt him to any kind of imitative action whatsoever.

From **Lisa Jardine, Reading Shakespeare Historically** (London: Routledge, 1996), pp. 150–7

Lisa Jardine's feminist criticism here combines a historicist precision about the cultural significance of certain terms in early modern England – here, the 'closet' – with psychoanalytical theory. She goes on to reach a conclusion about how the scene in which Hamlet confronts his mother (3.4) reveals something about the oppressive way in which the concept of the feminine is constructed in our culture.

Within the organisation of rooms in the English country house of the period, [. . .] as Alan Stewart has recently pointed out, [. . .]

The closet is thus constructed as a place of utter privacy, of total withdrawal from the public sphere of the household – but it simultaneously functions as a very *public* gesture of withdrawal, a very public sign of privacy.[1]

Of the domestic spaces occupied or traversed on a daily basis by the early modern gentlewoman, her closet was the sole place over which she ostensibly exercised total control, her one truly privy or private place.

Because what goes on in the closet, is, uniquely amongst the activities in the early modern gentrified household, customarily solitary, a suggestion of the illicit, the indiscreet, certainly the secretive, hovers over those infrequent occasions when men and women encounter one another there [. . .]. When Hamlet responds to his mother's summons and comes to her closet, he intrudes where customarily a woman would only entertain her husband or lover. For an adult son, intimations of erotic possibility are almost inevitable; the son crosses into the enclosure of his mother's privacy to encounter her as a sexualised subject.

---

9 Armstrong is referring to the puritans who argued that the theatre produced a 'copy cat effect' on its audience, inducing them to act out the vices which they saw portrayed on stage.

1 [Jardine's note.] Alan Stewart, 'The early modern closet discovered', *Representations*, 1995, vol. 50, p. 81.

The King of Denmark's close adviser and Councillor of State, Polonius, has no legitimate place within the intimate space of Gertrude's closet; his presence fatally confuses privacy with affairs of state. The erosion of privacy which has already been effected by the constant surveillance which has characterised Claudius and Polonius's management of the state of Denmark here reaches its logical conclusion: the state invades the Queen's inner sanctum, and in the ensuing confusion it is defiled by a botched and mistaken act of violence.

The instructions issued by Polonius to Gertrude are that she should reprimand her son for his behaviour towards Claudius [3.4.1–5] [. . .]

Performing before Polonius, Gertrude frames her reproach formally; believing himself alone, Hamlet responds familially. The upshot is that the language of public disapproval collides with that of personal hurt, coloured by the present reminders of maternal sexuality [3.4.8–16] [. . .]

Reproved for his offensive behaviour (with the familiar 'thou' of maternal scolding), Hamlet retaliates with the more grievous 'offence' against his deceased natural father of his mother's remarriage to his brother. The marriage is technically illicit, a serious matter under canon law; within the closet it takes on an aura of secrecy and deception, as if it has been 'discovered' by Hamlet (yet the marriage appears to bother no one else in the Court of Denmark). Whereas Hamlet, as he proceeds fully to reveal, continues to suffer the deeper smart of the usurped place of the two men whose part he takes – his father supplanted by Claudius in his mother's bed and himself supplanted on the throne by Claudius, who also now stands in affection between himself and his mother.

In a landmark essay on *Hamlet*, Jacqueline Rose suggested that Eliot's judgement of the play as an aesthetic failure ('Hamlet is up against the difficulty that his disgust is occasioned by his mother, but that his mother is not an adequate equivalent for it; his disgust envelops and exceeds her')[2] can be turned around – that the intensity of feeling produced in Hamlet by his mother's sexual inscrutability captures the essence of femininity. For Hamlet, Gertrude is unmanageable in the enigmatic and indecipherable quality of her sexuality, 'the Mona Lisa of literature' [. . .]

If we set this version of Hamlet's difficulty in relation to Gertrude within the context I have been describing, what do we get? In the terms of intimacy, privacy and enclosure away from the public domain which I have been exploring, the problem which confronts Hamlet in the closet scene is one of contradictory, inconsistent and incompatible messages. Hamlet is summoned to the intimate space into which his mother has (publicly) withdrawn: he crosses into what he believes to be the domestic sphere, expecting the entire secrecy of an intense conversation between mother and son. But the presence of an intruder means that privacy is already absent, his exchanges already coloured by public interpretation as they are uttered. The competing and conflicting signs which Hamlet receives from his mother are the product of an insecure separation of private and public domains, intimate and state spaces. The enigma of femininity (in Freud's [. . .]

2   [Jardine's note.] Jacqueline Rose, 'Hamlet – the Mona Lisa of Literature', Critical Quarterly, 1986, vol. 28, pp. 35–49. For Eliot, see Modern Criticism, pp. 53–5.

terms) lies in this insufficiently clear demarcation of discourses and domains – in the elision of the demands of social and secret (sexual) intercourse.

When the intimacies of the early modern closet are interpreted from a public perspective, the intimate transaction is perceived as erotically charged. Just as Hamlet's uncomprehending buffoonery in Ophelia's closet [2.1.77–100] was readily interpreted as thwarted eroticism, so Hamlet's retreat from his mother's closet – backwards, in disorder, dragging a dead body – implies an erotic situation he has been unable to deal with. In other words, I am suggesting that the physical spaces of intimacy in the early modern play readily lend themselves to a psycho-analytic interpretation – or rather a reinterpretation from the perspective of a world which no longer honours spatial thresholds between differing registers of publicness and privacy.

'Is it the King?' asks Hamlet [3.4.26], after he has run through with his rapier the figure concealed behind the tapestry hanging. And indeed, the only person Gertrude might reputably have entertained in her closet is her husband. As if to underscore this limitation, the ghost of Hamlet's father appears 'in his nightgown' [3.4.103 stage direction[3]] – in the kind of state of undress which only a woman's most intimate companion would be entitled to wear in such a place. In response, Hamlet fills the space of intimacy with an excess of sexually explicit accusation levelled against his mother in respect of her conduct with Claudius, accusations in which his constant invoking of the mismatch between brother and brother renders both men vividly present [3.4.53–67; see Key Passages, **p. 147**][. . .].

'[Hamlet's] disgust envelops and exceeds [his mother]', wrote Eliot. 'The fact that it is a woman who is seen as cause of the excess and deficiency in the play and again a woman who symbolises its aesthetic failure starts to look like a repetition', writes Rose. A troubling excess – emotions too large for the scale of the offences caused – has been a feature of all *Hamlet* criticism since Eliot's classic essay. Hamlet's 'excessive' feelings in terms of desire (inexpressible emotion) immediately make concrete and specific his mother as focus of attention for her guilt – she is pronounced guilty not as a judgement on her actions, but as a condition of her presence in the play in relation to Hamlet – faced with the impossibility of resolving the uncertainties surrounding his father's death Hamlet turns his attention instead upon his mother. If Hamlet's feeling is excessive it is because his sense of his mother's guilt exceeds what could possibly fit the facts of the plot. Or, as another critic puts it, the play's enigma is the gap between 'Hamlet's vehement disgust and the Gertrude who is neither vehement nor disgusting'.[4] [. . .]

There is, however, another source of 'excess' in *Hamlet*, which conforms intriguingly closely to Rose's suggestions that 'buffoonery, ecstasy, the excessive and unknowable [are] terms in which we have learnt to recognise (since Freud at least) something necessarily present in any act of writing . . . which only sup-presses them . . . at a cost'. The play-text of *Hamlet* with which we all, as critics, work is a conflation of three texts,[5] and at its most conflated in the closet scene.

---

3   This stage direction is only in the First Quarto Text; see Key Passages, **pp. 113–15**.
4   [Jardine's note.] Cedric Watts, *Harvester New Critical Introductions to Shakespeare: Hamlet* (Brighton: Harvester, 1988), pp. xxiv–xxv.
5   See Key Passages, **pp. 113–15**.

All modern editions of *Hamlet* use the second quarto of 1604 (Q2) as their core text, and incorporate material from the 1623 first folio (F), together with some material from the first 'bad' quarto of 1603. The result is a 'conflated' text[6] [. . .].

Excess is 'present in the act of writing' in *Hamlet* because the received text contains more than one version of the 'act of writing' the closet scene.[7] This should not, however, deter us in locating the emotional crux of the encounter between Gertrude and Hamlet here, in this scene. For we might well want to argue that it is precisely because the exchanges between them carry such a heavy emotional freight that the dramatist worked over and reworked them in successive stagings, or textual renderings of the play. In any case, it is a tribute to the critical ear of both Eliot and Rose that their insistence on the curiously repetitive and ecstatic nature of Hamlet's pronouncements is matched by the discovery that the text of *Hamlet* is at this point in the play literally excessive. [. . .]

[W]hy does Gertrude continue to carry the play's burden of guilt so recognisably – so convincingly – today?

I return, then, to my earlier question: what is it in our contemporary version of the tragic which [. . .] requires a blameless hero – a hero whose tragic predicament derives from fatal flaws in others?

I suggest that this critical shift mirrors, and perhaps takes its justification from, a prevailing political tendency to deny responsibility for the oppressed and disadvantaged of all races, genders and sexual preferences, and to transfer to them culpability for their own predicament.

From **John Kerrigan, *Revenge Tragedy*** (Oxford: Clarendon Press, 1996), pp. 184–91

In a wide-ranging and profound study of revenge in western literature, Kerrigan argues that it is Hamlet's need to remember, not to avenge, his father that is crucial in the play. Kerrigan begins with a psychoanalytical approach to the prince's melancholy: in all his relationships he yearns for his father, the one person who has never rejected him. The argument then develops into an explanation of the importance of theatricality in the play: only performance can meaningfully bring back the longed-for past; vengeance is inadequate because it merely recapitulates the past vainly in the present.

---

6   [Jardine's note.] [. . .] Twenty-seven lines in the second quarto version of the closet scene do not occur in the folio text, but are customarily returned to the text by the editor, thus increasing its length significantly. Almost all of these occur in Hamlet's outbursts against his mother. Largely reshaped in the folio version of the play, the restoration of the 'lost' lines from the second quarto has the effect of literally *repeating* many of the sentiments expressed. The excess and repetition to which both Eliot and Rose draw attention, in other words, are a feature of the editorial process of textual conflation and accretion as much as of the dramatist's original design. Every modern edition of *Hamlet* (including the one Eliot was using) has – literally – too much text in the scene between Hamlet and Gertrude; there is textual excess even before the critic sets to work on it. And lo and behold, what an outstandingly alert and sensitive reader like Eliot detects in the scene is excessive emotion – too much emotionally going on in the text to be sustained by the plot structure.

7   [Jardine's note.] We might add that the first quarto contains a further, almost entirely distinct version of the most emotionally complex component in this scene, the 'Look here upon this picture' speech [3.4.54]. [. . .]

[. . .] Ophelia's apparent rejection is one factor in Hamlet's distress: by returning his letters and refusing him access she throws his love back onto the father who has never (it would seem) emotionally betrayed him. Another is Claudius' refusal to let him return to school in Wittenberg: this leaves the prince surrounded by people and places which remorselessly remind him of the dead king. But most important, of course, is the injunction, 'Remember me!' With this command the ghost condemns Hamlet to an endless, fruitless 'yearning for the lost figure'. In the nunnery and closet scenes, we see the effect on his sanity.

'My lord,' says Ophelia, 'I have remembrances of yours | That I have longed long to redeliver. | I pray you now receive them' [3.1.93–5]. This confirms for Hamlet a suspicion bred of his mother's 'o'er-hasty marriage', that woman's love is brief and unworthy. It seems that Ophelia wants to divest herself of every shred of attachment. In this she is no better than Gertrude, glad to forget her first husband. Moreover, the girl's gesture, 'There, my lord' [3.1.102], recalls an earlier situation: Old Hamlet, like Ophelia, had pressed on the prince remembrances that were too much his already. In saying her farewells, Ophelia is, in effect, forcing him to remember (and no doubt, though an instrument of Polonius' plots, she *does* want to reclaim his attention). Through the loss of Ophelia, Hamlet feels that of his father—which is why the hysteria which follows is in excess of its apparent object. The sexuality which the prince denounces is that of his mother as well as Ophelia; Claudius, as well as he, is an 'arrant knave' [3.1.129]; and there is indeed a sad resonance to the question—whether or not Polonius' surveillance is suspected—'Where's your father?' [ll. 130–1]. 'Hysterics', wrote Freud and Breuer, '*suffer mainly from reminiscences*'.[1]

The queen triggers Hamlet's raving in her bedchamber by calling Claudius 'your father' [3.4.8]. Forced by this to compare one king with another, Hamlet insists that his mother do the same. As he shows her the counterfeit presentments, the pictures of her two husbands, that tormented, idealizing remembrance which had filled his first soliloquy overwhelms him [3.4.55–62; see Key Passages, p. 147] [. . .]

' 'A was a man, take him for all in all' [1.2.187]: the audience is carried back to that almost hallucinatory moment when Old Hamlet drifted into the prince's 'mind's eye' [1.2.185]. And this time the ghost, fancied even more vividly, appears, suspended between spiritual and imaginative existence. 'In melancholy men', writes Burton of the phantasy, 'this faculty is most powerful and strong, and often hurts, producing many monstrous and prodigious things, especially if it be stirred up by some terrible object, presented to it from . . . memory'.[2] Hamlet sees a prodigy, but Gertrude, who has forgotten, does not.

It may seem rash to define Hamlet's derangement in terms of remembrance when we have Polonius' warning that 'to define true madness, | What is't but to be nothing else but mad?' [2.2.93–4]. Yet this is, in fact, encouraging, for by its

1   [Kerrigan's note.] Sigmund Freud and Josef Breuer, *Studies on Hysteria* (1893–5), trans. James and Alix Strachey, in *The Standard Edition of the Complete Psychological Works of Sigmund Freud*, gen. ed. James Strachey, 24 vols (London, 1966–74), ii.7.

2   [Kerrigan's note.] *The Anatomy of Melancholy* [1621], ed. Holbrook Jackson (London, 1932), 159 (pt. 1, s. 1, mem. 2, subs. 7).

logic one character is amply qualified to offer a definition. In a tragedy largely dominated by assumed, or partly assumed, insanity, Ophelia's derangement is terminally authentic. And when, in a sequence which parallels the nunnery scene, she gives her brother, like Hamlet before him, remembrances, she says: 'There's rosemary, that's for remembrance; pray you, love, remember. And there is pansies, that's for thoughts' [4.5.174–5]. The language of these flowers is not left to speak for itself; Ophelia provides a gloss. And lest an audience overlook the allusion, Shakespeare spells out the moral. 'A document in madness,' Laertes translates, 'thoughts and remembrance fitted' [4.5.176–7].

Where does that leave revenge? In the body of the play, as in the first exchange with the ghost, it is far less important to Hamlet than is the impulse to remember. That imbalance is plainly dramatized in the performance of *The Murder of Gonzago*. 'Soliman and Perseda' was staged to effect Hieronimo's revenge,[3] but there is never any question of Claudius being killed in or at 'The Mousetrap'. Perhaps Hamlet does stage the play to test the word of the ghost. Presumably he is not simply rationalizing when he says that it will 'catch the conscience of the King' [2.2.601; see Key Passages, **p. 136**). But the crucial motive is revealed to Ophelia just before the show begins: 'O heavens, die two months ago, and not forgotten yet? Then there's hope a great man's memory may outlive his life half a year, but by'r lady, 'a must build churches then, or else shall 'a suffer not thinking on, with the hobby-horse, whose epitaph is, "For O, for O, the hobby-horse is forgot" ' [3.2.128–33]. Hamlet recovers the orchard as Hieronimo the arbour,[4] but the prince does so because he wants to see his father alive again and to help the 'great man's memory' survive. Revenge is so stifled by remembrance that, when the Player King announces 'Purpose is but the slave to memory' [3.2.183; see Key Passages, **p. 140**], he does more than gird unwittingly at Gertrude's forgetfulness of her husband: ironies spark from the prince's retrospective tardiness to the thought that, precisely by remembering his father, he neglects what Old Hamlet's spirit[5] wants him to do. Only the transformation of 'The Mousetrap's murderer from brother to nephew—making him the equivalent of Hamlet rather than Claudius—reveals the prince's guilty sense that if he could but abandon himself, become as crude and cruel as 'Lucianus, nephew to the king' [3.2.239; see Key Passages, **p. 142**], he could satisfy the ghost.

With characteristic audacity, Shakespeare gives Hamlet his best chance of killing the king (before the confusions of the denouement) immediately after 'The Mousetrap'. As he goes to see his mother in the bedchamber, the prince comes upon Claudius at prayer. Has he not just seen his father killed afresh, and been persuaded of his uncle's guilt by his reaction to the playlet? Now Hamlet can become Lucianus, and he takes up the role with relish, both in resolving to strike [3.3.73–4]—and in deciding against [3.3.87–93; see Key Passages, **p. 145**] [. . .]

Dr Johnson is not the only commentator to have been appalled by this. Others have spoken, more cautiously, of rationalization. What matters, however, is the

---

3   In Kyd's earlier revenge play *The Spanish Tragedy* (1587).
4   Where his son was murdered.
5   [Kerrigan's note.] The claim that the ghost may be a devil, impersonating the king – see e.g. Eleanor Prosser, *Hamlet and Revenge*, 2nd edn. (Stanford, Calif., 1971), chapters 4–5 – impinges on the play's histrionic concerns here, but does not otherwise greatly complicate its mnemonics.

emergence of these sentiments from thoughts of reciprocity. ' 'A took my father grossly, full of bread,' Hamlet says, 'With all his crimes broad blown, as flush as May' [3.3.80–81; see Key Passages, p. 145]. Now that the playlet has recovered the past, showing Old Hamlet asleep in his orchard, 'unhous'led, disappointed, unanel'd' [1.5.77; see Key Passages, p. 131], the punitive inadequacy of anything but complete retribution is freshly in mind. Through the Lucianus-like ruthlessness of his speech Hamlet registers a recognition that revenge is incoherent unless it possesses that recapitulative power which (*pace* Hieronimo) the passage of experience makes impossible. If the prince found Claudius gaming or swearing, he would want him asleep in an orchard, and not *now* but *then*. In other words, his prevarication anticipates problems about punishment in time [. . .]. Here, it is enough to notice that, in so far as *The Murder of Gonzago* stirs thoughts of the past, it not only compromises action by substituting remembrance for revenge but points up the incoherence of violence by staging a more persuasive recapitulation than stabbing in the back could contrive.

In any case, Hamlet cannot become a Lucianus, and so does not revenge his father. The weapons finally used to kill Claudius (the venomous rapier and celebratory, poisoned drink) mark the attack as spontaneous retaliation, not long-nurtured vengeance. The king dies for the murder of Gertrude and the prince, not for a poisoning in the orchard. Old Hamlet does not return to triumph over the corpses of his enemies, like the satisfied ghost of Andrea at the end of *The Spanish Tragedy*. Memory being private, the audience cannot even tell whether Hamlet is thinking about his father during these critical minutes. Old Hamlet is simply not mentioned in the turbulent last phase of the play—an omission which seems the more remarkable when Laertes, who is being hurried off by the fell sergeant death with yet more despatch than the prince, finds time to refer to Polonius. Hamlet knows that revenge would gratify the stern, militaristic father whom he loves, and he appears to want to please him; but he cannot overcome his radical sense of its pointlessness. Claudius has killed Old Hamlet and whored the queen. Neither evil can be undone. Revenge cannot bring back what has been lost. Only memory, with all its limitations, can do that. [. . .]

[. . .] If the graveyard focuses Hamlet's imagination on his approaching end, it also reminds him of the possibility of survival. That is why Horatio is so important to him in the final scene [5.2.339–45; see Key Passages, p. 168].

Yet, can Horatio report either Hamlet or his cause aright? His brief account to Fortinbras, with its 'carnal, bloody and unnatural acts . . . accidental judgements, casual slaughters' [5.2.386–7; see Key Passages, p. 169], suggests that he cannot, for everything that seems essential to Hamlet's tragedy is left out. Honest, compassionate, and intelligent though he is, Horatio is not equipped by circumstance to inform the yet unknowing world about the nunnery scene, Claudius's words to heaven, 'To be or not to be' [3.1.56; see Key Passages, p. 137] or, indeed, any of those perplexed soliloquies.[6] Only the play can report such things, which is why the dramatic imagery of Hamlet's speech is so interesting. [. . .]

---

6   [Kerrigan's note.] On the difficulty of Horatio's task, see Constantine Cavafy's poem, 'King Claudius'.

It should now be clear why the tragedians of the city are so prominent in *Hamlet*. Clearly the prince is interested in them because of his obsession with 'seeming' and 'being', and because they can act while divorcing themselves from their actions—which is what Hamlet would have to do if he were to revenge his father. They also interest him, however, because they make remembrance their profession. The prince must struggle to keep his promise to the ghost, to preserve his memory for only a few months against the tide of the world's indifference, but the first player can reach back effortlessly to the crash of 'senseless Ilium' [2.2.470] and the murder of Priam [2.2.464–93]. So vividly does he make the dead King of Troy live, that Hamlet has the players do the same for another dead king—his father—in *The Murder of Gonzago*. The most extended and public act of remembrance in *Hamlet*, 'The Mousetrap' moves on from Troy to dramatize the more immediate past of Vienna and, through that, Denmark, before melting into the present of the larger play, the murder in the orchard being effected and unpunished, the murderer being happily in possession of both crown and queen.

Throughout *Hamlet*, the prince's obsession with actors and acting, together with his allusions to revenge tragedy, work to divorce the character from the actor who represents him. When Burbage or Olivier[7] calls on those who are 'audience to this act' [5.2.340; see Key Passages, **p. 168**], members of the theatre audience are drawn within the scope of the hero's attention as surely as the pale and trembling Danes, but also made aware that, just as the squeaking boy is not Cleopatra,[8] so the actor is not the Hamlet which in another sense he is. The character seems to protest through the imagery that he is too elusively himself to be inhabited by another.

From **Kiernan Ryan, Shakespeare** (Basingstoke: Palgrave, third edition 2002), pp. 69–71

Like Holderness, Kiernan Ryan exposes the conservative assumptions which support much of the received twentieth-century Shakespearean critical tradition. For Ryan, Hamlet is a man who seems critically aware that the particular historical circumstances in which he lives are neither just nor right. History is a process; the human condition is not fixed. Hamlet will not accept the society in which he lives or its values, but he cannot escape either. Tragedy nevertheless shows us the possibility that the world can be changed for the better.

The notion that Shakespeare's tragedies depict as fixed and inexorable the destructive forces to which individuals find themselves subject, and that the wisdom they preach is submission to conditions human beings cannot change, crops up in a wide variety of critical guises. Its most common application turns the tragedies into timeless spiritual narratives of fall, sacrifice and redemption, or

---

7   Richard Burbage played the prince in the original production; Laurence Olivier on stage from 1937 and on film in 1948; see The Work in Performance, pp. 103–5.
8   [Kerrigan's note.] *Antony and Cleopatra*, 5.2.219–21.

temptation and damnation; or they are press ganged into labouring as secular parables, dramatized cautionary tales, which stress the prudence of obeying, and the folly of flouting, the unspoken rules that secure the way things are.

However sophisticated the phrasing, it is remarkable how much criticism boils down to this reductive, moralistic kind of reading. The myopic banality of such an approach is nowhere more apparent than in its infliction on *Hamlet*. Harry Levin has called *Hamlet* 'the most problematic play ever written by Shakespeare or any other playwright',[1] although critics seem to have had few qualms about recycling the same old solution to the problem decade after decade. Maynard Mack's essay of 1952 winds up with a Hamlet who at last 'accepts the world as it is, the world as a duel, in which, whether we know it or not, evil holds the poisoned rapier and the poisoned chalice waits; and in which, if we win at all, it costs not less than everything'.[2] And, thirty years later, Harold Jenkins concludes the introduction to his Arden edition of *Hamlet* in exactly the same vein:

> Johnson is well known to have said that Shakespeare 'seems to write without any moral purpose'; but this is perhaps a play in which a moral is implicit, both simple and profound. For it commends a man who, after questioning the meaning of creation, comes to accept a design in it beyond our comprehending, and who therefore, after seeking to withdraw from life through an abhorrence of all that is ugly and vicious in it, is finally – though tragically not until death approaches – content to live life as it is, able to acknowledge, in word and deed, 'The readiness is all'.[3]

Hamlet's task is seen here as the restoration of the status quo by exposing and killing Claudius, and thus executing the revenge commanded by the ghost of his father. The tragedy of the situation is construed as Hamlet's possession of moral and psychological flaws, however virtuous their origin, which prevent him from fulfilling his obligation without delay. 'We are forced to make the conclusion', as Willard Farnham puts it, 'that [Hamlet] might have escaped catastrophe if he had had narrower nobility', and had remained uncontaminated by 'a sort of deadly sin of sloth'.[4] If only, Jenkins clearly suggests, Hamlet had been able to perceive earlier the inescapable necessity of accepting one's appointed fate, of resting content with the mysterious way things are, no matter how 'ugly and vicious', the normal course of life might have been re-established and the tragedy need not have occurred.

But this misses the point of Shakespearean tragedy, which is to devise predicaments that cannot be accounted for, let alone resolved, by pinning the responsibility on the protagonist alone. Shakespeare's greatest tragedies compel us to probe beyond moralism, to analyse the attitudes that could trap such an individual in such a predicament in the first place. For the moralistic critic, the

1   [Ryan's note.] Quoted in *Hamlet*, New Arden Shakespeare, ed. Harold Jenkins (London: Methuen, 1982), p. 122.
2   [Ryan's note.] Maynard Mack, 'The World of Hamlet' in *Hamlet: A Selection of Critical Essays*, ed. John Jump (London: Macmillan, 1968).
3   [Ryan's note.] *Hamlet*, ed. Jenkins, p. 159.
4   [Ryan's note.] Willard Farnham, 'The Tragic Qualm' in *Shakespeare: The Tragedies*, ed. Alfred Harbage (Englewood Cliffs NJ: Prentice Hall, 1964), pp. 20, 21.

tragedy of Hamlet consists in his unfortunate, enigmatic failure to conform to the prescribed codes of behaviour from the start, although he is congratulated on seeing the need for resignation too late rather than never seeing it at all. But what if one proceeds on the opposite assumption? What if Hamlet's tormented reluctance to surrender to the role of revenging prince expresses a legitimate rejection of the whole way of life that festers in the 'prison' [2.2.243] Denmark has indeed become? In that case the tragedy turns out to be something quite different. It is the tragedy of having to live and die on the 'rotten' [1.4.90] terms of such a place at all, despite the knowledge that life could and should be otherwise, that human beings are not forever doomed to become the scoundrels, pawns and parasites that this sort of society moulds most of them into. Hamlet's belligerent withdrawal into the dramatic limbo and licensed discourse of his 'antic disposition' [1.5.180] functions, in fact, as a sustained estrangement-effect. It sabotages the revenge-play formula and thereby strikes at the social order whose validity that formula presupposes, and whose axioms it would otherwise smuggle through unchallenged. Only critics for whom compliance with convention is the plainest common sense could find Hamlet's failure to capitulate more promptly a source of endless puzzlement, and make this tragedy 'the most problematic play ever written'. But, once one has grasped that it is truly the time that is out of joint [1.5.196] and not Hamlet, the supposed central problem of the play melts away.

Most of the interpretations canonized in the standard editions an critical casebooks strive to defuse Shakespeare's tragedies. They habitually bleach out the plays' depiction of life as a changing social situation made, and hence transformable, by men and women. Time and again the tragedies' dynamic, concrete account of a particular person's history is obliterated. The plays are forced to testify instead to the underlying uniformity of human experience, which mocks social differences and historical development as delusions. Such criticism drains the tragedies of their power to expose the alterable causes of injustice, violence and despair, and expand our awareness of alternative fates hovering in the wings of what happens.

From **Stephen Greenblatt, Hamlet in Purgatory** (Princeton and Oxford: Princeton University Press, 2002), pp. 247–8; 251–4; 256–7

Stephen Greenblatt's book is a detailed study of the representation of the Catholic doctrine of purgatory in late mediaeval and early modern writing. Purgatory, the place where souls (like the Ghost) who do not deserve instant damnation go in order to be 'purged', is not mentioned in scripture but grew as a belief in the Middle Ages. Protestants, who only accepted what was sanctioned in the Bible, rejected it and mocked it (see Contextual Overview, **p.10**). Hamlet in Purgatory is not ultimately a study of purgatory, however; Greenblatt is leading to a striking conclusion. Hamlet's father's ghost on stage can be seen as a sort of secular substitute for the emotional functions which the pre-reformation institutions for remembering the dead once served. Many missed the Catholic rituals which had allowed the bereaved to feel that they could still have some contact with the dead: individuals who now only lived in the imagination of the living. The new public theatres, where figures at once real and imagined walked the stage, helped to fill the emotional void which the end of Catholic practices had left. The 'weirdness' of theatre was somehow close to the experience which religious practices had embodied.

Th[e] dispute over Ophelia's funeral ceremony [5.1.216–31] is an instance of an overarching phenomenon in *Hamlet*: the disruption or poisoning of virtually all rituals for managing grief, allaying personal and collective anxiety, and restoring order.

The source of this poisoning in the play is Claudius, who usurps not only the kingship but also the language of Protestant mourning. "Why should you shed tears immoderately for them who have all tears wiped from their eyes?" asked a seventeenth-century preacher in a typical funeral sermon [. . .]. "God allows us tears; Jacob wept over his dead father; tears give vent to grief," the preacher concedes, "but there is no reason we should grieve excessively for our pious friends, they receive a Crown, and shall we mourn when they have preferment?"[1] "To persever / In obstinate condolement," Claudius tells his nephew in similar accents,

> is a course
> Of impious stubbornness, 'tis unmanly grief' [. . .]
> [1.2.92–4]

In 1601, when Shakespeare wrote *Hamlet*, Protestant preachers had been saying words to this effect for fifty years, trying to wean their flock away from Purgatory and prayers for the dead and obstinate condolement. The argument seemed won: the chantries[2] were all silent. But why should Shakespeare—who sympathetically rehearses the same sentiments in *Twelfth Night*, albeit in the mouth of the fool [*Twelfth Night* 1.5.54–9]—have given the Protestant position to his arch-villain in *Hamlet*? And why should his Ghost—who might, after all, have simply croaked for revenge, like the Senecan ghosts in Kyd [see Contextual Overview, **pp. 8–9**] insist that he has come from a place where his crimes are being burned and purged away? [. . .]

[. . .] Shakespeare's *Hamlet* [. . .] probes precisely the fears, longings, and confusions that Foxe[3] attempts to ridicule. The Ghost comes from Purgatory bewailing his failure to receive full Christian last rites but then demands that his son avenge his death, thereby initiating a nightmare that will eventually destroy not only his usurping brother but also Polonius, Ophelia, Laertes, Rosencrantz, Guildenstern, Gertrude, and his own son. He tells Hamlet not to let "the royal bed of Denmark be / A couch for luxury and damnèd incest" [1.5.82–3; see Key Passages, **p. 131**] but then warns his son not to taint his mind or let his soul

---

1   [Greenblatt's note.] Thomas Watson, *The Fight of Faith Crowned: or, a Sermon Preached at the funeral of that Eminently Holy man Mr. Henry Stubs* (London: Joseph Coller, 1678).
2   Pre-Reformation Catholic chapels, in which prayers for the souls of the dead in purgatory were said.
3   A sixteenth-century Protestant writer who mocked the Catholic notion of purgatory.

contrive anything against his mother. Hamlet receives the most vivid confirmation of the nature of the afterlife, with its "sulph'rous and tormenting flames" [1.5.3], but then, in a spectacular and mysterious act of forgetting, speaks of death as the "undiscovered country from whose bourn / No traveller returns" [3.1.79–80; see Key Passages, p. 138]. These are the kinds of representational contradictions that Foxe mercilessly mocks. To notice, publish, and circulate them throughout the realm is to declare that key theological principles and emotional experiences cannot hold together, and that the institution that generated them is bankrupt, worthy only of contempt and laughter.

But in *Hamlet* the same contradictions that should lead to derision actually intensify the play's uncanny power. And it is precisely Foxe's comedy that helped make Shakespeare's tragedy possible. It did so by participating in a violent ideological struggle that turned negotiations with the dead from an institutional process governed by the church to a poetic process governed by guilt, projection, and imagination. Purgatory exists in the imaginary universe of *Hamlet*, but only as what the suffering prince, in a different context, calls "a dream of passion" [2.2.546; see Key Passages, p. 134]. Indeed, there is a striking link between Hamlet's description of the player who

> in a fiction, in a dream of passion,
> Could force his soul so to his whole conceit
> That from her working all his visage wanned,
> Tears in his eyes, distraction in's aspect,
> A broken voice, and his whole function suiting
> With forms to his conceit,
>
> [2.2.546–51]

and the Ghost's description of the effect that his tale of torment would have on Hamlet [1.5.15–20; see Key Passages, pp. 129–30] [. . .]

The link is the astonishingly palpable physiological effect of spectral fiction, dream, tale: "And all for nothing" [2.2.551].

Of course, within the play's fiction, Hamlet does not know that Purgatory is a fiction, as the state-sanctioned church of Shakespeare's time had declared it to be. On the contrary, he is desperate to establish the veracity of the Ghost's tale—"I'll take the Ghost's word for a thousand pound" [3.2.280–81], he exults after the play-within-the-play—and hence to establish that the Ghost is in reality his father's spirit and not the devil. But this reality is theatrical rather than theological; it can accommodate elements, such as a Senecan call for revenge, that would radically undermine church doctrine. At the same time, it can offer the viewer, in an unforgettably vivid dream of passion, many [. . .] deep imaginative experiences, the tangled longing, guilt, pity, and rage [. . .]. Does this mean that Shakespeare was participating in a secularization process, one in which the theatre offers a disenchanted version of what the cult of Purgatory once offered? Perhaps. But the palpable effect is something like the reverse: *Hamlet* immeasurably intensifies a sense of the weirdness of the theater, its proximity to certain experiences that had been organized and exploited by religious institutions and rituals.

Not all forms of energy in Shakespeare's theater, of course, have been transferred, openly or covertly, from the zone of the real to the zone of the imaginary. Plays can borrow, imitate, and reflect much of what passes for every-day reality without necessarily evacuating this reality or exposing it as made-up. But the power of Shakespeare's theatre is frequently linked to its appropriation of weakened or damaged institutional structures. It is conceivable that Shakespeare with his recusant[4] family background, his education in Stratford by teachers linked to Campion[5] and the Jesuits, his own possible links to the Lancashire recusants, felt a covert loyalty to these structures and a dismay that they were being gutted. [. . .]

We do not, however, need to believe that Shakespeare was himself a secret Catholic sympathizer; we need only to recognize how alert he was to the materials that were being made available to him. At a deep level there is something magnificently opportunistic, appropriative, absorptive, even cannibalistic about Shakespeare's art [. . .]. In the case of Purgatory, important forces had been busily struggling for decades to prepare the playwright's feast. And the struggle did not end with the performance of the play or the playwright's death. [. . .]

With the doctrine of Purgatory and the elaborate practices that grew up around it, the church had provided a powerful method of negotiating with the dead, or, rather, with those who were at once dead and yet, since they could still speak, appeal, and appall, not completely dead. The Protestant attack on the "middle state of souls" and the middle place those souls inhabited destroyed this method for most people in England, but it did not destroy the longings and fears that Catholic doctrine had focused and exploited. Instead, [. . .] the space of Purgatory becomes the space of the stage where old Hamlet's Ghost is doomed for a certain term to walk the night. That term has now lasted some four hundred years, and it has brought with it a cult of the dead that I and the readers of this book have been serving.

---

4   Catholics who refused the oath acknowledging the monarch's supremacy over the Church in England. There is evidence that Shakespeare's father John was just such a dissident; see, e.g., Park Honan, *Shakespeare: A Life* (Oxford: Oxford University Press, 1998), pp. 38–9.
5   Edmund Campion, a Catholic missionary to England executed in 1581. See Richard Wilson, *Secret Shakespeare* (Manchester: Manchester University Press, 2004), pp. 53–60.

The Work in Performance

Hamlet On Stage

Hamlet may well be the most performed play in world theatre. What follows is only an outline of notable productions in Europe and the USA since Betterton and Garrick (see Critical History, **pp. 29–31**).

Garrick's successor John Philip Kemble played the prince on the London stage from 1783 to 1817. Graceful, stately and noble in the role, Kemble brought a single interpretation to the whole performance, where earlier performers had regarded the part as a series of set piece speeches or scenes. Kemble displayed a 'natural melancholy, or rather pensiveness of manner'.[1] Some critics felt that his was a performance shaped by 'art' and not 'nature', but that was not a charge that could be brought against the electrifying Hamlet of Edmund Kean (who performed the role in London 1814–32). The critic William Hazlitt (see Early Critical Reception, **p. 46**) thought Kean not enough of the 'gentleman and the scholar'; indeed, there was a 'severity, approaching to virulence, in [his] common observations and answers'. But this was compensated by the 'force and animation' and 'extreme boldness' of his performance. Some of Kean's stage business delivered flashes of insight to the audience. For example, Hazlitt remarked on how Kean used his sword to prevent Horatio and Marcellus from accompanying him when he obeys the ghost's instruction (1.4.85–6), rather than point it towards the ghost as other Hamlets had done. Hazlitt also thought that 'the manner of his taking Rosencrantz and Guildenstern under each arm, under pretence of communicating his secret to them, when he means only to trifle with them, had the finest effect [presumably 2.2.249ff]'. In particular, 'the manner of his coming back after he has gone to the extremity of the stage, from a pang of parting tenderness to press his lips to Ophelia's hand [3.1.151] . . . had an electrifying effect on the house. It was the finest commentary that was ever made on Shakespeare. It explained the character at once.'[2] Yet if the apparently spontaneous natural passions of Kean made him the perfect Romantic Hamlet (see Critical History, **p. 31**), Kean

1   Mary Russell Mitford, quoted in *Shakespeare in Production: 'Hamlet'*, ed. Robert Hapgood (Cambridge: Cambridge University Press, 1999), p. 19.
2   William Hazlitt in *Shakespeare in the Theatre: An Anthology of Criticism*, ed. Stanley Wells (Oxford: Oxford University Press, 1997), pp. 41, 43, 42, 42, 42–3.

admitted to Garrick's widow that it was all 'premeditated and studied before-hand'.[3] William Charles Macready (took the role in London 1823–51) brought back some gentlemanly respectability to the role, as befited the high Victorian age. His Hamlet was a good man turned to pessimism, who eventually finds some peace through a trust in Providence.

The American actor Edwin Booth (see The Work in Performance, **pp. 95–7**) continued the romantic interpretation of the noble prince from 1860 to 1891 at a time when British Hamlets were, by contrast, fallibly human. Henry Irving's production filled the auditorium of the Lyceum in London from 1874 to 1885 with people of all classes. His Hamlet was a not an ideal prince but a 'real' human individual, intense, 'edgy', 'emotional rather than spiritual . . . mercurial and tormented . . . subject to real rather than feigned hysteria.'[4] A gangling, awkward man, his vulnerable individuality increased the melodrama of the prince's role. Irving disregarded the traditional gestures and bits of stage business and made the role his own. The journalist Clement Scott described the play scene (3.4; see Key Passages, **pp. 139–43**) as follows:

> He acted with an impulsive energy beyond all praise. Point after point was made in a whirlwind of excitement. He lured, he tempted, he trapped the King, he drove out his wicked uncle conscience-stricken and baffled, and with a hysterical yell of triumph he sank down . . . in the very throne . . . which his rival had just vacated.[5]

'Concentration on such small physical details gave the performance its nervous idiosyncrasy,' writes Dawson, 'and hence its reality for its cheering audience.'[6] All references to political events beyond Denmark were excised, and the focus was on a domestic Elsinore: 'Claudius's role was cut and shaped so that he resembled the melodramatic villain more than head of state.'[7] Irving was powerfully supported by the beautiful and plaintive Ellen Terry as Ophelia.

Johnston Forbes-Robertson's Hamlet (London, 1897) was a 'genial . . . human and loveable individual'.[8] 'Nothing half so charming has been seen by this generation,' wrote the playwright and critic George Bernard Shaw. Shaw also praised how Forbes Robertson 'plays as Shakespear[e] should be played, on the line and to the line, with the utterance and acting simultaneous, inseparable and in fact identical'.[9] This was not the way the American John Barrymore played the role (New York 1922, London 1925), and it offended Shaw.[10] Barrymore's many long pauses suggested that there was more going on the mind of Hamlet than his words suggested, but in fact Barrymore thought the role 'amazingly simple',[11] and there

3 Quoted in Hapgood (see note 1), p. 25.
4 Anthony B. Dawson, *Shakespeare in Performance: 'Hamlet'* (Manchester: Manchester University Press, 1995), p. 60.
5 Scott in Wells (see note 2), p. 109.
6 Dawson (see note 4), p. 62.
7 Dawson (see note 4), p. 64.
8 Review in *The Illustrated London News* quoted in *'Hamlet': New Critical Essays*, ed. Arthur F. Kinney (New York and London: Routledge, 2002), p. 51.
9 Shaw in Wells (see note 2), p. 150.
10 Dawson (see note 4), p. 70.
11 Hapgood (see note 1), p. 61.

was little development of character as the play progressed. Yet Barrymore's Hamlet was highly intelligent, 'tender and virile and witty and dangerous',[12] as well as handsome and athletic. His interpretation was as clear as his easy speaking of the verse. However, some felt his Hamlet was too reasonable and comprehensible. Notably, the production seems to have given the role of Gertrude (Constance Collier in 1925) some depth and sympathy.[13]

If Barrymore's performance looked back to the noble princes of the nineteenth century, the set for the production was ultra-modern: a single, versatile design of archway, platform and steps that served for all scenes of the play. William Poel had mounted an experimental London performance of the First Quarto text (see Key Passages, pp. 113–15) in 1914, on a bare thrust stage with Elizabethan costumes and a boy Ophelia. The twentieth century was to see many productions dominated by a single directorial 'concept' such as this, an idea which governed the design and the performance of the whole cast, rather than concentrating principally on the main character. Barry Jackson's *Hamlet* at the Birmingham Repertory Theatre in 1925 set the play in the present day, with the prince in plusfours; Ophelia was a cigarette-smoking 'flapper'. This was a fast-flowing production with judicious cuts. Hamlet himself was just one of many interesting, fully drawn characters on stage. Colin Keith-Johnston as the prince delivered his lines in an unpoetic, naturalistic way, with 'a caddishness born of despair' as one reviewer put it.[14] He appealed very much to the mood of post-war disillusionment among the young. Another reviewer, Hubert Griffith, identified the powerful impact of modern dress on audience response to the play:

> Who has ever cared before violently cared what Laertes does or thinks? And yet, once make him an ordinary decent undergraduate, warped by a rancorous hatred in his heart for the young man who he thinks has seduced his sister . . . I know that the Laertes of the trunk-hose[15] . . . is a creature I never want to endure again.[16]

Keith-Johnston's Hamlet was perhaps the first of the despairing, angry or disturbed Hamlets who dominated productions for the rest of the century. John Gielgud, who played the prince six times between 1930 and 1944, was noted for his beautiful, musical, lucid and intelligent speaking of the verse (the American director Lee Strasberg is supposed to have remarked that 'when Gielgud speaks the verse I can hear Shakespeare *thinking*').[17] Nevertheless, his 1930 prince was angry and disgusted; his 1939 Hamlet cynical, a 'coarse jester'.[18] When Richard Burton first played the prince in Edinburgh in 1953 he was thought to be 'angry, sturdy, athletic, unsubtle'.[19] Yet as the role developed after the production moved to London, Burton's performance attracted the audience by its emotional

12 Orson Welles quoted in Hapgood (see note 1), p. 62.
13 Dawson (see note 4), pp. 73–6.
14 *The Saturday Review*, quoted in Dawson (see note 4), p. 88.
15 Elizabethan costume worn around the lower body.
16 Griffith quoted in Wells (see note 2), p. 205.
17 Quoted in Hapgood (see note 1), p. 67.
18 Hapgood (see note 1), p. 66.
19 Hapgood (see note 1), p. 71.

unpredictability, as if Shakespeare 'actually put on stage in one character virtually every emotion of which a man is capable'.[20]

A similar dissolution of self, or loss of control over personal identity, became one of the dominant strands in late twentieth-century *Hamlets*. The set for the 1989 Royal Shakespeare Company (RSC) touring production, directed by Ron Daniels, had 'dizzyingly out-of-kilter window and walls' and 'the atmosphere of a mental institution'.[21] Mark Rylance's disturbed, lost, unhappy prince in a dysfunctional family nevertheless appealed to the audience; he used the soliloquies to confide intimately with them. Kevin Kline's 1990 New York Hamlet was 'antic and quixotic, prone to tears and somewhat emotionally unstable . . . he played on the fine line of jocularity and lunatic impulse'.[22]

The other dominant strand is a concentration on the political meanings of the play to a contemporary audience. Peter Hall's 1965 RSC production at Stratford and London cast the young David Warner as a voice of anti-establishment revolt (see The Work in Performance, **pp. 98–9**); Steven Pimlott in 2001, also for the RSC, cast Samuel West as a selfish zealot who is a danger to a flawed but well-functioning political system (see The Work in Performance, **pp. 100–1**). Richard Eyre's production at the Royal Court in London in 1980 contained both strands of interpretation. The ghost did not appear on stage, but possessed the prince (Jonathan Pryce), who spoke his lines in a 'violent, retching' manner. This was a dangerous, erratic prince who was also reasonable and lucid. The ingenious set meanwhile made Elsinore a place of spies and overhearing; Polonius was 'a bully, a sycophant'[23] and there was a sense of 'a nasty and brutish power structure'.[24] Harriet Walter's Ophelia was 'externally acquiescent but inwardly resentful, full of guilt', and her 'characterization complemented the general sense of political and social pressure'.[25]

Yet some recent London productions have been less fractured and more harmonious. The 1997 RSC production with Alex Jennings as the prince was remarkably apolitical and began with a home movie of the young prince playing in the snow with his father. The 2003–4 RSC Hamlet featured Toby Stephens as a clear-headed man of action in the John Barrymore mode. Peter Brook directed Adrian Lester at the Young Vic in London in 2001 in a production which sought to reveal the 'inner myth' beneath the surface of the play, in the patterns of the protagonists' emotions.

Brook's vision of the play has echoes of the ideas of the avant-garde British designer Edward Gordon Craig, who worked on the Moscow Arts Theatre production of 1912. The play has always been culturally significant in eastern Europe. Craig envisaged a still Hamlet on stage throughout who 'embodies the mystical powers of the spirit'.[26] The director, Konstantin Stanislavsky, ensured

---

20 Richard L. Sterne quoted in Hapgood (see note 1), p. 72.
21 Hapgood (see note 1), p. 83.
22 Mary Z. Maher, *Modern Hamlets and their Soliloquies* (Iowa City: University of Iowa Press, 2003), pp. 183–4.
23 John Carey quoted in Dawson (see note 4), p. 162.
24 Dawson (see note 4), p. 162.
25 Dawson (see note 4), p. 167.
26 Hapgood (see note 1), p. 58. Craig originally wanted the 'entire court covered by a single golden cape, with the characters' heads protruding through holes in it' (p. 57).

instead that Vasili Kachalov's Hamlet was intense, mobile and psychologically convincing. In communist eastern Europe later in the century, Hamlet, the intellectual who is challenged to take action against tyranny, became a politically controversial figure. Roman Zawistowski's production at Cracow in 1956 was 'full of pain and hatred against Stalinist oppression and surveillance'.[27] Yuri Lyubimov's *Hamlet* for his Taganka Theatre ran from 1971 until his death in 1980. The set was dominated a by a huge woollen curtain, moving around the actors

> like a giant monster . . . setting the pace, and holding within its folds the symbols and tools of power – black armbands, swords, goblets, thrones edged with knives. It envelops Ophelia, intimidates Polonius, protects Gertrude, supports Claudius and threatens Hamlet. Finally its sweeps the stage clean, and moves towards the audience as though to destroy it, too.[28]

It was 'the sign of the prison house, Denmark as Gulag', perhaps the Soviet system itself. Josef Svoboda's 1978 Prague *Hamlet* oscillated between 'farce and tragedy'[29] – a comment on what had become of communist idealism – as the gravediggers, dressed as clowns, intervened in the action and dominated the whole ending of the play.

This survey of *Hamlet* on stage should also mention the plays which have grown out of its celebrity in the modern theatre. Tom Stoppard's absurdist comedy *Rosencrantz and Guildenstern are Dead* (1967)[30] puts the two courtiers at the uncomprehending centre of their own tragedy, while Shakespeare's play intrudes comically and puzzlingly on the action. Heiner Müller's 1984 *Hamletmachine* is a disturbing, violent collage, fragments of the play embodied in a chaotic theatrical experience intended to resist our dominant view of reality.[31] The Canadian director Robert Lepage has adapted the play as *Elsinore* (1995), a dazzling one-man show using multimedia technology to enable us 'to see the colour of Hamlet's despair'.[32]

There follow a few detailed glimpses of key productions of *Hamlet*. They show, just as the foregoing account has demonstrated, that this iconic tragedy continues to have something important to say to us at very different historical moments.

Edwin Booth (1860–91): From *Shakespeare in Production: 'Hamlet'*, ed. Robert Hapgood (Cambridge: Cambridge University Press, 1999), pp. 33–6

Edwin Booth was perhaps the first great American Hamlet. He succeeded in creating a genuinely romantic interpretation of the role which portrayed the prince as a tortured intelligence in a fallen world. Booth's performance proved

27 Zednek Stríbny, *Shakespeare and Eastern Europe* (Oxford: Oxford University Press, 2000), p. 100; quoted in Kinney (see note 8), p. 57.
28 M. Croyden, quoted in Dawson (see note 4), p. 236.
29 Stríbny (see note 27), p. 118, quoted in Kinney (see note 8), p. 58.
30 *Rosencrantz and Guildenstern are Dead* (London: Faber and Faber, 1967).
31 Heiner Müller, 'Hamletmachine', in *Theatremachine*, trans. and ed. Marc von Henning (London: Faber and Faber, 1995).
32 http://www.changeperformingarts.it/Lepage/elsinore.html

very attractive with audiences in the USA, even if its sentimentality did not endear itself in Britain. Robert Hapgood's edition of the play (from which this extract comes) provides a history of *Hamlet*'s performance history and also a commentary on the way that each scene has been played on stage and screen over the centuries.

No Hamlet has been more 'refined and gentle' than America's Edwin Booth. He was not the first Hamlet to inherit the part from his father (Junius Brutus) – Charles Kean had given a notable portrayal. Nor was he to be the last – H. B. and Laurence Irving would also follow their father, Henry. But Edwin Booth is the only Hamlet to have surpassed his father in the role. [. . .]

Booth put his own touch on the general Romantic reading of the character (he had read both Goethe and Hazlitt) [see Early Critical Reception, **pp. 46–7**]. He portrayed a Prince 'of a reflective, sensitive, gentle, generous nature, tormented, borne down and made miserable by an occasion . . . to which it is not equal' (New York *Herald*, 28 November 1864). Amid the corrupt materialism of the gilded age in America, he may well have seemed to contemporaries the very reverse of the vulgar and reckless yet strong-willed and all-conquering robber barons of industry and business. To Charles Clarke, whose handwritten columns provide an extraordinarily detailed manuscript account of Booth's 1870 production,[1] Booth's prince was 'a man of first-class intellect but second-class will' (col. 129), resolute in minor matters yet irresolute in major ones. Clarke finds these traits illustrated again and again in the performance. For instance, Booth skilfully mousetraps the king with the play-within-a-play, yet is so overcome by his success that he fails to capitalize on his advantage and follow through to the fulfilment of his revenge. When the Ghost appears in the closet scene, Booth combined 'doubt, anxiety, apprehension, and awe' with 'a new and agonizing fear that he will now be forced to some act at which his soul revolts' (*New York World*, 9 January 1876), thus subverting the impact of the Ghost's call to arms. And when he actually does kill Claudius, after a moment of 'mad exultation' he looks at the King with a 'stare of horror, then reels and falters down the steps of the throne' (col. 199); as Clarke concludes: 'his conscientiousness was outraged. His will was appalled, for it had overdone itself' (col. 202). Thus did Booth find a way to include Hamlet's violently decisive actions yet show them to be contrary to his true Romantic nature. He spoke 'O cursed spite / That ever I was born to set it right' [1.5.196–8] as to himself, emphasizing 'cursed', 'I', and 'born': he explained that 'Tis the groan of his overburthened soul'.[2]

Booth's Hamlet was 'every inch the noble Prince and true-born gentleman;

---

1   [Hapgood's reference.] Charles Clarke, unpublished columns of commentary on Edwin Booth's *Hamlet* in the Folger Shakespeare Library.

2   [Hapgood's reference.] Charles H. Shattuck, *The Hamlet of Edwin Booth* (Urbana and London: University of Illinois Press, 1969), p. 158.

strong, pure, and refined, in soul and senses'.³ [. . .] Consistently, Booth found ways to soften the sharp edges of Hamlet's scorn for Rosencrantz and Guildenstern, Polonius, his mother, Osric. The gravediggers' lack of refinement contrasted with his gentility.

The social decorum of Booth's student prince was matched by the artistic decorum of his impersonation. [. . .] His assumed madness was conveyed 'more by insinuation . . . than through intense outbreak' (Clarke, col. 73). Stone discerns the artistry by which Booth gave full value to the early scenes yet held himself 'within bounds' in order to build a 'reserve power' for more intense moments to come.⁴ The expression of this power could be quite subtle. She remarks on how Booth conveys a 'tension of nerves' when Hamlet is with other people and the subsequent relaxation when left alone, or with Horatio.⁵ She points out how with Horatio in the graveyard scene 'The appearance of anguish of soul is *intensified*, and this is done not by an increase of demonstrativeness, but by an increase of *restrainedness*' (p. 121). [. . .]

Occasional lapses in restraint on Booth's part were deplored, which he as a consequence toned down. On the other hand, some felt that Booth was too tame. In 1883 a German critic commented that Booth 'stirs us in many a moment of moving pathos, but he never sweeps us off our feet with tragic passion'.⁶ While acknowledging a general 'want of fire and *electricity*', a more sympathetic observer found in Booth's interpretation not 'flashes of lightning' but 'a steady light'⁷ [. . .].

Various commentators found affinities between Booth himself and Hamlet. [. . .]

It was in his devotion to his father that Booth was most deeply kin to Prince Hamlet. When his wife died in 1863, he took up spiritualism and received messages not only from her but from his father. It was a miniature of his own father that as Hamlet he wore on a neck-chain, and he sometimes fancied he could hear his father's voice in that of the Ghost.⁸

By 1870, Booth was acclaimed 'the accepted Hamlet of the American stage' *(New York Herald*, 6 January 1870). Partly his success was personal. Partly it came from favouring cultural trends. Booth's approach was in accord with the general 'feminization' of American culture, as clergy and women writers and readers celebrated such sentimental values as gentleness and a depth and delicacy of feeling. [. . .] Especially in the 1870 production in Booth Theatre, Booth's *Hamlet* also took part in the 'sacralization' of the arts (opera, classical music, and the fine arts as well as drama and literature) that was separating high brow from low brow culture in America at this time. The souvenir brochure for the new theatre promised that the play would glorify 'our too mundane souls with some of its higher, more heavenly attributes'.⁹

3 [Hapgood's reference.] *Edwin Booth's Performance: The Mary Isabella Stone Commentaries*, ed. D. Watermeier (Ann Arbor: University of Michigan Press, 1990).
4 [Hapgood's reference.] Ibid., pp. 118–19.
5 [Hapgood's reference.] Ibid., p. 136.
6 [Hapgood's reference.] Shattuck (see note 2), p. 298.
7 [Hapgood's reference.] Ibid., p. 91.
8 [Hapgood's reference.] Ibid., p. 7.
9 [Hapgood's reference.] Ibid., p. 72.

David Warner (1965): From **Ronald Bryden, The Unfinished Hero and Other Essays** (London: Faber, 1969), pp. 63–6

Peter Hall became the director of Britain's Royal Shakespeare Company in 1960 at the age of only twenty-nine and transformed what had been an annual Shakespeare festival at Stratford-upon-Avon into a major national cultural institution. A colleague, Trevor Nunn, reported that Hall insisted that 'whenever they did a play by Shakespeare, they should do it because the play was relevant, because the play made some demand upon our current attention';[1] Hall's RSC would challenge the conservative British establishment and its oppressive values. In casting the gangling twenty-four-year-old David Warner as the prince, Hall caught the spirit of 1960s youthful rebellion. 'For our decade,' wrote Hall in the programme, 'I think the play will be about the disillusionment which produces an apathy of the will so deep that commitment to politics, to religion or to life is impossible.'[2] Warner was a Hamlet who was not afraid of appearing ridiculous as he made his own protest against the world as he found it.

[. . .] Offering a radical and complex new reading of the play, Hall has taken apart and reassembled each line so that the audience can see how it's done. [. . .] It finds something genuinely original to say about the play, not by scissoring about the text but by exploring and illumining dead corners of it.

It succeeds against my expectation, for all Hall's emphasis in his published statements of intent has been on contemporaneity. [. . .]

The more important debt, it seems to me, is to Eliot's suggestion that the play is unsatisfactory because its plot offered Shakespeare an inadequate 'objective correlative' for the emotions he wished to vent [see Modern Criticism, **p. 54**]. Hall redeems the play by turning the unsatisfactoriness back into character. He has imagined a Hamlet himself in search of an objective correlative, a cloud of immature and unfocused emotions in search of means to express them. His revenge is inadequate to his disgust because he is not yet adequate for his revenge. Hamlet's buffoonery, said Eliot, is the outlet for an emotion which can find no relief in action. In this Hamlet, it is the buffoonery of adolescent self-disgust [. . .]. This is a prince who must goad himself to princeliness, to a mature magnificence and ruthlessness for which he is not yet fitted. [. . .] His failure to become king speaks a dual failure in kingliness—he is both too slight for the role and insufficiently narrow. He is an incomplete Machiavel because an incomplete prince. In Hall's production, *Hamlet* is no longer the imperfect tragedy Eliot saw. It's the perfected tragedy of an unfinished hero.

For the revenge he really wishes, and achieves, is on himself for not being the great Hamlet his father was. The key to every *Hamlet* is its ghost. A solid ghost demands an active, believing hero, thwarted by events; an insubstantial

---

1   Ralph Berry, *On Directing Shakespeare* (London: Croom Helm, 1977), p. 56.
2   Quoted in Anthony B. Dawson, *Shakespeare in Performance: 'Hamlet'* (Manchester: Manchester University Press, 1995) p. 133.

one, all light-effects and echoes, a brainsick prince, nerveless and Oedipal. The apparition which swims above the walls of [designer] John Bury's Elsinore (a superb inferno of bitumen ramparts and lakes of black marble, whose throne-room swarms with faded frescoes of sad grey Rubens flesh like a wax museum of elderly lasciviousness) is something new: a giant, helmeted shadow ten feet tall which dwarfs his shuddering child in a dark, commanding embrace. 'This was a man,' Hamlet tells Horatio enviously: for once we are shown the other side of the Oedipus complex. This Hamlet is less jealous of his mother's bedfellow than of his father's stature. As the hollow voice beneath the stage cries 'Swear!' [1.5.157], his son lovingly measures his length on the ground, as if on a grave; but the voice moves, he cannot cover it. Clutching violently at his mother on her bed, he looks up to find the huge presence of his father towering between them. Every recollection of his mission is a reminder of his sonship, his immaturity.

His pretence of madness is half an admission of this. He shelters in childishness, seeking to appear not merely too insane to be responsible for his actions, but too young. His disguise is not just dishevelment but the wilful untidiness of an under-graduate, the half-baked impertinence of the adolescent who would test his parents' love to the limit of tolerance. He slops ostentatiously through the castle in a greenish, moth-eaten student's gown, peering owlishly over his spectacles to cheek his elders. He knows his position as heir to the throne protects him, and abuses it as far as he can. The easiest disguise for an adolescent with a problem too big for him is that of a problem adolescent.

It's a conception which requires a special kind of actor, young enough to play both buffoon and tragedian. The image may have been Hall's, but clearly it shaped itself around the peculiar talents of David Warner [. . .] an angelically gawky Danish stork, [. . .] who tries on ideas and emotions for size as he tries on the Player King's crown—it slips down over his nose. As he denounces the firma-ment to Rosencrantz and Guildenstern for a foul and pestilent congregation of vapours [2.2.302–3], he watches to see if they find his pessimism as impressive as it sounds. Do they believe it? Does he? Or are his emotions as false as theirs? They laugh, swinging teasingly on his long student's scarf, and he turns chastened to the arriving players, to test his rage and grief against those of Pyrrhus and Hecuba. [. . .]

[. . .] Ultimately, I'd say, its inspiration is Brechtian.[3] For Hamlet and Ophelia, things might have gone otherwise. They might have grown differently, taken other roles. Life need not have turned them into legends. The most familiar master-piece in English becomes new and unforeseeable again. So for the first time in years there can be a Hamlet who voluntarily embraces his destiny, achieving it with a sense both of triumph and of loss.

---

3 The German Marxist dramatist Bertolt Brecht (1898–1956) exerted a considerable influence on British theatre in the 1960s. One of his beliefs was that the theatre should show that the world can be changed; that we have the power to alter our historical circumstances.

Samuel West (2001): From **Steven Pimlott,** interviewed by the sourcebook editor (2002).

Steven Pimlott directed a production for the Royal Shakespeare Company that opened at Stratford-upon-Avon on 31 March 2001 with Samuel West as the prince. The production was set in the present day, and was performed on an empty stage enclosed by a high-walled grey box set, with a steel walkway into the audience. Pimlott's frank and lucid opinions are an excellent illustration of how a theatre director approaches the play very differently from a literary critic. Sam West's Hamlet is not an attractive rebel, but a man whose self-righteous moral certainty makes him a danger to those who are trying to make things work in a complex and difficult political world.[1] It was an exciting, visually striking production which caught the spirit of the times as effectively as Hall's did in 1965, if without the public acclaim. My footnotes illustrate Pimlott's ideas by referring to production details.

I always wanted to direct *Hamlet*. When I was about twelve I played Gertrude, and I'd heard the story at primary school. It's a play that's personally close to me: it's so much about our lives. The audience don't have leaps of understanding to make; there's nothing you have to fill in for them.

I didn't start with a fixed idea of what the play's about. It's a play of questions. I wanted the actors involved in all decisions from the start, on their feet. There seems no reason not to give it a contemporary setting. I wanted a political context – I don't think that it's first and foremost a play about families. As soon as you say that, the perspective becomes your own political perspective. We decided to give it a US, not a UK, setting. Denmark is clearly a major power, and the foreign setting gave it an objectivity, as it did for Shakespeare. And it gave us a user-friendly Elsinore: civil, agreeable, open, apparently democratic. Claudius is under the sort of pressures a US president faces. We used the television series *The West Wing* as a sort of touchstone in our thinking. Of course, there's always a pressure at Stratford to do 'heritage' theatre. But once you have period costume the audience settles back into Madame Tussaud mode. You don't want that: in this play you want to convey existential arguments, the awfulness of life. Our society is still so similar to Shakespeare's; the play still speaks – or rather, asks us questions; it's a questions play.

Claudius is Shakespeare's most intelligently drawn 'villain', but the real villain is Hamlet. Claudius is a man of the world with his eye on the ball, not a bad man. He really does love Gertrude[2]: he gives his motivation when he says 'my crown, mine own ambition and my queen' (3.3.55; see Key Passages, **p. 144**). He's good at his job and he has no conscience. To that end we cut his aside about the harlot's cheek (3.1.49–54). He only acquires a conscience when he's found out. In the final

---

1   The interview took place in late September 2001, when the recent terrorist attacks in the United States, by his own admission, had made Pimlott even less sympathetic to the figure of the moral zealot as avenger.
2   Claudius was utterly shocked when she drank the poison (5.2.295 s.d.; see Key Passages, **p. 166**), and crawled across the floor when mortally wounded to try to die with her.

fencing match we made it him who exchanges the rapiers (5.2.306 s.d.; see Key Passages, **p. 167**) out of a sense of guilt.

In Shakespeare's time it's clear that Hamlet would have been seen as the real villain. Our sympathy for his personal search has to be put against unbelievable levels of destruction, and the handing over of Denmark to Norway. And yet he is too close to our hearts: we don't see that his moral honesty, his endless probing, hurts everyone he touches, including himself.[3] The problem of the play is that Shakespeare can't make up his mind about him, but remains unsentimental. In many ways he's like the traditional 'Vice' figure – witty, amusing, destructive, bad.[4] He treats Ophelia appallingly and kills Rosencrantz and Guildenstern but doesn't realize what he's done. We made Horatio walk off stage in disgust – but return – when he hears what Hamlet did to them (5.2.56).[5] Claudius is a man who gets on with life. In comparison to Hamlet he is humane, witty and generous.

We didn't play Polonius as a fool; why would a fool have such a responsible job? In rehearsal on the scene with Reynaldo we discovered that he's a man who's started to become forgetful and lose his inner confidence (2.1.50–4). He creates the world in his own image as a way of coping with the fact that he's losing touch with things.

I wanted the section where Hamlet gives his instruction to the actors (3.2.1–45) to be a scene about acting. The auditorium was painted the same grey colour as the set. We turned the lights on in the auditorium at the beginning, and lit the stage in a totally flat way. We didn't block it at all.[6] I just told the actors playing the travelling players to go on 'as themselves', in their own clothes. The actors and audience were left looking at each other. It was by far the hardest scene to do.

All the doubling up was significant. The actor playing Polonius doubled with the Gravedigger; First Player with Fortinbras. Hamlet projects himself onto both of them; in fact, Fortinbras is more a projection than anything else. He's all things: a pirate and a shark, and a delicate and tender prince. I wanted the audience to think 'Who's this? How does he manage to clean up at the end?' The final action, when the courtiers applaud their new ruler too frantically, indicated the unease they felt. He is the perfect Machiavel (see Contextual Overview, **pp. 10–11**): he doesn't give anything anyway. He reminds us of Claudius. We can see that there's no such thing as the perfect prince: power corrupts.

Hamlet On Film

The first sight of *Hamlet* on film was at the Paris Exposition of 1900, where Sarah Bernhardt played the prince in a performance of the duel from Act 5,

---

3   It was clear that suicide was on his mind from when he held a pistol to his own head during the first soliloquy (1.2.132; see Key Passages, **p. 127**). His 'antic disposition' was just mental instability and incomprehension.

4   'A perversely popular character, often a minor imp or devil, in the morality plays and interludes of the late-fifteenth and sixteenth centuries. He [. . .] specialised in tempting the audience, with whom he often interacted directly' (Simon Trussler, *Shakespearean Concepts* [London: Methuen, 1989]), p. 176.

5   He also tries to pass off the killing of Polonius by making jokes about it (3.4.213–9).

6   'Blocking' means planning, implementing and recording the dispositions and movements of the actors around the stage.

Scene 2.[1] There followed at least four silent feature films of the play.[2] In 1948 the British actor and director Laurence Olivier produced perhaps the most influential screen version. Olivier's cutting of the text and his focus on the Hamlet–Gertrude relationship are particularly evident in Franco Zeffirelli's 1990 Hollywood film (see The Work in Performance, **pp. 103–5** and **pp. 105–7**).

The Russian director Grigori Kozintsev was also inspired by Olivier, but produced a very different film. He said of his remarkable black and white, widescreen 1964 *Hamlet* that 'the tragedy must be played in sixteenth-century costumes but must be comprehended as a modern story.'[3] The modern story for Kozintsev was of a man who has the moral strength to take a stand against totalitarian oppression. Taking advantage of the temporary relaxation of state control of the arts in the years following the death of the dictator Josef Stalin in the USSR (1953), Kozintsev shows Denmark to be, indeed, a prison (2.2.243). A great portcullis slams shut on the prince as he enters Elsinore on horseback at the beginning of the film. He only leaves at the end, mortally wounded, to die by the crashing waves of the sea, an image that has symbolized freedom throughout the film. Hamlet speaks to Ophelia (3.1.90–151) through a balustrade which recalls prison bars. Symbolism is carefully deployed throughout. Ophelia is shown being trained in mechanical dance steps, and she is seen being enclosed in a rigid metal cage which will support her mourning dress. There are spies and informers everywhere. Hamlet's denunciation of Rosencrantz and Guildenstern in the 'recorders' speech (3.2.354–63), 'which many critics thought the climax of the film',[4] was where Innokenti Smoktunovski's prince was at his most energetic and powerful, denouncing those who had been his friends but who were now government informers, 'a shift all too familiar to those who had lived through the Stalinist years.'[5] Politics is central to the film. Huge statues of Claudius in the film refer to the dictator's own cult of personality. Where Olivier's Elsinore is a series of empty rooms to focus attention on the prince's mind, Kozintsev's castle is full of courtiers and armed men. Hamlet speaks his first soliloquy (1.2.129–59; see Key Passages, **pp. 127–8**) as a voice-over as he walks through courtiers and diplomats discussing Claudius's opening proclamation (1.2.1–39) in several languages. We also see Claudius's speech being read to the ordinary people outside the castle; Laertes's rebellion and Fortinbras are important parts of the action. Hamlet is a brave dissident who acts not just for himself but for a whole society. Pasternak's translation and Shostakovich's music also contribute enormously to making Kozintsev's film a coherent and powerful reading of the play.

Notable versions since Kozintsev include the 1969 film of the London Round House stage production, with Nicol Williamson as a particularly sardonic but tortured prince in a decadent and sensual Elsinore. The 1980 BBC TV version is a

1   *Walking Shadows: Shakespeare in the National Film and Television Archive*, eds Luke McKernan and Olwen Terris (London: BFI, 1994), p. 62.
2   McKernan and Terris (see note 1), pp. 45–8.
3   Quoted in Mark Sokolyansky, 'Grigori Kozintsev's *Hamlet* and *King Lear*' in *The Cambridge Companion to Shakespeare on Film*, ed. Russell Jackson (Cambridge: Cambridge University Press, 2000), p. 203.
4   Sokolyansky (see note 3), p. 203.
5   Anthony B. Dawson, *Shakespeare in Performance: 'Hamlet'* (Manchester: Manchester University Press, 1997), p. 189.

full script with powerful performances from Derek Jacobi as Hamlet and Patrick Stewart as Claudius, even if both are constrained by a cluttered interior set and by gaudy renaissance costumes. The major film of the last forty years is Kenneth Branagh's 1996 epic, although Michael Almereyda's version set amidst the corporate politics of contemporary New York (2000) has a clarity of vision which Branagh's film might lack (see The Work in Performance, **pp. 107–10**).

As an icon in western culture, *Hamlet* has also been central to scores of other films as a satirical target, motif or narrative, from the 1919 cartoon parody *Oh'Phelia* to Oliver Stone's *JFK* (1991)[6] and Disney's 1994 *The Lion King*.[7]

Directed by Laurence Olivier (1948): From **Anthony B. Dawson, Shakespeare in Performance: 'Hamlet'** (Manchester: Manchester University Press, 1995), pp. 173–5; 179–80

Having played the role on stage in 1937, Olivier directed himself as the prince on film in 1948. Dawson explains how Olivier turned a Freudian reading of the play (see Modern Criticism, **pp. 48–9**) into cinema. In doing so, he stripped the play of its political elements and instead presented Hamlet as an alienated and hollow individualist. Such a version of the play seemed to spring from the exhausted European political situation in the years immediately following the Second World War. The film won the Oscar for best picture in 1948.

The cinema, it now seemed to Olivier, offered a way, at once more intimate and more detached than was possible in the theatre, of rendering the unconscious visible. The obvious method would be a series of cuts establishing a chain of associations, but Olivier chose a different route: the serpentine tracking of the camera through Elsinore, up and down the ubiquitous staircases, past Romanesque columns and shadowy passageways, pausing here and there to gaze at, and then dolly expectantly towards, some salient feature, before retreating again to continue its interminable search. Of its various points of pause, none is more suggestive, nor more blatant, than the vast, slightly tousled, bed that *is* his mother's chamber. With its vaginal shaped canopy[1] and dark recesses, its symbolic emphasis seems almost comic, especially given the dearth of furniture in the rest of the castle. In the long establishing sequence following the first scene, the camera lavishes its slow, gradually advancing attention on it, before dissolving to an image of the King drinking from a huge chalice. Such is the prelude to our first sight of Hamlet, the prowling of the camera through the arched corridors of the castle clearly analogous to the restless wanderings of the melancholy prince, registering not his thoughts exactly, but his unconscious conflicts. In fact our view of him is withheld until it cannot be avoided ('But now, my cousin Hamlet, and my son . . .'

6   McKernan and Terris (see note 1, page 102), pp. 47, 64.
7   See '*Hamlet*': *New Critical Essays*, ed. Arthur F. Kinney (New York and London: Routledge, 2002), pp. 65–6.

1   [Dawson's reference.] Peter S. Donaldson, *Shakespearean Films/Shakespearean Directors* (Boston and London: Unwin Hyman, 1990), p. 31.

[1.2.64; see Key Passages, p. 125]), so that the first section of the court scene [1.2] is shot from Hamlet's point of view, sometimes literally (i.e. the camera occupies the space we later see is his), sometimes figuratively (as in the vaguely repellent portrayal of the 'bloat', and somewhat inebriated, King); this helps to establish the fluid but essential links between individual psychology and the camera.

All in all the inexorable tracking camera makes the castle – sparse, stony, and almost devoid of furniture – into a purely inner space, the inside of Hamlet's cranium; frequent shots, from the back, of Olivier's own blond head corroborate this sense. The most famous of these occurs immediately before the 'To be or not to be' soliloquy when Hamlet, high on the vertiginous parapet that seems to represent the apex of both his isolation and his vulnerability, is seen from above and behind, the camera gradually zooming in on the whorled crown of his hair and seeming to penetrate his skull – there ensues a misty, barely identifiable image of what looks like a human brain, before the camera moves around for a shot of his knitted brow and the beckoning beach far below (to which, a moment later, he lets his ineffectually phallic dagger fall). The inner space thus created seems the logical extension of an essentially theatrical evolution, developed in the nineteenth century and continuing through Barrymore, Gielgud and Olivier himself. Cinematic means are used to achieve what are, from the point of view of theatrical history, essentially conservative goals, focusing exclusively on Hamlet's psychology.

The psychoanalytic framework produces a way of privileging individual consciousness as the ultimate measure of reality. Again we find a development here of elements that had inhered in the *Hamlet* project for generations. Like so many of his predecessors, Olivier eliminated all traces of a *political* world, not just the international scene with Fortinbras and the various ambassadors, but Laertes' abortive rebellion as well: Laertes and Claudius are first heard and then seen from a distance in a large empty hall, all the while our attention being haunted by Ophelia's gentle madness and vacant wanderings. We thus focus on her inner plight and, briefly, Laertes' troubled personal reaction to it, the action remaining safely within the confines of mental, not political, disorder. Rosencrantz and Guildenstern also disappear totally from the action, robbing Hamlet of most of his opportunities to display his sardonic wit and lightning-fast perceptions of motive. But more importantly, their disappearance also reduces the political world of the play; what spying remains is purely personal (Polonius and Claudius behind the arras, Polonius in the Queen's closet). There is no sense of a network of spying, no 'secret service', no probing of Hamlet's 'ambition' in II.ii [2.2.252–65], little of the careful fawning before the King that is the sign of getting ahead at court. A key moment after the King breaks up the play with his call for lights might seem to contradict what I have just said, but in fact confirms it. The court explodes with horrified movement as the King rushes out in a whirlwind of fear and guilt, but the moment is purely symbolic; it does not register any actual social relations, but works as an allegory, an externalization of the King's feelings and Hamlet's elated response to the success of his plan. [. . .]

[. . .] More important, like Booth [see The Work in Performance, **pp. 95–7**] and a host of others, he avoided hysteria and madness, interpreting them as play-acted rather than real, and replaced them with brooding melancholy. The play-acting is evident, for instance, in the interpolated scene which accompanies

Ophelia's description of Hamlet's visit to her in her chamber. One of several 'tableaux' designed to flesh out the poetry with visual cues, this one shows Hamlet going through the motions of hand to brow, perusal of Ophelia's face and shaking of her arm, all in an exaggerated theatrical manner calculated to alert us to his ploys.

If acting mad provides a refuge, the theatrical mode also helps to rescue this Hamlet from himself. What I mean is that there is a continuous edge of self-conscious play-acting in the presentation of the tortured inner life, a sense of pose and deliberate showiness that combines with the arty camera-work to render the self paradoxically hollow as well as full. These indeed 'are actions that a man might play' [1.2.84; see Key Passsages, p. 125]. Olivier seems ambivalent about this element – he eliminates almost the whole of the 'O what a rogue and peasant slave' soliloquy in which Hamlet ruminates on the deeply illusory basis of his own 'reality' and along with that most of the scene with the Players, including the whole of the Player's speech about Hecuba. All that remains is the famous final couplet of the soliloquy, 'The play's the thing / Wherein I'll catch the conscience of the king' [2.2.600–01; see Key Passages, p. 136], which is thus detached not only from any clear plan or motivation on Hamlet's part, but from the anguished self-analysis that in the text leads up to his resolution. Olivier's Hamlet, despite the impulsions of Freudianism, is externalized and theatrical rather than intro-spective. The delivery of the couplet is extravagantly stagy: the prince gets a gleeful look in his eye, rushes down a pillared passage and up on to a raised dais that will serve as a stage for 'The Mousetrap' (the Players' props and masks are bunched carefully at the side), and shouts out the lines while performing an excited pirouette in a gradually narrowing spotlight, as the stirring show music builds to a climax.

The theatrical thread adds an odd texture to the film and its rendering of interiority. It is as though the psychoanalytic categories and insights are them-selves theatrical constructs, put into play by the confrontation of actor and text. Interiority is something to be staged. This is where the element of modernism is most salient, where, despite the many throwbacks to Victorian staging and emo-tion, a more fragmented and alienated sense of personhood emerges, the self watching itself. A telling sign of the transformation of interiority into theatricality is the fact that in some prints of the film the fleeting view of a human brain before 'To be or not to be' gives way to an image of the masks of comedy and tragedy. The post-war period, marked by the recent experience of European deracination and the subsequent emergence of existentialism, produced a troubled individualism, one linked to Olivier's split vision.

Directed by Franco Zeffirelli (1990): From Neil Taylor, 'The Films of Hamlet' in Shakespeare and the Moving Image, eds Anthony Davies and Stanley Wells (Cambridge: Cambridge University Press, 1994), pp. 192–3

Taylor explains how the impact of Zeffirelli's film was very much the product of its use of contemporary film-genre and star-casting. These factors are, of course, important in the meaning of any mainstream film, but in the case of the

1990 *Hamlet* they are clearly dominant. Though the film may be an undistinguished, perhaps even perverse, reading of the play, the presence of major Hollywood stars ensured that this version of *Hamlet* is the one that has, perhaps, been seen by more people than any other.

Zeffirelli [. . .] adopted the shooting style and, to some extent the narrative conventions, of [. . .] 1980s cinema and television action movies. In such films a slightly antisocial, often humorous, male hero (or pair of buddies) challenges a corrupt and evil male villain, finally outwitting and then killing him after scenes of extraordinary violence. The text of *Hamlet* can release such a story but only with some directorial manipulation. Zeffirelli is by far the most radical reshaper of the text. His 129-minute film contains only thirty-one per cent of the lines, but he cavalierly re-organizes the order of the text that remains, advancing and delaying speeches in a bewildering manner. The longer speeches and scenes are broken down into bite-sized pieces. This process of segmentation complements his shooting style, which involves frequent changes of image. Zeffirelli moves the camera very little but uses far more shots per minute than any of the other directors – his average shot lasts less than six seconds.

Such an interventionist directorial style affects the power-relations between characters (cutting to reaction shots can divert attention from the character whom Shakespeare's language would prioritize on stage) and between actors and audience (the effect of rapid cutting on a soliloquy like 'To be or not to be' [3.1.56–88; see Key Passages, **pp. 137–8**], which involves sixteen different shots, is to prioritize the role of the director over the character). [. . .] Zeffirelli's prime purpose is to simplify the narrative. 'To be or not to be', being in voiceover, can be disentangled from the question of being overheard by Ophelia, Polonius or Claudius, and is delivered later in its own discrete scene. Next, Mel Gibson's Hamlet follows the conventions of Beverly Hills cops and rides out of town into the open countryside in order to commune with nature. Only then does he meet Rosencrantz and Guildenstern, whom he treats to a cook-out and a few beers. This sub-scene itself precedes a truncated version of 'O what a rogue' which, ending as it does with the decision to put on a play, leads directly into the play scene.

Here is a Hamlet who can make up his mind,[1] and who is, in the words of the video blurb, 'more macho than melancholy'.[2] Zeffirelli saw him in Richard Donner's 1987 film, *Lethal Weapon*, in which Gibson plays a suicidal young detective. 'There was a scene in which there's a kind of "to be or not to be" speech. Mel Gibson is sitting there with a gun in his mouth but he can't pull the trigger. When I saw that I said *This* is *Hamlet! This boy is Hamlet!*'.[3] And this Hamlet is 'a man who likes sex, likes to drink, likes riding horses . . .', but who suffers from the modern condition of being unable to find God.[4]

---

1   Olivier's 1948 film began with the voice-over: 'This is the tragedy of a man who could not make up his mind.'
2   [Taylor's note.] Alasdair Brown, *Hamlet* (London: 1990), p. 9.
3   [Taylor's note.] Ibid., p. 8.
4   [Taylor's note.] Ibid., p. 8.

Perhaps because of the frequent cross-cutting between shots, Mel Gibson appears in a smaller proportion of shots than any of the other Hamlets in these five films (only forty per cent). Gibson's acting is psychologically unexpressive, but his function in the simplified Zeffirelli narrative, combined with his star status, reasserts his prioritized role in the film. At the same time, the casting of Glenn Close as Gertrude encourages the reading into her performance of both an unusual importance [. . .] and a sexual authority derived, at least for early audiences of the film, from her roles in Adrian Lyne's *Fatal Attraction* (1987) and Stephen Frears's *Dangerous Liaisons* (1988).[5] Murray Biggs asserts that 'Zeffirelli makes no bones about translating the Oedipal theme into a full-blown, vulgarized, traditional screen romance between coevals,[6] in which the viewer is less aware of Shakespeare's mother and son than of the Hollywood stars who have transformed them into other types altogether.'[7]

Directed by Kenneth Branagh (1996): From Julie Sanders, 'The End of History and the Last Man' in *Shakespeare, Film and Fin de Siècle,* eds Mark Thornton Burnett and Ramona Way (Basingstoke: Macmillan, 2000), pp. 149–51; 152–3; 153–4; 155–6

Branagh had made two very successful Shakespeare films before undertaking *Hamlet*. For this project he assembled an impressive array of British theatrical talent and international stars. His use of widescreen 70mm film gave the production an epic quality. Remarkably, he shot an entire conflated text (see Key Passages, **pp. 113–15**) of the play (although a shorter, edited version was also released). His Elsinore was Blenheim Palace, a vast eighteenth-century English stately home near Oxford. Though Branagh set his production in the mid-nineteenth century, Julie Sanders places Branagh's film in the context of Britain at the end of the 1990s, and sees it as a reflection of contemporary anxieties about political and family authority. In particular, she looks at the film's presentation of royalty at a time of crisis for Britain's own royal family. She finds Branagh's approach to be incoherent but revealing.

[There are] specific parallels between the film's themes and contemporary society's concerns, [. . .] such as a widespread anxiety about political tyranny and the oppression of human rights, the breakdown of the family as a social unit [. . .] and the extreme pressure on individuals, which manifests itself in physical and psychological disorders [. . .].

Branagh finds in the [. . .] crisis of the British monarchy in the 1990s, and in the figure of Princess Diana in particular, a facilitating idea for exploring these themes, as he finds them, in *Hamlet*. [. . .] Integral to Branagh's exploration of the fate of the modern monarchy in his interpretation [. . .] is an examination of a

---

5   In both films Close played an amoral, sexually voracious older woman.
6   Of the same age.
7   [Taylor's note.] Murray Biggs, ' "He's Going to his Mother's Closet": Hamlet and Gertrude on Screen' in Stanley Wells, ed. *Shakespeare Survey 45*, pp. 61–2.

world in which the lines and demarcations between private and public life prove dangerously blurred. This [. . .] is most evident in his treatment of the character of Ophelia, whose trajectory in the film – from secret lover of Hamlet to betrayed partner and daughter to very public psychological breakdown – undoubtedly conjures the popular press images of Princess Diana. The royal family, in this respect (in the play, film and contemporary life), becomes a metonym for the fate of the family unit in society at large, depicted, as it is, as under duress and dysfunctioning to the point of disappearance. [. . .]

The crisis of the monarchy in the 1990s is inextricably connected to the perils of increased media exposure [. . .]. This was a decade in which the private lives of the royals were made public in ways scarcely imagined by deferential preceding generations. [. . .] Diana symbolized for the 1990s the public/private debate in a very unique way. Branagh finds a parallel figure for this in his film in the character of Ophelia, subjecting her to a series of voyeuristic intrusions: for example, the reading aloud to the court of Hamlet's love letter to her (an action she is initially forced to undertake, her father stepping in only when her own voice falters) and the selfconscious spectating of her mental disintegration in a padded cell.

Ophelia is not, however, the only victim of this 'culture of intimacy'.[1] The claustrophobia of the duel scene, which sees the court crowded into the central hall and the doors locked against the outside world, is telling. This is the culminating image of a series of court 'shows' which commences with Claudius' post-marriage address [1.2.1–39] (staged as a 'performance' applauded by courtiers) and continues with the vertiginous seating of the audience for *The Mousetrap* (a spatial decision, which ensures that every word exchanged between members of the Royal Family can be heard). A recurring element of Branagh's *Hamlet* is the sense that royal families have no private life, and the director has explained the mirror motif of the film in the following terms: these are 'people forever being watched or forever watching themselves'.[2]

The film's millennial anxieties are played out through various linked ideas and images of a monarchy under threat or decline. [. . .]

Branagh's *mise-en-scène* [. . .] prove[s] central to an exploration of the contradictory treatment of monarchy in the film. The palatial setting and its snowbound landscape, with Blenheim Palace operating as Elsinore, evoke a series of complex associations with monarchy and absolutist power [. . .]. Branagh's Denmark has a distinctly English imperialist air. The exterior scenes of the film were shot at Blenheim Palace, the resonances of whose epic architecture were not lost on Branagh or his reviewers.[3] [. . .] [M]y concern here is ostensibly with the latter observations on the role that Blenheim plays in constructing, and to a certain

---

1   [Sanders' note.] This phrase was used persistently in newspaper reports during the week after Diana's death.

2   [Sanders' note.] In 'The Making of *Hamlet*' Open University Television Production, BBC2, December 1997. (For example, Branagh speaks the 'To be or not to be' soliloquy [3.1.56–89] into a mirrored door.)

3   [Sanders' note.] In his film diary, appended to Branagh's published screenplay, Russell Jackson's entry for Tuesday, 13 February, records: 'Cold wet morning in the grounds of Blenheim Palace. Our first set-up is outside the side gate of the extraordinary piece of English early eighteenth-century baroque that was the (enormously expensive) reward of a grateful nation for the military prowess of the first Duke of Marlborough (Kenneth Branagh, *'Hamlet' by William Shakespeare: Screenplay, Introduction and Film Diary* [London: Chatto and Windus, 1996]), p. 192.

extent deconstructing, a sense of a Royal Family, both that of the play and that of Britain in the 1990s.

Undoubtedly, by reinserting the political scenes excised by both Laurence Olivier's and Franco Zeffirelli's film versions (1948 and 1990 respectively), Branagh invites his audiences to make associations of this kind. The new political world of might and expediency that Fortinbras represents at the end of the play could be identified with the secular power of a Churchill[4] in the twentieth century, and the Churchillian referents are expanded on by Branagh in the screenplay.[5] But in Branagh's film, Fortinbras (played by Rufus Sewell as a sulky victor), though he may slouch in the throne of Denmark, does put on the crown, thereby associating himself with sovereignty, however ill-fitting or uncomfortable that might appear. So what is the political point being made here? That royal families, once over-thrown, are only replaced by new tyrants? The problematic and potentially con-tradictory images of the final few minutes of the film do leave us uncertain as to the future that lies ahead for Elsinore. [. . .]

The murder of Old Hamlet becomes, accordingly, a site both of nostalgia and of confused critique. [. . .] [Sanders refers here to the pulling down of statues of communist leaders after the collapse of totalitarian regimes in eastern Europe in 1989 and just afterwards.] Branagh's *Hamlet* chooses to open and close with a monumental statue of its own, that of Old Hamlet, which is placed on the thresh-old of Elsinore. The film commences with a striking emphasis on text – the stone lettering of the name 'Hamlet' on the statue's plinth. This enables a clever trick whereby we move into 'reality' as the camera pans sideways and we realize we are at the gates of the palace. The image also suggests something of the stature of Old Hamlet, preparing us for the significance of his ghostly apparition. It is important that Old Hamlet's ghost appears as the statue come to life in full military armour; this is no flesh-and-blood patriarch but a ruler of a warring nation, an emblem and a myth. This all seems to tally with a film in which the director seeks to win sympathy for his protagonist's, and his nation's, plight.

The closing invocation is more ambiguous. Branagh elects to end his film not with the heartstring-pulling image of Hamlet's corpse borne aloft (Christ-like though the image is)[6] but with Fortinbras' foot soldiers hammering away at the edifice of Old Hamlet's statue. As the chipping away at this image of power provides a poignant close-up, what questions are we meant to pose? Is the action meant to suggest the desecration of something great, or is it, as I am suggesting, almost unavoidably, meant to remind audiences of those fallen statues of Stalin and of others? If the latter is true, then the conclusion must be that Old Hamlet was a tyrant, one whose representational apparatus needs to be dismantled for history to truly find and 'end'.[7] [. . .]

---

4 Winston Churchill, Prime Minister of Britain 1940–45 and 1951–5, was born in Blenheim Palace; the Duke of Marlborough was his ancestor, and the current Duke played a small role in the film.
5 [Sanders' note.] Claudius is described as speaking with a 'Churchillian focus' (Branagh, '*Hamlet*', p. 16). Elsewhere, allusions are made to US [first] Gulf War General, Norman Schwarzkopf, as if to emphasize the twentieth-century applications of the scene.
6 Branagh's posture is also a direct quotation from the same moment in Olivier's film.
7 Elsewhere in the article Sanders writes of the idea current in the 1990s among some liberal historians, such as Francis Fukuyama, that the fall of communism brought an 'end' to history, produced by the final 'triumph' of capitalist democracy.

[. . .] Branagh's choice of a sentimental musical overlay at this point in the film confuses the effect upon watching audiences. The politics of this *fin-de-siècle* rumination are incoherent at their heart and at their close. Branagh seems at turns appalled and enticed by the power invested in a figure such as Old Hamlet. As a result, his film effects as its only certainty an implicit association between the *fin-de-siècle* moment and a crisis of political authority. [. . .]

[. . .] [T]his is perhaps true of the film as a whole: sentimentality seems to overtake any political concerns staked out by the opening sections. [. . .]

In that final court scene in the film, everyone's focus is on the ultimate emblem of royal rule, a red carpet. As if to emphasize the inward-turned and restricted vision of the Elsinore community, whilst the court's attention is consumed by events unfolding themselves on that carpet, the scene for the cinema audience is punctuated by images of Fortinbras' army, advancing through the snows, breaking down the barriers between them and the seat of power (doors and thresholds, which have played a considerable role in the construction of the court throughout the film) and finally crashing through the windows in the central hall. Something is indeed rotten in this state of Denmark: this is an unsustainable world, which has eaten itself apart with corruption and betrayal, yet it is also one that Branagh's film seems inexplicably nostalgic and sentimental towards. This is the fundamental incoherence of the film's ruminations on power and royalty [. . .].

3

Key Passages

Introduction

The Texts of *Hamlet*

The original performance of *Hamlet* was probably in 1601. The play first appeared in print in 1603, in an unauthorized form known as the First Quarto. A quarto was a small, paper-covered pamphlet-size edition. This version of the play is considerably shorter than the other two contemporary texts which we possess and only takes two hours to play. In 1604 and then again in 1605 another quarto edition appeared. Not only does it contain many more lines than the First Quarto; those lines often differ greatly, and are much more polished. Certain speeches are placed differently in the text (most notably the soliloquy 'To be or not to be' [3.1.56–88], which appeared before Hamlet meets either Rosencrantz and Guildenstern or the players in the First Quarto). In 1623, seven years after his death, Shakespeare's friends John Hemmings and Henry Condell published a collected edition of his poetry and thirty-six plays in a large book known as the First Folio. The text of *Hamlet* in this volume is a little shorter than the Second Quarto and differs from it in many details, especially in that certain passages from the Second Quarto are omitted in the Folio text.

There are, then, three different versions of the play all published within twenty years of each other. They differ substantially. The Hamlet of the First Quarto is different from the prince of the Second Quarto or the Folio. He lacks, for example, 'nearly all the language of sexual loathing',[1] including some of his crude remarks to Ophelia before *The Murder of Gonzago* (3.2.110–19) and his comparison of his mother's 'enseamed' bed to a nasty 'sty' (3.4.91–4; see **p. 148**). He is far less melancholic, too. The world is not a 'pestilent congregation of vapours' (2.2.302–3) to him, nor does he tell Polonius that is he weary of his life (2.2.217). He is much more a convinced Christian (for the discussion of the First Quarto's version of the 'To be or not to be' soliloquy [3.1.56–88], see Key Passages, **pp. 137–8**); he dies asking heaven to receive his soul.[2] The Hamlet of the Second Quarto can also be seen to be a different prince from that of the Folio. The

---

1 Leah S. Marcus, *Unediting the Renaissance: Shakespeare, Marlowe, Milton* (London: Routledge, 1996), p. 141.
2 *The First Quarto of Hamlet*, ed. Kathleen O. Irace (Cambridge: Cambridge University Press, 1998), 17.104. Compare 5.2.363 (see Key Passages, **p. 168**).

soliloquy beginning 'How all occasions do inform against me' (4.4.32–66) is in the Second Quarto, but not the Folio. In that speech Hamlet resolves to follow Fortinbras's example; he will stop being reflective and cynically follow the culture of honour, for he lives in 'a world where action feels arbitrary and meaningless'.[3] In the Folio text, however, Hamlet acts out of a desire for salvation through revenge. 'Is't not perfect conscience / To quit him with this arm? Is't not to be damned', he asks only in the Folio, 'To let this canker of our nature [Claudius] come / In further evil?' (5.2.67–70). Other changes reinforce this new clarity of motivation in the Folio text.[4]

For many years the different texts of *Hamlet* have posed a worrying problem for critics who wanted to know what Shakespeare *really* wrote. It was felt that there must have been a single original manuscript in Shakespeare's hand, now lost, which was the 'true' copy and the source of the three printed versions with their varying 'corruption'. Consequently editors set out to produce an edition which reconstructed what they thought that 'true' copy must have been on the basis of the evidence of the three texts. Just such an edition is that used in this sourcebook: the text edited by Harold Jenkins for the second series of the Arden Shakespeare.[5] Jenkins follows the work of Dover Wilson[6] in assuming that the Second Quarto was Shakespeare's original manuscript. The additions and cuts in the Folio text, thought Dover Wilson, were errors in the scribal transmission process between 1605 and 1623. Although they do not correspond to any printed text in the early seventeenth century, 'conflated' texts, like the one used in this sourcebook, still enjoy considerable currency and are the most likely form in which readers will encounter the play, even if the case for their authenticity is far from convincing.

Other important modern editors have wished to assert the difference between the Second Quarto and Folio text. Philip Edwards uses the Folio as his principal text but includes the excised passages from the Second Quarto in square brackets.[7] G. R. Hibbard, following Stanley Wells and Gary Taylor, regards the Folio as Shakespeare's personal revision of the Second Quarto, and relegates those passages unique to the Second Quarto to a separate appendix.[8]

It was once thought that the First Quarto was a 'pirated' version of the 'true' text, based on an actor's faulty memory, or was Shakespeare's early draft (perhaps the ur-*Hamlet* itself; see Contextual Overview, **p. 7**), or was a cut-down touring version. The First Quarto has been discovered to work very well on stage, even if it is less poetic and philosophical than the longer versions of the play.[9] It has only a minor influence, however, on the texts normally used today.

3   James Shapiro, *1599: A Year in the Life of William Shakespeare* (London: Faber and Faber, 2005), p. 351.
4   Shapiro (see note 3), pp. 342–53, develops this argument further.
5   *Hamlet*, ed. Harold Jenkins (London: Thomson, 1982).
6   John Dover Wilson, *The Manuscript of Shakespeare's 'Hamlet' and the Problems of its Transmission*, 2 vols (Cambridge: Cambridge University Press, 1934).
7   *Hamlet*, ed. Philip Edwards (Cambridge: Cambridge University Press, 1985).
8   Stanley Wells and Gary Taylor, *William Shakespeare: A Textual Companion* (Oxford: Clarendon Press, 1987); *Hamlet*, ed. G. R. Hibbard (Oxford: Oxford University Press, 1987).
9   Marcus (see note 1), pp. 145–6; *The First Quarto of Hamlet*, ed. Kathleen O. Irace (Cambridge: Cambridge University Press, 1993), pp. 20–7; *The Tragicall Historie of Hamlet Prince of Denmarke*, eds Graham Holderness and Bryan Loughrey (Hemel Hempstead: Harvester Wheatsheaf, 1992), pp. 24–7.

Critics no longer regard a Shakespeare text to be a direct contact with the mind of an individual genius. Consequently the search for the 'true' text of *Hamlet* has been called off. Today critics stress that plays are created not just in the study, but in rehearsal, and in live contact with different audiences in different spaces and at different times. The third series Arden edition of the play, edited by Ann Thompson, will publish modern editions of all the versions in one volume, giving all three equal status. 'Recently,' writes Paul Werstine, 'both textual critics and editors have come to realize that they neither can know nor need to know what kind of manuscripts served as a printer's copy for the earliest printings of Shakespeare's plays.'[10] Critics are free to choose the version, or multiplicity of versions, which suit their argument best (see, for example, Modern Criticism, **pp. 59, 73, 80–1**). There are many *Hamlets*, and many Hamlets.

Plot Summary

Hamlet is one of the best-known of Shakespeare's works. There follows, nevertheless, a brief reminder of the play's events, indicating which important passages are reproduced and discussed in the rest of this section of the book.

Act I

(1.1) Two guards, Marcellus and Barnardo, nervously take up sentry duty guarding the king of Denmark's palace (**pp. 120–1**). Marcellus has brought along the scholar Horatio, who is sceptical about the sentries' reports that they have seen what appeared to be the ghost of the recently deceased king Hamlet on the 'platform' the previous night. To Horatio's astonishment the ghost appears again, twice. In the meantime Horatio tells of the threat to Denmark from the forces of the Norwegian adventurer Fortinbras (**pp. 121–4**). They resolve to tell young Hamlet, the dead king's son, what they have seen.

(1.2) Denmark's new king is the old king's brother, Claudius. He has married king Hamlet's widow, Gertrude. Before the Danish court the prince makes clear his grief for his dead father (**pp. 124–5**). Claudius asks Hamlet not to return to his studies in Germany, and at his mother's request Hamlet agrees. After a soliloquy in which the depth of Hamlet's feelings about his mother's hasty marriage to his uncle becomes plain (**pp. 126–8**), the sentries and Horatio tell the prince of the ghost's appearance. Hamlet resolves to accompany them on their watch that night.

(1.3) Claudius's chief minister, Polonius, has a son, Laertes, and a daughter, Ophelia. Laertes is travelling to Paris and is bidding farewell to his family. Laertes is concerned that Hamlet has been courting his sister, and he warns her that she cannot expect to marry a prince; she should beware his advances. Polonius blesses his son before he leaves, and then reinforces Laertes's advice to Ophelia: he commands his daughter not to see Hamlet again.

10 Paul Werstine, ' "The Cause of This Defect": *Hamlet*'s Editors', in '*Hamlet*': *New Critical Essays*, ed. Arthur F. Kinney (New York and London: Routledge, 2002), p. 131.

(1.4) That night the ghost appears again.

(1.5) Hamlet follows the ghost to a private place where it tells him that Claudius poisoned old Hamlet while he slept. The ghost asks his son to avenge his death, but to take no retaliation on Gertrude (**pp. 128–32**). Hamlet undertakes to do so. When the ghost departs the guards catch up with the prince. Hamlet makes them swear an oath never to reveal what they have seen. He also warns them that he may appear to be mad in the days to come. If so, they should not give any indication that they know why Hamlet is behaving in this way.

Key Passages
Act 1, Scene 1, lines 1–22: sentry duty at Elsinore (**pp. 120–1**)
Act 1, Scene 1, lines 61–119: news of Fortinbras; Horatio addresses the ghost (**pp. 121–4**)
Act 1, Scene 2, lines 64–86: Claudius and Hamlet's first exchange (**pp. 124–5**)
Act 1, Scene 2, lines 129–59: first soliloquy – Hamlet's private grief (**pp. 126–8**)
Act 1, Scene 5, lines 9–112: the Ghost speaks to Hamlet (**pp. 128–32**)

Act 2

(2.1) Polonius, having dispatched one of his servants to spy on Laertes's activities in Paris, hears from Ophelia that Hamlet had entered her room in a state of great agitation, but did not speak to her. Polonius concludes that Hamlet is mad with frustrated love for her.

(2.2) The king has sent for two old friends of Hamlet, Rosencrantz and Guildenstern, to see if they can find out why he is acting so strangely. They are only too pleased to help. Claudius, having heard that his ambassadors have persuaded the king of Norway to rein in Fortinbras and send the young adventurer off on a mission against Poland, hears Polonius's theory about the source of Hamlet's madness. To prove his point Polonius says he will arrange for the king and him to overhear a meeting between Ophelia and Hamlet from a hiding place. Hamlet sees through Rosencrantz and Guildenstern straight away and makes them admit they are acting as the king's spies. Hamlet becomes more animated when his friends tell him that a familiar group of travelling players are about to visit the court. When they arrive, Hamlet asks the actors to perform a speech about the killing of Priam, the old king of Troy. Privately he asks them to insert a speech he will write into the play the following evening. Once alone (**pp. 132–6**), he reflects on the power of the actor to arouse his emotions in a way that his genuine predicament cannot. He tells us that he will get the players to re-enact the Ghost's account of his father's murder. Claudius's response will reveal his guilt, one way or the other.

Key Passage
Act 2, Scene 2, lines 544–601: second soliloquy – Hamlet's response to the Player's speech (**pp. 132–6**)

Act 3

(3.1) Rosencrantz and Guildenstern report back to the king and queen. Claudius and Polonius hide themselves and overhear Hamlet contemplating suicide (**pp. 136–8**). As arranged, Ophelia meets the prince. He abuses her. When the eavesdroppers emerge, the king does not believe Hamlet is in love, but regards him as dangerous; he will exile him to England.

(3.2) Having instructed the players in how they should perform, Hamlet takes his place in the audience for the play. He becomes increasingly excited as the performance progresses. Claudius storms out, perhaps because he recognizes his crime being re-enacted on stage (**pp. 139–43**). Hamlet is convinced that the king's reaction is proof that the ghost told him the truth. Polonius then tells Hamlet that the queen wishes to see her son privately.

(3.3) Claudius orders Rosencrantz and Guildenstern to accompany Hamlet to England. Polonius says he will hide secretly in Gertrude's 'closet' to overhear the meeting with Hamlet. In a soliloquy, Claudius admits his guilt to the audience. He tries to pray for forgiveness. Hamlet enters unseen, and is about to stab his uncle when he decides that he would rather kill him at a moment when Claudius's behaviour was more damnable (**pp. 143–5**).

(3.4) In her private apartments, Hamlet angrily accuses his mother of complicity in the murder. Frightened, she cries out. Polonius, who is hiding behind a wall hanging, calls out for help. Hamlet stabs through the hanging, thinking that he is killing his uncle, and soon discovers his mistake. Hamlet continues his diatribe against his mother, but is interrupted by the reappearance of the ghost, whom only he can see. The ghost reminds him of his unfulfilled duty (**pp. 146–50**). Gertrude is convinced of her son's madness, but, in distress, does promise not to reveal any of their conversation to the king. Hamlet drags Polonius's body out of her chamber to hide it somewhere.

Key Passages
Act 3, Scene 1, lines 56–88: Hamlet's third soliloquy (**pp. 136–8**)
Act 3, Scene 2, lines 181–264: the performance of *The Murder of Gonzago* (**pp. 139–43**)
Act 3, Scene 3, lines 36–98: Claudius prays; Hamlet's opportunity to strike (**pp. 143–5**)
Act 3, Scene 4, lines 53–160: the central part of the 'closet' scene – Hamlet and Gertrude alone together (**pp. 146–50**)

Act 4

(4.1) The king enters and discovers what has happened. He sends Rosencrantz and Guildenstern after Hamlet.

(4.2) When they find the prince, he abuses them wittily.

(4.3) When the king arrives he gets the same treatment. Hamlet reveals where the body is hidden, and learns of his journey to England. Claudius tells the audience that he will instruct the king of England to execute Hamlet on the prince's arrival.

(4.4) On their way out of the kingdom, Hamlet and his companions meet Fortinbras's army marching, as yet unauthorized, through Denmark on its way to Poland. In a soliloquy Hamlet compares his own lack of decisive action to Fortinbras's pride, daring and energy.

(4.5) Ophelia has become mad and speaks to the king and queen in a distracted manner. Laertes returns from France at the head of a rebellious mob. They cry that Laertes should be king, but he says that he seeks only vengeance for his father's hushed-up death. Claudius confronts him bravely, and promises him the chance of vengeance against the guilty party. Ophelia enters, and Laertes becomes distressed at her state (pp. 115–16).

(4.6) Horatio receives a letter from Hamlet. Hamlet had been taken prisoner by pirates but is now back in Denmark. Rosencrantz and Guildenstern were not seized and are still bound for England.

(4.7) As Claudius is explaining to Laertes why he could not punish Hamlet publicly for Polonius's death, a message comes from Hamlet announcing his return. Laertes and the king hatch a plot to entice Hamlet into a fencing match where either a poisoned sword or a deadly cup of wine will cause his death. The queen brings news that Ophelia has drowned.

Key Passage
Act 4, Scene 5, lines 16–168: Ophelia's madness and Laertes's rebellion (pp. 151–6)

Act 5

(5.1) Horatio and Hamlet come across the gravediggers who are preparing what is discovered to be Ophelia's grave (pp. 157–62). Her funeral procession arrives. Hamlet watches unseen for a while, and then tussles with Laertes over Ophelia's body, protesting his love for her. Claudius sets Horatio to 'wait upon him'.

(5.2) Hamlet tells Horatio how he secretly altered Rosencrantz and Guildenstern's commission from Claudius so that they will now be put to death instead of the prince. A verbose courtier, Osric, delivers Laertes's challenge to a fencing match to take place in front of the court. Against Horatio's advice, Hamlet accepts. Hamlet is winning the contest when Laertes stabs him while not at play. In the angry scuffle which follows, the swords are exchanged and Hamlet wounds Laertes with the poisoned rapier. Laertes, knowing he is doomed, reveals the plot to Hamlet and tells him he too must shortly die. Meanwhile, the queen has drunk, in ignorance, the poisoned cup and collapses, dying. Hamlet kills Claudius and dies just as Fortinbras arrives on stage with his army, claiming the right to the now vacant throne (pp. 162–70).

Key Passages
Act 5, Scene 1, lines 1–118: the gravediggers (**pp. 157–62**)
Act 5, Scene 2, lines 213–408: the final duel; the deaths of Gertrude, Claudius, Laertes and Hamlet and the entry of Fortinbras (**pp. 162–70**).

A Note on the Passages

With such a dense and complex play as *Hamlet*, any selection of passages for discussion at the expense of others will seem idiosyncratic, as some aspect of the play will be stressed at the neglect of others. My selection perhaps displays a bias towards the political and theatrical aspects of the play, but I hope that the crucial moments of the play for most approaches are nevertheless represented here. Thus, the first section is included to show how, famously, Shakespeare's stagecraft operates to create a certain mood as well as raising some significant intellectual questions. Horatio's account of Old and Young Fortinbras, and Old Hamlet, followed by his encounter with the ghost, serves to underline important political and historical issues in the text, as does the confrontation between Claudius and Laertes in Act 4. The interaction between language and power is a concern of the text which is represented in the exchanges between Claudius and Hamlet in Act 1 and between Hamlet and the gravedigger in Act 5. The play's concern with its own theatricality, and with the role of the theatre in the real world, arises in Hamlet's second soliloquy and the performance of *The Murder of Gonzago*. The so-called closet scene between Hamlet and Gertrude, and Ophelia's first 'mad' scene are important in any discussion of the representation of women and female sexuality in the play.

The tinted boxes before each passage offer a comment on what I take to be key critical issues in the lines which follow, with cross-references in bold type to the contextual and critical extracts which appear in earlier sections when relevant. They are not intended to be anything like a definitive interpretation of the scene; nor are the glosses which appear in the footnotes intended to be the last word on that point in the text, but merely, I hope, an aid to understanding one or more readings of that line. I have also included in both headnotes and footnotes some account of how that moment of the text has been played in stage and film realizations of the play, as a means of stressing once again that *Hamlet* was written to be a blueprint for live performances, each one as different as the time and place in which it is produced. In my notes I draw on three important modern editions of the play (those of Edwards, Hibbard and Jenkins) (see Key Passages, **p. 114**) and on two detailed histories of *Hamlet* in performance (Dawson and Hapgood) (see Further Reading, **p. 175**).

Key Passages

Act 1, Scene 1, lines 1–22: sentry duty at Elsinore

The opening lines of *Hamlet* are dramatically striking. They also reveal a great deal about the concerns of the play to come. It is clear that the action takes place in the dark, as the different sentries struggle to recognize one another. More strangely, the first challenge is given by Barnardo, the relieving sentry, rather than by Francisco, the soldier who is still on duty (lines 1–2). Not only is there a sense of suppressed panic and fear in all of these opening exchanges, preparing the mood for the arrival of the ghost, but people in Denmark do not seem to be confident in carrying out their allotted roles. The precise nature of personal identity is also a matter of question here (lines 2 and 21 in particular), as it will be in a more profound sense later in the play. Twice (lines 3 and 16) the king's name (but which king?) is used as a means to authenticate identity and loyalty: the issue of allegiance to the king as a stable political concept in Denmark will also be interrogated in the drama to follow. The play will also end with armed men arriving in Elsinore. This is a country under external military threat, a serious political matter which Hamlet neglects in his struggle with Claudius.

Enter BARNARDO *and* FRANCISCO, *two Sentinels.*

BARNARDO Who's there?
FRANCISCO Nay, answer me. Stand and unfold yourself.[1]
BARNARDO Long live the King!
FRANCISCO Barnardo?
BARNARDO He.   5
FRANCISCO You come most carefully upon your hour.
BARNARDO 'Tis now struck twelve. Get thee to bed, Francisco.

---

1   This is a blank verse line, but the uneasy opening means that the play does not stutter into something like consistent verse until line 12.

FRANCISCO For this relief much thanks. 'Tis bitter cold
And I am sick at heart.[2]
BARNARDO Have you had quiet guard?[3]   10
FRANCISCO Not a mouse stirring.
BARNARDO Well, good night.
If you do meet Horatio and Marcellus,
The rivals[4] of my watch, bid them make haste.
FRANCISCO I think I hear them.

Enter HORATIO *and* MARCELLUS.

Stand, ho! Who is there?   15
HORATIO Friends to this ground.
MARCELLUS   And liegemen to the Dane.
FRANCISCO Give you good night.
MARCELLUS O, farewell honest soldier, who hath reliev'd you?
FRANCISCO Barnardo hath my place. Give you good night.[5]   *Exit.*
MARCELLUS Holla, Barnardo!   20
BARNARDO Say, what, is Horatio there?
HORATIO A piece of him.

Act 1, Scene 1, lines 61–119: news of Fortinbras

This dialogue takes place between the two appearances of the ghost, who has walked past the sentries and ignored both their questions and their attempts to strike him. Apparitions who return to earth to demand revenge for their murder seem to be staples of the revenge tragedy tradition, one of whose sources was the grisly work of the Roman writer Seneca (c. 4BC–AD65) (see Contextual Overview, p. 8). In this scene the ghost seems to have come from a *feudal* past distant in time from Claudius's machiavellian court (see Contextual Overview, pp. 10–11). Not only is the notion of a king engaging in single combat (lines 85–96) in order to settle a territorial dispute with another monarch pre-modern, but much of the language in this part of Horatio's speech is archaic ('moiety competent', 'gaged') and refers to chivalric regulations and ideas already historical in Shakespeare's lifetime. Claudius seeks to settle the dispute with Fortinbras by the modern method of diplomacy, not by single combat

---

2 Exactly what ails Francisco is never revealed, but it adds to the air of unease. We never see him again in the play. John Laurie, in Olivier's 1949 film, said the line as if he could not himself understand why he felt this way. John Dover Wilson said it 'foreshadows Hamlet' (*Hamlet*, ed. John Dover Wilson [Cambridge: Cambridge University Press, 1934], p. 144). In Olivier's film the battlements are foggy, and the action takes place next to a cannon which is well provided with ammunition.
3 In several productions the actor has paused fearfully before 'quiet guard' because he is trying to find out if Francisco has seen the ghost without admitting that he has seen it himself; *Shakespeare in Production: 'Hamlet'*, ed. Robert Hapgood (Cambridge: Cambridge University Press, 1999), p. 99.
4 Partners; but there is also a sense of mistrust here.
5 i.e. 'God give . . .'

(1.2.17–41). The idea that the modern, sceptical Hamlet is called upon to enact a feudal revenge in a state, like Elizabeth I's, where private revenge has been taken out of the hands of individual nobles and placed under royal jurisdiction, prompts materialist critics to examine the position of Hamlet in his historical moment. Holderness (see Modern Criticism, **pp. 65–6**) sees him tragically torn between two incompatible ideologies, feudal and modern. Ryan (see **pp. 85–7**) describes him as an intellectual who refuses to accept the morality and politics of a society whose 'time is out of joint' (1.5.188).

Marcellus's account of a country where Sunday can no longer be separated from the working week, nor the night from the day (lines 79 and 81), is part of an overall pattern of uncertainty and shifting focus in this scene, where characters like Francisco come and go, explanations are broken off incomplete (1.1.42, 128) – or are not given at all in the case of the ghost. A ghost is itself a marginal and uncertain figure: is it alive, or dead, or neither? This sense of uncertainty about political authority, historical location, personal identity and the nature of theatre itself is characteristic of contemporary writers such as Montaigne (see Contextual Overview, **p. 11**) and of what is to follow.

The reference to Julius Caesar (lines 116–9) may well serve to remind the Globe audience of the recent performance (1599) of Shakespeare's work of that name in the same theatre. The reference introduces that sense of self-awareness in the play which is so crucial an element of *Hamlet*'s own examination of theatricality and its connection with 'reality'. But it also serves dramatically to remind the audience that the good of the people might sometimes require the assassination of an autocrat (see Contextual Overview, **p. 9**), as Caesar's killers claimed. In 44BC Caesar was felt by Roman republicans to be on the verge of becoming a tyrant. The leader of the conspiracy against him, Brutus, was a Stoic and thus espoused a system of beliefs which applauded tyrannicide. Horatio is also praised by Hamlet for his Stoic beliefs (3.2.65–74) and the prince himself expounds Stoic ideas ('there is nothing either good or bad, but thinking makes it so'; see also 2.2.149–50: 'There is special providence in the fall of a sparrow . . .' (5.2.215–20) (see Modern Criticism, **pp. 70–5**).

MARCELLUS	Is it not like the King?

HORATIO As thou art to thyself.
　　　　Such was the very armour he had on
　　　　When he th'ambitious Norway[1] combated.
　　　　So frown'd he once, when in an angry parle[2]　　　　　　　65
　　　　He smote the sledded Polacks on the ice.
　　　　'Tis strange.
MARCELLUS Thus twice before, and just at this dead hour,
　　　　With martial stalk hath he gone by our watch.
HORATIO In what particular thought to work on I know not,　　　70

---

1 The King of Norway.
2 Conference.

But in the scope and gross of my opinion[3]
This bodes some strange eruption to our state.
MARCELLUS Good now, sit down, and tell me, he that knows,
Why this same strict and most observant watch
So nightly toils the subject of the land,   75
And why such daily cast of brazen cannon
And foreign mart[4] for implements of war,
Why such impress[5] of shipwrights, whose sore task
Does not divide the Sunday from the week.
What might be toward that this sweaty haste   80
Doth make the night joint-labourer with the day,
Who is't can inform me?
HORATIO   That can I.
At least the whisper goes so: our last King,
Whose image even now appear'd to us,
Was as you know by Fortinbras of Norway,   85
Thereto prick'd on by a most emulate pride,[6]
Dar'd to the combat; in which our valiant Hamlet
(For so this side of our known world esteem'd him)
Did slay this Fortinbras; who by a seal'd compact,
Well ratified by law and heraldry[7]   90
Did forfeit, with his life, all those his lands
Which he stood seiz'd of[8] to the conqueror;
Against the which a moiety competent[9]
Was gaged[10] by our King, which had return'd
To the inheritance of Fortinbras,   95
Had he been vanquisher; as, by the same cov'nant
And carriage of the article design'd,
His fell to Hamlet. Now, sir, young Fortinbras,
Of unimproved mettle, hot and full,
Hath in the skirts[11] of Norway here and there   100
Shark'd up a list of lawless resolutes
For food and diet to some enterprise
That hath a stomach in't,[12] which is no other,
As it doth well appear unto our state,
But to recover of us by strong hand   105
And terms compulsatory those foresaid lands
So by his father lost. And this, I take it,
Is the main motive of our preparations,

---

3 Horatio is not sure exactly why the ghost has appeared, but he has a general notion.
4 Trading.
5 Conscription.
6 Provoked by a proud self-esteem.
7 An agreed deal which was ratified both by law and chivalric custom.
8 Was the legal owner of – another archaic expression.
9 Adequate portion; it sounds like Norman-French legal language.
10 Promised, perhaps by the knightly act of pledging his gauntlet ('gage').
11 Outlying provinces.
12 The military adventure will both feed these landless men and require some courage ('stomach').

The source of this our watch, and the chief head
Of this post-haste and rummage[13] in the land.   110
BARNARDO I think it be no other but e'en so.
Well may it sort that this portentous figure
Comes armed through our watch so like the King
That was and is the question of these wars.
HORATIO A mote it is to trouble the mind's eye.[14]   115
In the most high and palmy[15] state of Rome,
A little ere the mightiest Julius fell,
The graves stood tenantless and the sheeted dead
Did squeak and gibber in the Roman streets [. . .]

Act 1, Scene 2, lines 64–86: Claudius and Hamlet's first exchange

In this scene, Claudius has just addressed the assembled Danish court and thanked them on behalf of himself and his new wife for their support (in Branagh's 1996 film Gertrude is in her wedding dress and they exit through a storm of white confetti petals – see the Work In Performance, **pp. 107–10**). Hamlet stands out from the rest of the court because he is dressed in black (line 78) and is usually at the side of the stage rather than in the centre with the king, where a prince would conventionally be placed (in the Second Quarto text he is last on the list of characters who enter). The exercise of power through spectacle (see Contextual Overview, **pp. 12–13**) is obvious in this scene, the opening stage directions in the Folio text indicating a grand procession accompanied by fanfares. Hamlet's obvious refusal to join in the spectacle makes its political point too. After first giving his permission for Laertes to return to France, Claudius finally turns to his nephew (this is a slight, as Laertes is merely the son of his chief minister). Hamlet's answers are riddling and evasive: he refuses, as he will later, to speak in a language which Claudius will be able to comprehend completely. It is another act of insolent resistance. In refusing to speak as clearly and politely as Claudius would wish he is perhaps recognizing the role which language plays in conscripting us into agreement with the thinking of the powerful. Like this language, which slips between different meanings, throughout the play Hamlet will slip uncertainly between different roles: madman and sane man, courtier and clown, inside the action of the play and standing outside it.

In lines 76–86 the prince claims that he is feeling something which no performance of external signs ('actions that a man might play') could ever communicate. This would seem to suggest that no actor could possibly convey his true feeling, which 'passes show'. Of course an actor is speaking these lines –

---

13 Frantic activity and bustling commotion.
14 An irritating thing which stops the mind from seeing clearly.
15 Flourishing, triumphant.

lines which deny the possibility of their own effective communication. It raises the question whether the theatre can ever tell us the truth about ourselves, or show us the truth of our lives. Ironically, Hamlet seems to think so when he stages *The Murder Of Gonzago*: 'the play's the thing / Wherein I'll catch the conscience of the king' (2.2.605–6). The play is again very aware of its own theatricality.

KING But now, my cousin Hamlet, and my son—
HAMLET A little more than kin, and less than kind.[1]   65
KING How is it that the clouds still hang on you?
HAMLET Not so, my lord, I am too much in the sun.[2]
QUEEN Good Hamlet, cast thy nighted colour[3] off,
    And let thine eye look like a friend on Denmark.
    Do not forever with thy vailed lids[4]   70
    Seek for thy noble father in the dust.
    Thou know'st 'tis common: all that lives must die,
    Passing through nature to eternity.
HAMLET Ay, madam, it is common.[5]
QUEEN   If it be,
    Why seems it so particular with thee?   75
HAMLET Seems, madam? Nay, it is, I know not 'seems'.
    'Tis not alone my inky cloak, good mother,
    Nor customary suits of solemn black,
    Nor windy suspiration of forc'd breath,[6]
    No, nor the fruitful river in the eye,   80
    Nor the dejected haviour of the visage,[7]
    Together with all forms, moods,[8] shapes of grief,
    That can denote me truly. These indeed seem,
    For they are actions that a man might play;
    But I have that within which passes show,[9]   85
    These but the trappings and the suits of woe.

1 'Hamlet's first utterance is a riddle, like his character' (*What Happens in 'Hamlet'*, ed. John Dover Wilson (Cambridge: Cambridge University Press 1935), p. 150). He means 'I am more than just a kinsman now you've married my mother, but I'm not your son, nor do I share any mutual feelings with you.' If it is an aside, then it immediately establishes the importance to the play of Hamlet's relationship with the audience; if not, it is a barbed and publicly rude reply to Claudius.
2 Another punning reply: 'I don't like being called "son" by you.'
3 His black mourning clothes, but also his disposition and mood, or even disguise.
4 Downcast eyes, but veils were also worn by female mourners.
5 A cliché, but with perhaps a glance at 'common' applied to women who were sexually available.
6 Forced sighing.
7 Facial expression.
8 External appearances.
9 Goes beyond mere display. 'In the Branagh film, the crowd whispers . . . "They're witnessing a scene that should take place behind closed doors" (*Screenplay*, p. 15)' (*Shakespeare in Production: 'Hamlet'* in ed. Robert Hapgood (Cambridge: Cambridge University Press, 1999) p. 113). In the 1969 Tony Richardson film Hamlet confronts Claudius face to face in this scene, suggesting the king's own hypocrisy in mourning.

Act 1, Scene 2, lines 129–59: first soliloquy – Hamlet's private grief

Hamlet agrees, after his mother's pleading, to stay in Denmark and not to return to university at Wittenburg in Germany. The court then departs the stage, leaving Hamlet alone for the first of his soliloquies. The four long speeches which Hamlet addresses to the audience are a remarkable feature of the play, especially in performance. They ensure that the audience develop an emotional contact, or even identification, with the prince, and this is a crucial aspect of the play's impact in the theatre.

In a passionate speech whose broken syntax conveys the character's mental disturbance, he sees the world as a neglected garden grown foul (lines 135–7), and portrays his father as a god compared to the bestial and lecherous Claudius (lines 151–2). He censures his mother's moral weakness as a woman (line 146). Psychoanalytic critics have found much of interest in the image of the Garden of Eden polluted by the treachery of Eve, the first mother. They also note the hero-worshipping of his father and the depiction of his uncle (the man who carried out Hamlet's own conjectural oedipal fantasies) as a sexually predatory figure (see Modern Criticism, **pp. 48–9**). We see here a disgust in his mother's sexual nature (line 157; see also 3.4.68–93; 184–190), which has been read by Freudian critics as a symptom of his own ambiguously possessive feelings towards Gertrude. At the very least this speech shows Hamlet to be a man who is very far from being emotionally independent of his parents.

The prince's misogynistic attitude throughout the play – see, for example, his treatment of Ophelia in the 'nunnery' scene (3.1.88–151) – might seem a response to a mother who has betrayed his feelings so painfully. It is worth considering feminist arguments, however, which emphasize the play's presentation of the rigid patriarchal constraint under which Ophelia lives (see Modern Criticism, **pp. 62–5** and **66–70**). Close examination of the lines Gertrude actually speaks in the play also suggest a woman whose principal concern is the welfare and feelings of others, including Ophelia, rather than the raddled and lascivious figure of some twentieth-century productions (see Critical History, **p. 38 note 36**).

The English critic Caroline Spurgeon pointed out in her book *Shakespeare's Imagery and What it Tells Us* (1935) that the text is patterned with recurring images of disease and decay, such as we find here (lines 133, 135–6). A powerful, almost subliminal current is set up in the audience's mind of corruption in a once wholesome body: the political corruption at the heart of the state of Denmark (1.4.90). This image pattern is further commented on in the next headnote.

HAMLET O[1] that this too too sullied[2] flesh would melt,
Thaw and resolve itself into a dew,   130
Or that the Everlasting had not fix'd
His canon[3] 'gainst self-slaughter. O God! God!
How weary, stale, flat, and unprofitable
Seem to me all the uses[4] of this world!
Fie on it, ah fie, 'tis an unweeded garden   135
That grows to seed; things rank and gross in nature
Possess it merely.[5] That it should come to this!
But two months dead—nay, not so much, not two—
So excellent a king, that was to this
Hyperion to a satyr,[6] so loving to my mother   140
That he might not beteem[7] the winds of heaven
To visit her face too roughly. Heaven and earth,
Must I remember? Why, she would hang on him
As if increase of appetite had grown
By what it fed on; and yet within a month—   145
Let me not think on't!—Frailty, thy name is woman—
A little month or ere those shoes were old
With which she follow'd my poor father's body,
Like Niobe,[8] all tears—why she, even she—
O God, a beast that wants discourse of reason[9]   150
Would have mourn'd longer—married with my uncle,
My father's brother—but no more like my father

1 This 'O' has been a great 'bubbling out' (Jacobi, 1977/80) of emotion for many actors. Irving
   (1874) breathed the whole line with great yearning; for Pryce (1980) it was a long, heartfelt sigh
   that became the 'O' (*Shakespeare in Production: 'Hamlet'*, ed. Robert Hapgood (Cambridge:
   Cambridge University Press, 1999), p. 115). In his 1964 film Grigori Kozintsev made the soliloquy
   a voice-over in Hamlet's head as he walked among the busy courtiers, emphasizing how the prince
   was isolated from all around him. Kevin Kline (1990) had wept throughout the preceding part of
   the scene and only began to compose himself when alone with the audience.
2 The Folio Text has 'solid', The First and Second Quartos 'sallied'. Jenkins follows John Dover
   Wilson (*What Happens in 'Hamlet'* (Cambridge: Cambridge University Press, 1935), p. 151), who
   took 'sallied' as a misprint for 'sullied': ' "sullied flesh" is the key to the soliloquy and tells us that
   Ham. is thinking of the 'kindless' . . . incestuous marriage as a personal defilement'. Until Dover
   Wilson (1934) all editors had 'solid'. As Philip Edwards (*Hamlet* (Cambridge: Cambridge University Press, 1985), p. 383–4) points out, this has the authority of the Folio text, but 'most
   importantly of all, solidity is associated with earth . . . It is the flesh, the solid earthly part of himself
   that Hamlet wants to shed' because it is the preponderance bodily elements of earth and water
   which oppress him with melancholy. This famous textual 'crux' is a good example of how a
   modern text can be the product of an editor's critical preferences.
3 Law. Sam West in Steven Pimlott's 2001 production pulled out a gun from his leather jacket at this
   moment.
4 Ways, activities.
5 Totally.
6 Hyperion was the sun god; a satyr was half-goat, half-man, associated with drunkenness and
   lechery. Garrick (1742–76) could only mouth the words 'so excellent a king' as he struggled to be
   manly and keep his emotions in check (Anthony B. Dawson, *Shakespeare in Performance: 'Hamlet'*
   (Manchester: Manchester University Press, 1995), p. 35).
7 Allow.
8 In Ovid's poem *Metamorphoses* (VI.143–346) Niobe still wept despite having been turned to stone
   lamenting the death of her fourteen children slain by Apollo and Artemis. She had boasted of her
   fertility compared to that of their mother, Leto.
9 Lacks the ability to think logically.

Than I to Hercules.[10] Within a month,
Ere yet the salt of most unrighteous tears
Had left the flushing of her galled eyes,[11]   155
She married—O most wicked speed! To post
With such dexterity to incestuous sheets![12]
It is not, nor it cannot come to good.
But break, my heart, for I must hold my tongue.

Act 1, Scene 5, lines 9–112: the Ghost speaks to Hamlet

Following Hamlet's soliloquy, Horatio, Marcellus and Barnardo break the news of the ghost's appearance on the 'platform' (1.2.213) the previous night, and its resemblance to the dead king. Hamlet resolves to watch with them that night. After a scene in which Laertes bids farewell to his sister Ophelia and warns her not to become involved with Hamlet, whose princely status means they could never marry – a message underlined by Polonius, who orders her not to speak to him again – the scene shifts to the battlements that night. The ghost duly appears and summons Hamlet to accompany it to 'more removed ground' (1.4.61). Horatio and Marcellus try to prevent Hamlet from doing so, fearing for his life, but he cannot be restrained by them. Once he is alone with the apparition, it speaks.

The ghost of the unavenged victim of murder was a convention of the revenge tragedy genre, and of its precursor in Seneca's plays (see **p. 8**). This apparition is obviously a Catholic who has failed to take the last sacraments (line 77) and is now paying for his unabsolved sins in purgatory (lines 10–13). There was a mediaeval tradition of souls from purgatory coming back to ask those on earth to pray for them. Like Denmark, England in 1601 was officially Protestant (see Contextual Overview, **p. 10**), and for seventy years the Church of England had done its best to wipe out belief in purgatory, which it saw as a superstition without biblical authority which was exploited by the Catholic Church for its own purposes. For critical explanations of this eruption of Catholic ideas in the text, see the extract from Greenblatt (Modern Criticism, **pp. 87–90**). Many educated Protestants doubted whether ghosts existed at all (for example Horatio at 1.1.23–5); if there were such things, given the non-existence of purgatory, it was argued that they must be demons sent to tempt

---

10 Hercules was not just heroic and strong; he rid the world of many wicked men and monsters. Acting the role of Hamlet, Henry Irving (1874) and Mark Rylance (1988) paused to think before the word to stress how un-Hercules-like is Hamlet in appearance in so many productions (Hapgood (see note 1), p. 116).
11 Before the salt of her insincere tears had gone from her reddened eyes.
12 To race with such nimbleness to incestuous sex. In the Bible a woman who has intercourse with her husband's brother is thus condemned (Leviticus 18.16; 20.21). Such a union was also regarded as incestuous in English law in 1601. When Kevin Kline's 1990 New York Hamlet spoke this line 'the sibilant consonants were hissed out with rancour' (Mary Z. Maher, *Modern Hamlets and their Soliloquies* (Iowa City: University of Iowa Press, 2003), p. 187).

Christian souls to their doom. This is a concern of both Horatio and Hamlet (1.4.40–42; 69–74; 2.2.509–604).

The recurring image of Hamlet's parents being in blissful Edenic state before Gertrude's 'fall' is evident again here in the account of Claudius being like a serpent in the garden (lines 35–6; 'orchard' (line 59) is often glossed by editors as 'garden'). Old Hamlet's body is figured as a city through which an invading force runs destructively (lines 63–7), emphasizing the political impact on the whole country of Claudius's treason. This image of internal corruption (here caused by poison) becoming apparent by external symptoms (lines 71–3) stands in contrast to the image of a secretly corrupt court whose internal disease is not manifested on the surface at 3.4.140–42. As noted in the head-note to the previous passage (p. 126), disease imagery is prevalent in the play. The image of Claudius as something diseased is used by Hamlet at 3.3.96 and 3.4.65–6. Claudius, interestingly, also regards Hamlet as a hidden disease in himself (4.1.21–3; 4.3.9–11; 4.3.65–6).

In the earliest stagings of the play the ghost may have appeared in full armour from the centre-stage trapdoor. Modern productions vary in their interpret-ations. John Barrymore's Hamlet (New York 1922; London 1925; see The Work in Performance, p. 93) spoke to 'a vague greenish light on the backdrop . . . it flickered and faded, then formed a brief, spectral image of an armoured king, the whole vision being accompanied by the "moaning and whistling of the wind" (promptbook) while the voice came from off stage'. As Dawson also notes, 'the Ghost's injunctions thus became potentially more ambiguous and unsettling than they traditionally had been, more implicated in the puzzle of contradictory interpretations that are the mark of a modern understanding of the play'.[1] It was clear that the ghost was some sort of internal psychological disturbance in Jonathan Pryce's 1980 Hamlet at the Royal Court in London ('he croaked the voice from his own solar plexus as if possessed').[2] In Tony Richardson's 1969 film the ghost was an unseen reverberating recording of Hamlet's own voice, only evident as a bright light shining on the prince's face (Nicol Williamson). In Steven Pimlott's 2001 Royal Shakespeare Company production Hamlet closely embraced a very natural-looking but gaunt and dishevelled ghost (see The Work in Performance, pp. 100–1). This staging emphasized the pathos of father and son's longing for each other very strongly.

GHOST I am thy father's spirit,
    Doom'd for a certain term to walk the night,   10
    And for the day confin'd to fast in fires,
    Till the foul crimes done in my days of nature
    Are burnt and purg'd away. But that I am forbid
    To tell the secrets of my prison-house,
    I could a tale unfold whose lightest word   15

1 Anthony B. Dawson, *Shakespeare in Performance: 'Hamlet'* (Manchester: Manchester University Press, 1995), p. 81.
2 *Shakespeare in Production: 'Hamlet'*, ed. Robert Hapgood (Cambridge: Cambridge University Press, 1999, p. 137; see The Work in Performance, p. 95.

Would harrow up thy soul, freeze thy young blood,
Make thy two eyes like stars start from their spheres,[3]
Thy knotted and combined locks[4] to part
And each particular hair to stand an end
Like quills upon the fretful porpentine.[5]   20
But this eternal blazon[6] must not be
To ears of flesh and blood. List, list, O list!
If thou didst ever thy dear father love—

HAMLET O God!

GHOST Revenge his foul and most unnatural murder.   25

HAMLET Murder!

GHOST Murder most foul, as in the best it is,
But this most foul, strange and unnatural.

HAMLET Haste me to know 't, that I, with wings as swift
As meditation[7] or the thoughts of love   30
May sweep to my revenge.

GHOST   I find thee apt.
And duller[8] shouldst thou be than the fat weed
That roots itself in ease on Lethe wharf,[9]
Wouldst thou not stir in this. Now, Hamlet, hear.
'Tis given out that, sleeping in my orchard,   35
A serpent stung me—so the whole ear of Denmark
Is by a forged process of my death
Rankly abus'd[10]—but know, thou noble youth,
The serpent that did sting thy father's life
Now wears his crown.   40

HAMLET O my prophetic soul! My uncle!

GHOST Ay, that incestuous, that adulterate[11] beast,
With witchcraft of his wit, with traitorous gifts—
O wicked wit, and gifts, that have the power
So to seduce!—won to his shameful lust   45
The will[12] of my most seeming-virtuous queen.
O Hamlet, what a falling-off[13] was there,
From me, whose love was of that dignity[14]
That it went hand in hand even with the vow
I made to her in marriage, and to decline[15]   50

3 Make your eyes jump from their sockets like stars unnaturally leaving their orbits.
4 'Hair carefully and intricately arranged, possibly in curls. During the first act Hamlet should be
   "The glass [mirror] of fashion" [3.1.153]' (Hamlet, ed. G. R. Hibbard (Oxford: Oxford University
   Press, 1987), p. 186).
5 Porcupine.
6 Proclamation of the secrets of eternity.
7 Thought.
8 More slothful.
9 The bank of the river of forgetfulness in the mythological underworld.
10 Foully deceived.
11 Adulterous.
12 Assent, but the word could also mean sexual desire.
13 Betrayal and deterioration.
14 Worth.
15 Sink down.

Upon a wretch whose natural gifts were poor
To those of mine.
But virtue, as it never will be mov'd,
Though lewdness court it in a shape of heaven,[16]
So lust, though to a radiant angel link'd,   55
Will sate[17] itself in a celestial bed
And prey on garbage.
But soft, methinks I scent the morning air:
Brief let me be.[18] Sleeping within my orchard,
My custom always of the afternoon,   60
Upon my secure[19] hour thy uncle stole
With juice of cursed hebenon[20] in a vial,
And in the porches of my ears did pour
The leperous[21] distilment, whose effect
Holds such an enmity with blood of man   65
That swift as quicksilver it courses through
The natural gates and alleys of the body,
And with a sudden vigour it doth posset[22]
And curd, like eager[23] droppings into milk,
The thin and wholesome blood. So did it mine,   70
And a most instant tetter[24] bark'd about,
Most lazar[25]-like, with vile and loathsome crust
All my smooth body.
Thus was I, sleeping, by a brother's hand
Of life, of crown, of queen, at once dispatch'd,   75
Cut off even in the blossoms of my sin,
Unhousel'd, disappointed, unanel'd,[26]
No reck'ning[27] made, but sent to my account
With all my imperfections on my head.
O horrible! O horrible! most horrible!   80
If thou hast nature in thee, bear it not,
Let not the royal bed of Denmark be
A couch for luxury[28] and damned incest.

16 Even if an appearance of heavenly beauty tries to seduce it.
17 Satiate.
18 In the 1948 Olivier film (see The Work in Performance, **pp. 103–5**) a flashback of the murder
   appears, which the shot indicates should be understood as happening in Hamlet's imagination. In
   Branagh's 1996 film (see The Work in Performance, **pp. 107–110**) both the murder and a scene
   in which Claudius is flirtatious with Gertrude are shown in a conventional flashback. In indicating
   that everything that the ghost says is literally true the film closes down many dramatic possibilities
   early in the action.
19 Free from care.
20 A poison, but the reference remains obscure.
21 Causing leprosy.
22 Curdle, congeal.
23 Acidic.
24 Skin disease.
25 Leper.
26 Not having taken communion, nor having been prepared for death (through confession), nor
   having been anointed (according to sacramental Catholic rite of 'extreme unction').
27 'Rendering an account to God of one's life and conduct' (Hibbard (see note 4), p. 189).
28 Lechery.

But howsomever thou pursuest this act,
Taint not thy mind nor let thy soul contrive   85
Against thy mother aught. Leave her to heaven,
And to those thorns that in her bosom lodge
To prick and sting her. Fare thee well at once:
The glow-worm shows the matin to be near
And gins to pale his uneffectual fire.[29]   90
Adieu, adieu, adieu. Remember me.   *Exit.*
HAMLET O all you host of heaven! O earth! What else?
And shall I couple hell? O fie! Hold,[30] hold, my heart,
And you, my sinews, grow not instant old,
But bear me stiffly up. Remember thee?   95
Ay, thou poor ghost, whiles memory holds a seat
In this distracted globe.[31] Remember thee?
Yea, from the table[32] of my memory
I'll wipe away all trivial fond[33] records,
All saws[34] of books, all forms, all pressures[35] past   100
That youth and observation copied there,
And thy commandment all alone shall live
Within the book and volume of my brain,
Unmix'd with baser matter. Yes, by heaven!
O most pernicious woman!   105
O villain, villain, smiling, damned villain!
My tables.[36] Meet it is I set it down
That one may smile, and smile, and be a villain—
At least I'm sure it may be so in Denmark.   *[Writes.]*
So, uncle, there you are. Now to my word.   110
It is 'Adieu, adieu, remember me.'
I have sworn't.[37]

Act 2, Scene 2, lines 544–601: second soliloquy – Hamlet's response to the Player's speech

In this second long soliloquy Hamlet reflects on the nature of theatre and devises a plan to test Claudius's guilt. Told of the ghost's appearances by

---

29 Dim his fire that no longer gives off light.
30 Be firm.
31 Confused world, or head, or even theatre; but Philip Edwards (*Hamlet* (Cambridge: Cambridge University Press, 1985)) writes that 'it only dilutes the strength of this passage to find a triple pun here' (p. 109).
32 Slate.
33 Foolish, pointless.
34 Common sayings.
35 Impressions upon my memory.
36 Notebook.
37 Mark Rylance's 1988 Royal Shakespeare Company Hamlet at this point 'cut his hand and smeared the blood on his forehead' (Hapgood (see note 2), p. 140).

Horatio and Barnardo, he encounters it on the 'platform' and hears it tell of his father's secret poisoning by Claudius. He resolves to put on 'an antic disposition': a strange manner of behaviour, perhaps to make him seem distracted and thus not a danger to the king. Polonius, the king's chief minister, is convinced that Hamlet's 'madness' is caused by his love for Ophelia, Polonius's daughter. Claudius asks two of Hamlet's old university friends, Rosencrantz and Guildenstern, to try to find out the true cause of his behaviour. They receive only Hamlet's contempt, but the prince seems cheered when they announce that a troop of players are about to arrive in court. Hamlet greets them with enthusiasm, and asks for a recital of a speech from a play about the fall of Troy and the killing of its king, Priam, by the son of the Greek warrior Achilles as an act of vengeance for his own father's death. The speech serves as a reminder to Hamlet of the need to play the role of the heroic avenger, and depicts Pyrrhus in a much more positive light than its obvious source, Christopher Marlowe's play *Dido, Queen of Carthage*.[1]

In the soliloquy Hamlet tells the audience what was going through his mind as he listened to the speech. In being amazed at how an actor can be more moved by a fictional situation than he can be by his current predicament (lines 545–54), the audience's attention is called to the fact that a work of art – such as the one that they are now watching – has the capacity to condense and perhaps simplify emotion in a powerful way that enables us to see reality in a new, perhaps clearer perspective. At the same time the very conventionality of the generic forms that art takes can lead us to adopt its crafted language and to see the world in its condensed and perhaps simplified terms. Hamlet speaks in what sounds like the inflated and absurd register of the stage avenger in lines 566–77. Perhaps in order to motivate himself, he inhabits this textual role, with life imitating art, only immediately to see through it and to condemn the tragedian's discourse as that of a prostitute, mere words said for money, not out of genuine feeling (lines 582–3). As so often in this play, the action reminds us of the fictionality of what we are watching in order, paradoxically, to undermine, from the stage, drama's claim to interpret the world for its audience, politically and morally (see Contextual Overview, **pp. 12–13**). And yet it will be through drama that Hamlet hopes to produce the moral impact on the king which will give him the evidence he needs to take the political step of regicide (lines 600–01). The question remains: what will be the political impact of *Hamlet* on its audience?

There is clear reference here to the Catholic tradition that ghosts who were apparently returners from purgatory might actually be devils in disguise (lines 594–9). In considering the reasons for Hamlet's apparent delay in taking his revenge his real doubts on this question would have been eminently reasonable to many in the contemporary audience.

---

1   Christopher Marlowe, *Dido, Queen of Carthage* (printed 1594), ed. H. J. Oliver with *The Massacre at Paris* (London, Methuen, 1968), 2.1.221–64.

HAMLET O what a rogue and peasant slave am I!
   Is it not monstrous that this player here,   545
   But in a fiction, in a dream of passion,[2]
   Could force his soul so to his whole conceit
   That from her working all his visage wann'd,[3]
   Tears in his eyes, distraction in his aspect,[4]
   A broken voice, and his whole function suiting   550
   With forms to his conceit? And all for nothing!
   For Hecuba![5]
   What's Hecuba to him, or he to her,
   That he should weep for her? What would he do
   Had he the motive and the cue for passion   555
   That I have? He would drown the stage with tears,
   And cleave the general ear with horrid speech,[6]
   Make mad the guilty and appal the free,[7]
   Confound the ignorant, and amaze indeed
   The very faculties of eyes and ears.   560
   Yet I,
   A dull and muddy-mettled[8] rascal, peak
   Like John-a-dreams, unpregnant of my cause,[9]
   And can say nothing—no, not for a king,
   Upon whose property and most dear life   565
   A damn'd defeat was made. Am I a coward?[10]
   Who calls me villain, breaks my pate[11] across,
   Plucks off my beard and blows it in my face,
   Tweaks me by the nose, gives me the lie i'th' throat
   As deep as to the lungs[12]—who does me this?   570
   Ha!
   'Swounds,[13] I should take it: for it cannot be
   But I am pigeon-liver'd, and lack gall
   To make oppression bitter, or ere this
   I should ha' fatted all the region kites   575

2 Violent emotion at a fictional event.
3 Could, through the workings of his imagination, so affect his soul that his face went pale.
4 A disturbed look on his face.
5 Hecuba was the queen of Troy, whose grief has been piteously described in the player's speech which Hamlet has just heard. Peter O'Toole's Hamlet (1963) could hardly speak for guffawing at the absurdity of the situation at this point (*Shakespeare in Production: 'Hamlet'*, ed. Robert Hapgood (Cambridge: Cambridge University Press, 1999), p. 171).
6 Split everyone's eardrums with language that would make your hair stand on end ('horrid').
7 Guiltless.
8 Dull-spirited.
9 This may mean 'mope about like a dreamy person, not quick to respond to my grievance', but it has been suggested that Hamlet is accusing himself of behaving in masturbatory way.
10 David Warner's Hamlet (1965) was stunned to be heckled by an audience member who called out 'yes!' at this point, and then replied with their own name to his following question (Hapgood (see note 5), p. 172); but this event gives a clue to Hamlet's need to interact with the audience in soliloquy in order to define himself and his ideas.
11 Head.
12 Very deliberately and loudly calls me a liar.
13 By God's wounds (i.e. on the cross; a swearword).

With this slave's offal.[14] Bloody, bawdy villain!
Remorseless, treacherous, lecherous, kindless[15] villain!
Why, what an ass am I! This is most brave,
That I the son of a dear father murder'd,
Prompted to my revenge by heaven and hell,   580
Must like a whore unpack my heart with words,
And fall a-cursing like a very drab,[16]
A scullion![17] Fie upon't! Foh!
About, my brains. Hum—I have heard
That guilty creatures sitting at a play   585
Have, by the very cunning of the scene,[18]
Been struck so to the soul, that presently
They have proclaim'd their malefactions.[19]
For murder, thought it have no tongue, will speak
With most miraculous organ. I'll have the players   590
Play something like the murder of my father
Before mine uncle. I'll observe his looks;
I'll tent him to the quick.[20] If a do blench,[21]
I know my course. The spirit that I have seen
May be a devil, and the devil hath power   595
T'assume a pleasing shape, yea, and perhaps,
Out of my weakness and my melancholy,
As he is very potent with such spirits,
Abuses me to damn me. I'll have grounds

14 I must have the liver of a pigeon, and lack the gall to make injustice feel bitter, or else I would have
    made fat all the birds of prey around here with this slave's (Claudius's) guts.
15 Unnatural. Derek Jacobi's BBC Hamlet (1980) 'hurled out' this line 'with drawn sword held high,
    as though he were about to lunge, while at the same time the whole gesture was undercut by a
    knowing, self-consciously theatrical look' (Anthony B. Dawson, Shakespeare in Performance:
    'Hamlet' (Manchester: Manchester University Press, 1995), p. 220). Kevin Kline (1990) performed
    this part of the speech with a mannered theatricality verging on parody, then on hysteria, before
    realising the absurdity of his behaviour on 'O, vengeance!', a short line following l. 577 in the
    Folio text but not in the Second Quarto. Jenkins (Hamlet, ed. Harold Jenkins (London: Methuen,
    1982), p. 272, felt that line 'has all the marks of an actor's addition'; Hamlet is reproaching himself
    here and only considers revenge later (l. 584). But the line makes sense in Kline's reading, and in
    that of Michael Pennington's 1980 Hamlet, who used the cloak and sword of the first player, as he
    'whirled and tossed, flung down the cloak, brandished the sword, and then, crouching, suddenly
    caught himself in the embarrassment of playing the part of the conventional wild revenger'
    (Dawson, p. 153). There was no theatrical self-awareness in the way John Gielgud (1930) delivered
    these lines however: he was 'trembling with fury, his body shaking, his voice high' (Hapgood
    (see note 5), p. 172).
16 A prostitute.
17 A rough kitchen maid. The Second Quarto text has 'stallyon', a male prostitute, which stresses the
    thought of the previous line but the implied homosexuality was perhaps too much for some editors.
18 The very skill of the performance.
19 Misdeeds. A Norfolk woman, according to a 1599 play, 'saw a play in which a wife murdered her
    husband, and was so affected by it that she promptly confessed to having done the same thing
    herself' (Hamlet, ed. G. R. Hibbard (Oxford: Oxford University Press, 1987), p. 235).
20 Probe him to where it hurts.
21 Flinch.

More relative than this.[22] The play's the thing   600
Wherein I'll catch the conscience of the King.[23]   *Exit.*

Act 3, Scene 1, lines 56–88: Hamlet's third soliloquy

This speech's opening is so familiar to the audience that actors have struggled to make its first lines fresh (see Introduction, **p. 1**). Simon Russell Beale's 2001 National Theatre Hamlet was seen to have written his conclusion down in his notebook before he began the speech.[1] The Russian actor Pavel Mochalov (Moscow, 1837) dashed onto the stage excitedly and shouted the first half of the first line, then slumped into an armchair and was silent for some time before despairingly calling out 'that is the question'.[2]

In the First Quarto the soliloquy comes after Polonius ('Corambis' in that text) reads the letter that Hamlet sends to Ophelia and the king agrees to 'loose' her on the prince while they observe unseen (2.2.162). Hamlet's misery and despair make more dramatic sense here than at the beginning of Act 3 (as in the Second Quarto and the Folio), when he has already decided he will use the play to test the ghost's word. Some productions, including Tony Richardson's film version (1969), use the First Quarto placing.

Wherever it is positioned, it is a puzzling soliloquy in some ways. It is striking that in a speech that expresses such doubts about the existence of the after life Hamlet should not even mention the traveller who *does* seem to have returned (line 80) from that 'undiscovered country' – his father's ghost (see Modern Criticism, **p. 89**). It is a very unchristian speech in a play full of Christian ideas and references, and once more rehearses the Stoic ideal of resisting suffering through control of the emotions (lines 57–8) (see Modern Criticism, **pp. 70–1**). The reasons that Hamlet gives for life not being worth living (lines 70–74) can be seen to refer to the contempt with which he feels he has been treated by the king and Polonius, and the lack of justice for his father's death (if this is what 'the law's delay' in line 72 means). On the other hand, it also sounds as if he thinks that some of the worst things in life are being patronized by pompous people and officious 'jobsworths'. The 'pangs of [despised] love' (line 72) must refer to the fact that Ophelia is now shunning him at her father's behest (1.3.131–6), but in the immediately following lines we see a much more hurtful despising of a lover in the way he treats Ophelia (3.1.95–151).

---

22 Evidence more solid than the ghost's word.
23 Derek Jacobi's 1977 Hamlet at the Old Vic at this point fell into 'a fit of hysterical laughter, a sense of ironic futility undermining his plan even as he devised it. Such moves served to reduce Hamlet to actorly self-parody instead of establishing differing ways of looking at or reading the character' (Dawson (see note 15), p. 220).

---

1 Mary Z. Maher, *Modern Hamlets and their Soliloquies* (Iowa City: University of Iowa Press, 2003), p. 240.
2 *Shakespeare in Production: 'Hamlet'*, ed. Robert Hapgood, Cambridge: Cambridge University Press, 1999, p. 178.

HAMLET To be, or not to be, that is the question:[3]
Whether 'tis nobler in the mind to suffer
The slings[4] and arrows of outrageous fortune,
Or to take arms against a sea of troubles
And by opposing end them.[5] To die—to sleep,　　　　　　60
No more;[6] and by a sleep to say we end
The heart-ache and the thousand natural shocks
That flesh is heir to: 'tis a consummation[7]
Devoutly to be wish'd. To die, to sleep;
To sleep, perchance to dream—ay, there's the rub:[8]　　　65
For in that sleep of death what dreams may come,
When we have shuffled off this mortal coil,[9]
Must give us pause—there's the respect[10]
That makes calamity of so long life.
For who would bear the whips and scorns of time,[11]　　　70
Th'oppressor's wrong, the proud man's contumely,[12]
The pangs of dispriz'd love, the law's delay,
The insolence of office,[13] and the spurns
That patient merit of th'unworthy takes,
When he himself might his quietus[14] make　　　　　　75
With a bare bodkin?[15] Who would fardels[16] bear,
To grunt and sweat under a weary life,
But that the dread of something after death,

3　In Kevin Kline's 1990 New York Hamlet, 'Kline came onto the playing area and completely circled the platform stage once without speaking. Occasionally, his hands would flutter down toward it, indicating that his mind was still on the players and playacting. He seemed to be working out something very difficult for himself . . . He stopped at the center front . . . and delivered quietly . . . [this line]. He did not make contact with the audience – this was an inner dialogue' (Maher (see note 1), pp. 190–91). In Olivier's 1948 film the camera swirled around alarmingly to discover the prince sitting on a rocky outcrop of the castle overlooking a precipitous drop, before the camera seemed to penetrate the back of his head: we are entering into Hamlet's inmost thoughts. In Almereyda's 2000 film Ethan Hawke's prince walked up the aisle of the 'Action' section of a New York *Blockbusters* video store, glancing at a killing from an action film on multiple screens, cleverly emphasizing the idea that revenge is a (popular) cultural narrative, not necessarily any kind of moral absolute.
4　Slingshots, missiles.
5　To die in the process of opposing one's troubles, or perhaps to kill oneself in an act of defiance against them. 'Hamlet no longer talks of setting right a world that is out of joint' (Philip Edwards, *Hamlet* (Cambridge: Cambridge University Press, 1985), p. 146).
6　Death is no more than a sleep.
7　Appropriate end.
8　Obstacle (a metaphor from the game of bowls).
9　Slipped out of this mortal body (like a snake shedding its skin); but 'coil' also means fuss, trouble.
10　Consideration.
11　'Life is thought of as a beadle [constable] whipping us through the streets, like the vagabond or the whore, with jeering mobs around' (*Hamlet*, ed. John Dover Wilson (Cambridge: Cambridge University Press, 1934), p. 192). The line might perhaps also refer to ageing.
12　Insolent treatment.
13　Those in positions of (petty) authority.
14　Sign off from life: *quietus est* was written on an account to signify "paid"' (*Hamlet*, ed. G. R. Hibbard (Oxford: Oxford University Press, 1987), p. 240). *Quietus* also means 'inactive, at peace' in Latin.
15　A dagger not much more significant than a darning needle. In his 1996 film Branagh, who had been delivering his soliloquy into a two-way mirror, pulled out his dagger to startle the king and Polonius hidden on the other side.
16　Burdens.

The undiscover'd country from whose bourn[17]
No traveller returns,[18] puzzles[19] the will,   80
And makes us rather bear those ills we have
Than fly to others that we know not of?
Thus conscience[20] does make cowards of us all,
And thus the native hue of resolution
Is sicklied o'er with the pale cast of thought,[21]   85
And enterprises of great pitch and moment[22]
With this regard their currents turn awry[23]
And lose the name of action. [. . .]

From **The First Quarto version of the 'To be or not to be'
soliloquy,** from *The First Quarto of 'Hamlet'* (1603) (Scene 7, lines 114–35),
ed. Kathleen O. Irace (Cambridge: Cambridge University Press, 1998), pp. 58–9

Scholars are notoriously divided about this 'quarto' text (see Key Passages,
pp. 113–15) which was first discovered in 1823. Whatever its origins, this
version of the soliloquy is much less uncertain and philosophically speculative
than the more familiar text. In the First Quarto in general, Hamlet is much more
of a clear-headed man of action. Here he adheres to the conventional Christian
belief in judgement after death (lines 117–21). In the Second Quarto and Folio
texts (see 3.1.78–82) Hamlet is unsure about the existence of the after life at all.
The list of reasons which make life a burden in the two later versions (3.1.70–74)
are more personal and less political than here (lines 122–6). This is a much less
introspective and self-absorbed Hamlet, and one who interacts more with the
spectators. The opening line, according to a modern actor (Christopher
McCullough) who performed the role in the First Quarto version, 'only made
sense if I said it *to the audience'.* The American critic Leah S. Marcus observes
that for actors 'there was something indefinable about [the First Quart text]
that made it appear more faithful to Elizabethan theatrical practice than either
of the more polished texts [the Second Quarto and Folio]'.[1]

17 Boundary.
18 'One of the great commonplaces of about death: that the road leading to it is a one-way street'
    (Hibbard (see note 14), p. 241). 'Ham. has given up all belief in the "honesty" of the Ghost, and . . .
    Sh. wrote the lines to make this clear to the audience' (Dover Wilson (see note 11), p. 192).
19 Confuses. John Gielgud's 1930 Hamlet made these words the hinge and key idea of the whole
    speech (Anthony B. Dawson, *Shakespeare in Performance: 'Hamlet'* (Manchester: Manchester
    University Press, 1995), p. 100). At this point 'he began to pace about the stage' (Maher
    (see note 51), p. 10). He seemed to have 'a mind magnetized by the need to examine the void' (Ibid.,
    pp. 9–10).
20 Sense of right and wrong. Kevin Kline's 1990 Hamlet stressed 'does' and 'cowards' in this line,
    making it clear he had come to a conclusion at the end of the speech (Maher (see note 1), p. 191).
21 Our natural healthy colour turns pale and sickly when we think rather than act.
22 Weight and importance.
23 Because of this are diverted from their objective.

1   Leah S. Marcus, *Unediting the Renaissance: Shakespeare, Marlowe, Milton* (London: Routledge,
    1996), pp. 153–4.

HAMLET To be, or not to be; ay, there's the point.
　　　To die, to sleep: is that all? Ay, all.   115
　　　No, to sleep, to dream; ay, marry, there it goes.
　　　For in that dream of death, when we awake
　　　And borne before an everlasting judge
　　　From whence no passenger ever returned,
　　　The undiscovered country at whose sight   120
　　　The happy smile and the accursed damned –
　　　But for this, the joyful hope of this,
　　　Who'd bear the scorns and flattery of the world,
　　　Scorned by the right rich, the rich cursed of the poor,
　　　The widow being oppressed, the orphan wronged,   125
　　　The taste of hunger or a tyrant's reign,
　　　And thousand more calamities besides,
　　　To grunt and sweat under this weary life,
　　　When that he may his full quietus make
　　　With a bare bodkin?[2] Who would this endure   130
　　　But for a hope of something after death,
　　　Which puzzles the brain and doth confound the sense,
　　　Which makes us rather bear those evils we have
　　　Than fly to others that we know not of?
　　　Ay, that. O, this conscience makes cowards of us all. –   135

Act 3, Scene 2, lines 181–264: the performance of *The Murder of Gonzago*

This section is the conclusion of the play, *The Murder of Gonzago*, performed before the court by means of which Hamlet intends to 'catch the conscience of the king' (2.2.601). Since the last soliloquy, Hamlet has addressed the audience again, contemplating suicide. Secretly observed by Claudius and Polonius, he has also callously and crudely dismissed Ophelia, who had been sent to him by her father. Having instructed the players on how they should act, and praised Horatio for his stoical control of his emotions, as the court await the performance, Hamlet makes a series of satirical barbs aimed at those around him, including some crude and suggestive remarks to Ophelia which in some productions cause her public embarrassment. Following a dumb show, the play begins with a King telling a Queen that he does not think he has long to live. She in turn promises that she will never remarry after his death.

　　The cunning irony of the Player King's speech lies in the fact that he is offering advice which Hamlet himself would perhaps be well-advised to take: promises made in the heat of passion do not remain valid when that powerful emotion has ended (lines 187–190). Hamlet is staging the play in order to provoke a damning public reaction from Claudius as his guilty conscience causes him to react to the re-enactment of his brother's murder: but Hamlet pays no attention to the words of the play and is unaffected himself. Further, the Player King tells us that 'purpose is but the slave to memory' (line 183). But we do not and cannot remember everything; what we remember is often very subjective and varies from person to person according their interests and needs. The political function of memory, and the implied question of what we should forget because of what the future demands of us, is also a key issue in the play. Nothing in the world remains still: Hamlet should accept that no promise, no emotion, can bind us irrevocably (lines 193–8) (See Bacon in Contemporary Documents, **pp. 25–6**). And, finally, the Player King prophetically points out that since we can never draw a line under the consequences of our actions (lines 205–8), the traditional avenger may well be fundamentally misconceived in thinking that his act of vengeance can result in a just and conclusive end-state.

The dramatic power of the central section of this passage is partly produced by the discomfort felt by the audience at Hamlet's sarcastic comments aimed at his mother and uncle (lines 219–38); even though we know Claudius's guilt, Hamlet still comes across here as embarrassingly out of control, especially in his crude sexual banter with Ophelia (lines 241–4).

In Laurence Olivier's 1948 film Claudius was increasingly and dramatically distressed at the players' revelation of his crime, much to the obvious concern of the court. In Adrian Noble's 1992 production 'an overtly symbolic and very bright spotlight was trained on him from the side, and he [Claudius] stumbled off in terror' (Dawson, p. 16).[1] But there is no textual evidence here or later on that Claudius's decision to call for lights and to leave is actually the result of guilt-induced panic rather than merely embarrassment at the prince's constant interruptions and uncivil behaviour (see Modern Criticism, **p. 56**). If so, a doubt may be raised in this scene about the power of theatre to intervene politically in the world.

PLAYER KING *I do believe you think what now you speak;*
But what we do determine, oft we break.
Purpose is but the slave to memory,
Of violent birth but poor validity,[2]
Which now, like fruit unripe, sticks on the tree,   185
But fall unshaken when they mellow be.
Most necessary 'tis that we forget
To pay ourselves what to ourselves is debt.
What to ourselves in passion we propose,
The passion ending, doth the purpose lose.   190
The violence of either grief or joy

---

1   Anthony B. Dawson, *Shakespeare in Performance: 'Hamlet'* (Manchester: Manchester University Press, 1995), p. 16.
2   Our intentions are entirely dependent on what we remember; the passion that initially motivates us is powerful, but doesn't last long. Lines 194–5 repeat the sentiment.

Their own enactures with themselves destroy.[3]
Where joy most revels grief doth most lament;
Grief joys, joy grieves, on slender accident.[4]
This world is not for aye, nor 'tis not strange   195
That even our loves should with our fortunes change,[5]
For 'tis a question left us yet to prove,[6]
Whether love lead fortune, or else fortune love.
The great man down, you mark his favourite flies;
The poor advanc'd makes friends of enemies;   200
And hitherto doth love on fortune tend:
For who not needs[7] shall never lack a friend,
And who in want a hollow friend doth try
Directly seasons him his enemy.
But orderly to end where I begun,   205
Our wills and fates do so contrary run
That our devices[8] still are overthrown:
Our thoughts are ours, their ends[9] none of our own.[10]
So think thou wilt no second husband wed,
But die thy thoughts when thy first lord is dead.   210
PLAYER QUEEN Nor earth to me give food, nor heaven light,
Sport and repose lock from me day and night,
To desperation turn my trust and hope,
An anchor's cheer[11] in prison be my scope,
Each opposite, that blanks the face of joy,   215
Meet what I would have well and it destroy,[12]
Both here and hence pursue me lasting strife,
If, once a widow, ever I be a wife.
HAMLET If she should break it now.
PLAYER KING 'Tis deeply sworn. Sweet, leave me here awhile.   220
My spirits grow dull, and fain I would beguile
The tedious day with sleep.
PLAYER QUEEN   Sleep rock thy brain,
And never come mischance between us twain!

                                                           Exit. He sleeps.

---

3 When either grief or joy goes to an extreme, both the emotion and the need to act upon it thereupon
   pass away.
4 At the slightest excuse.
5 Nothing lasts for ever in this world, and we should not find it strange when love changes according
   to changing events.
6 Discover, work out.
7 Is wealthy.
8 Plans, schemes.
9 Outcomes.
10 Lines 211–13 were made the final lines of Michael Almereyda's 2000 film, put into the mouth of
   the news anchorman reporting the royal deaths. They seemed to the director to have a 'centrality
   in Shakespeare's long view of things' (Michael Almereyda, William Shakespeare's 'Hamlet':
   A Screenplay Adaptation (London: Faber and Faber, 2000), p. 143.
11 A hermit's way of life.
12 Let everything that cancels out joy come to wipe out all my hopes.

HAMLET Madam, how like you this play?
QUEEN The lady doth protest too much, methinks.[13]   225
HAMLET O, but she'll keep her word.
KING Have you heard the argument?[14] Is there no offence
in't?
HAMLET No, no, they do but jest[15]—poison in jest. No offence
i'th' world.   230
KING What do you call the play?
HAMLET *The Mousetrap*—marry, how tropically![16] This play
is the image of a murder done in Vienna—Gonzago
is the duke's name, his wife, Baptista—you shall see
anon. 'Tis a knavish piece of work, but what o' that?   235
Your Majesty, and we that have free souls, it touches
us not. Let the galled jade wince, our withers are
unwrung.[17]

Enter LUCIANUS.

This is one Lucianus, nephew to the King.
OPHELIA You are as good as a chorus,[18] my lord.   240
HAMLET I could interpret between you and your love, if I
could see the puppets dallying.[19]
OPHELIA You are keen, my lord, you are keen.
HAMLET It would cost you a groaning to take off my edge.[20]
OPHELIA Still better, and worse.   245
HAMLET So you mis-take your husbands.[21]—Begin, mur-
derer. Leave thy damnable faces and begin. Come,
the croaking raven doth bellow for revenge.
LUCIANUS *Thoughts black, hands apt, drugs fit, and time agreeing,*
Confederate season,[22] else no creature seeing,   250
Thou mixture rank, of midnight weeds collected,
With Hecate's ban[23] thrice blasted, thrice infected,
Thy natural magic and dire property
On wholesome life usurp immediately.
Pours the poison in the sleeper's ears.

---

13 Too much protesting makes the sentiment sound insincere.
14 Plot, storyline.
15 i.e. it's only a play.
16 How metaphorically appropriate.
17 'Let the horse with a sore back wince when you put a saddle on it; we won't react' (because our
    consciences are clear of wrongdoing).
18 An explainer or interpreter of the play's action. In Kenneth Branagh's 1996 film Hamlet gets on
    stage next to Lucianus and holds up to Lucianus's poison bottle, staring savagely at Claudius;
    'I make little doubt that Lucianus should be dressed like Hamlet' (*Hamlet*, ed. John Dover Wilson
    (Cambridge: Cambridge University Press, 1934), p. 204).
19 'I know exactly what you'd say to your lover, like a puppet-master who provides the dialogue for
    the puppets he controls.' He is very indirectly accusing her of being sexually available to another.
20 Ophelia tells Hamlet he is bitterly witty; Hamlet interprets her words to mean that he is so 'sharp'
    that she would cry out in pain if he satisfied his sexual appetite with her.
21 Betray them by sleeping with someone else.
22 The occasion itself is my ally.
23 The curse of the goddess of witchcraft.

HAMLET He poisons him i'th' garden for his estate. His name's   255
Gonzago. The story is extant, and written in very
choice Italian. You shall see anon how the murderer
gets the love of Gonzago's wife.
OPHELIA The King rises.
HAMLET What, frighted with false fire?[24]   260
QUEEN How fares my lord?
POLONIUS Give o'er the play.
KING Give me some light. Away.
POLONIUS Lights, lights, lights.

Act 3, Scene 3, lines 36–98: Claudius prays; Hamlet's opportunity to strike

After the play breaks up in chaos, Hamlet is summoned to a meeting with his mother, who is astonished at his behaviour. He tells the audience that he will 'speak daggers to her, but use none' (3.2.396). Claudius tells Rosencrantz and Guildenstern that they will shortly accompany Hamlet on a journey to England. Polonius says he will hide in Gertrude's room to overhear Hamlet's imminent interview with him. Claudius is then left alone on stage.

One modern editor writes that: 'In this scene the arrogance of the man who is trying to effect justice is strongly contrasted with the Christian humility of the man who has done murder.'[1] Though the context of the scene is perhaps the most religious in the entire play – in both Olivier's and Branagh's films it is set in Elsinore's chapel – it is striking how ultimately *un*christian both 'mighty opposites' are. By the end of the scene Claudius has apparently accepted his damnation, knowing that he cannot give up his worldly power and love (lines 53–5). There seems to be no self-deception or prevarication in Claudius's soliloquy. How sincere his religious feeling appears is up to the director: the king never refers to it again. Hamlet, for his part, thinks he should be able to choose what happens to Claudius's soul after death, in lines which Samuel Johnson (see Early Critical Reception, **pp. 43–4**) found 'too terrible to be read or uttered'. This scene is powerful because of the density, vividness and colour of its imagery, its visual construction, and its sheer theatrical tension: will Claudius die now? Is there not some reversal of audience sympathy here? The scene stands at the centre of the play, often just before or just after the interval in modern productions. Modern, secular political pragmatism stands in contrast to a primitive revenge code. Hamlet's tragedy has been seen by some materialist critics to be the result of being caught in the middle of that very opposition (see Holderness in Modern Criticism, **pp. 65–6**).

---

24 Scared of a blank-firing gun? (It's only make-believe . . .)

1   *Hamlet*, ed. Philip Edwards (Cambridge: Cambridge University Press, 1985), p. 54.

KING[2] O, my offence is rank, it smells to heaven;
It hath the primal eldest curse upon't—
A brother's murder. Pray can I not,
Though inclination be as sharp as will,
My stronger guilt defeats my strong intent,   40
And, like a man to double business bound,
I stand in pause where I shall first begin,
And both neglect. What if this cursed hand
Were thicker than itself with brother's blood,
Is there not rain enough in the sweet heavens   45
To wash it white as snow? Whereto serves mercy
But to confront the visage of offence?[3]
And what's in prayer but this twofold force,
To be forestalled ere we come to fall,
Or pardon'd being down?[4] Then I'll look up.   50
My fault is past[5]—But O, what form of prayer
Can serve my turn? 'Forgive me my foul murder?'
That cannot be, since I am still possess'd
Of those effects for which I did the murder—
My crown, mine own ambition, and my queen.   55
May one be pardon'd and retain th'offence?[6]
In the corrupted currents of this world
Offence's gilded hand may shove by justice,
And oft 'tis seen the wicked prize itself
Buys out the law.[7] But 'tis not so above: 60
There is no shuffling, there the action lies
In his true nature; and we ourselves compell'd
Even to the teeth and forehead of our faults
To give in evidence.[8] What then? What rests?
Try what repentance can. What can it not?   65
Yet what can it, when one can not repent?
Oh wretched state! Oh bosom black as death!
Oh limed soul, that struggling to be free

---

2 According to the Bible, the first murder was that of a brother: Cain killed Abel (Genesis 4.8).
   Timothy West, playing Claudius opposite Derek Jacobi on stage in 1977, 'gave this speech as a dog-
   tired worrying away at an old, incurable obsession, packed with self-mockery and self-contempt,
   the last testament of a man who was already evolved from despair to a deadly cynicism' (*Shakespeare in Production: 'Hamlet'*, ed. Robert Hapgood (Cambridge: Cambridge University Press,
   1999), pp. 205–6). In Steven Pimlott's 2001 production, however, Larry Lamb's worldly Claudius,
   who loved both his queen and his political achievements, pragmatically and calmly reminded
   himself of why he could find no Christian guilt for what he done. In Kozintsev's 1964 film Claudius
   spoke the soliloquy to a mirror, honestly examining his own conscience.
3 'What is mercy for, except to meet crime face to face?' (Edwards (see note 1), p. 171).
4 A reference to the Lord's Prayer: 'Lead us not into temptation, but deliver us from evil' (Matthew
   6.13).
5 'I'll be hopeful (and pray); I have a sin to be pardoned.'
6 Keep what was gained from the crime.
7 'In the corrupt course of things, the guilty hand full of gold may bribe away justice; often the
   ill-gotten gains purchase the law itself.'
8 Face to face (with God) we will have to give evidence against ourselves.

Art more engag'd!⁹ Help, angels! Make assay.
Bow, stubborn knees; and heart with strings of steel,   70
Be soft as sinews of the new-born babe.
All may be well.   *He kneels.*

Enter HAMLET.

HAMLET Now might I do it pat,¹⁰ now a¹¹ is a-praying.
And now I'll do't.   [*Draws his sword.*]
          And so he goes to heaven;
And so am I reveng'd. That would be scann'd:¹²   75
A villain kills my father, and for that
I, his sole son, do this same villain send
To heaven.
Why, this is hire and salary, not revenge.
A took my father grossly, full of bread,   80
With all his crimes broad blown,¹³ as flush as May;
And how his audit stands who knows save heaven?
But in our circumstance and course of thought
'Tis heavy with him. And am I then reveng'd,
To take him in the purging of his soul,   85
When he is fit and season'd for his passage?
No.
Up, sword, and know thou a more horrid hent:¹⁴
When he is drunk asleep, or in his rage,¹⁵
Or in th'incestuous pleasure of his bed,   90
At game a-swearing, or about some act
That has no relish of salvation in't,
Then trip him, that his heels may kick at heaven
And that his soul may be as damn'd and black
As hell, whereto it goes. My mother stays.   95
This physic¹⁶ but prolongs thy sickly days.   *Exit.*
KING My words fly up, my thoughts remain below.
Words without thoughts never to heaven go.   *Exit.*

---

9 Birds were caught by attaching a sticky substance ('lime') to the branches of a tree.
10 Very conveniently.
11 He.
12 Considered carefully.
13 'In full blossom' Edwards (see note 1), p. 173).
14 Occasion.
15 'Uncontrollable sexual desire' (*Hamlet*, ed. G. R. Hibbard (Oxford: Oxford University Press, 1987), p. 275).
16 Both the 'medicine' of Claudius's prayer and the life-giving stay of execution which Hamlet grants.

Act 3, Scene 4, lines 53–160: the central part of the 'closet' scene – Hamlet and Gertrude alone together

Hamlet finds his mother in her 'closet' (3.2.322; a private room, not usually a bedroom).[1] He is angry, and seizes her to prevent her calling for others. She panics and calls out. Polonius, who is hiding behind a wall-hanging ('arras'), echoes her call. Hamlet, thinking, it seems, that it is Claudius, draws his sword and stabs him dead through the hanging. No one answers her calls for help, and Hamlet tells his mother how he will now tell her the full nature of her offences.

The striking nature of the imagery and the density of the syntax in this section powerfully convey Hamlet's obsessions, passions and intellectual turmoil. The image of his father as a combination of classical gods (lines 55–62) is yet again (see 1.2.139–40) contrasted with the depiction of Claudius, who is associated with something filthy and diseased (lines 64–5; 146–51; 170). There seems to be no middle ground in much of Hamlet's thought. He does not seem to be a man who can make any kind of compromise in his thinking. Yet many critics and audience members have found some redeeming qualities in Claudius (see the preceding and succeeding extracts). The language also conveys a powerful sense of Hamlet's disgust at the idea of his mother being sexually active, especially with Claudius, and becomes graphic and sensual, albeit in a grotesque way (lines 81–8, 91–4).

This obsession with his mother's sexuality has been taken by psychoanalytic critics as the 'key' to understanding his behaviour (see Critical History, **pp. 34–6** and Modern Criticism, **pp. 48–9**). Many twentieth-century productions deployed this interpretation very powerfully. In Olivier's deliberately Freudian 1948 film (see the Work in Performance, **pp. 103–5**), Hamlet's parting from his mother is marked by a lingering kiss on the lips after he has been cradled in her lap. In Zeffirelli's 1990 film (see the Work in Performance, **pp. 105–7**), Mel Gibson's Hamlet appears to be simulating some sort of rape on his mother (Glenn Close) in the early, angry part of the scene. It ends with her kissing him.[2] The puzzling 'emotion' which Hamlet shows 'is in excess of the facts as they appear' was taken by T. S. Eliot (see Modern Criticism, **pp. 53–5**) as the reason why the play was an 'artistic failure'. But the prince's attitudes can also be read as part of a general misogynistic fear of female sexuality ('rebellious hell', line 82), which some feminist critics have seen as part of the early modern tendency to depict the sexualised mature female as a threat to patriarchal power (see Modern Criticism, **pp. 62–5**). A society in which most property was passed on to the first-born legitimate heir insisted on strict female chastity among the

---

1   Under the influence of Freud's reading of the play (see Modern Criticism, **pp. 48–9**), since 1927 the scene has often been set in Gertrude's bedroom; see Stanley Wells, *Looking for Sex in Shakespeare* (Cambridge: Cambridge University Press, 2004), p. 24; but see also Modern Criticism, **p. 78**.

2   Anthony B. Dawson, *Shakespeare in Performance: 'Hamlet'* (Manchester: Manchester University Press, 1995), pp. 206–7.

property-owning classes and found any independent expression of female desire to be a threat (see Contextual Overview, **p. 13**).

The ghost in his nightgown in the First Quarto text echoed a mediaeval Catholic belief that subsequent apparitions of souls in purgatory were often dressed in white to show the increasing purification of their souls: Hamlet's father's angry ghost, like his desire to effect revenge (lines 107–9; 127–30), is fading away in time. Dover Wilson draws on a theatrical and cultural tradition to argue that Gertrude cannot see the ghost because the guilty are blind to such phenomena; when the ghost realizes this he is horrified (lines 125–9) and ' "steals away" in shame'.[3]

HAMLET Look here upon this picture, and on this,
    The counterfeit presentment of two brothers.[4]
    See what a grace was seated on this brow,   55
    Hyperion's curls, the front[5] of Jove himself,
    An eye like Mars to threaten and command,
    A station[6] like the herald Mercury
    New-lighted on a heaven-kissing hill,
    A combination and a form indeed   60
    Where every god did seem to set his seal
    To give the world assurance of a man.
    This was your husband. Look you now what follows.
    Here is your husband, like a mildew'd ear
    Blasting[7] his wholesome brother. Have you eyes?   65
    Could you on this fair mountain leave to feed
    And batten on this moor?[8] Ha, have you eyes?
    You cannot call it love, for at your age
    The heyday[9] in the blood is tame, it's humble,
    And waits upon the judgment, and what judgment   70
    Would step from this to this? Sense sure you have,
    Else could you not have motion; but sure that sense
    Is apoplex'd, for madness would not err
    Nor sense to ecstasy[10] was ne'er so thrall'd
    But it reserv'd some quantity of choice   75
    To serve in such a difference. What devil was't

3 *Hamlet*, ed. John Dover Wilson (Cambridge: Cambridge University Press, 1934), p. 214.
4 In some productions, such as Olivier's 1948 and Tony Richardson's 1969 films, Hamlet compares the picture of his father which he wears in a locket around his neck to the picture of Claudius which hangs around his mother's. In others there are portraits of both on the wall. The latter is evident in the 1709 engraving for Rowe's edition, which seems to be based on Betterton's Hamlet (1661–1709). Jonathan Pryce's 1980 Hamlet thrust, with bloody hand, two different coins, one from each reign, in front of a 'whooping, groaning' queen (Dawson (see note 2), p. 166; see also *Hamlet*, ed. Robert Hapgood (Cambridge: Cambridge University Press, 1999), p. 211).
5 Forehead; Hyperion was the Titanic sun-god (see **p. 127**).
6 Way of standing.
7 Spreading disease to.
8 Could you stop feeding on this fair mountain and grow fat on this moor?
9 Excitement.
10 Hallucination.

That thus hath cozen'd you at hoodman-blind?[11]
Eyes without feeling, feeling without sight,
Ears without hands or eyes, smelling sans[12] all,
Or but a sickly part of one true sense   80
Could not so mope.[13] O shame, where is thy blush?
Rebellious hell,[14]
If thou canst mutine[15] in a matron's bones,
To flaming youth let virtue be as wax
And melt in her own fire; proclaim no shame   85
When the compulsive ardour gives the charge,[16]
Since frost itself as actively doth burn
And reason panders will.[17]

QUEEN   O Hamlet, speak no more.
Thou turn'st mine eyes into my very soul,
And there I see such black and grained spots   90
As will not leave their tinct.[18]

HAMLET   Nay, but to live
In the rank sweat of an enseamed[19] bed,
Stew'd[20] in corruption, honeying and making love[21]
Over the nasty sty!

QUEEN   Oh, speak to me no more.
These words like daggers enter in my ears.   95
No more, sweet Hamlet.

HAMLET   A murderer and a villain,
A slave that is not twentieth part the tithe[22]
Of your precedent lord, a vice[23] of kings,
A cutpurse[24] of the empire and the rule,
That from a shelf the precious diadem stole   100
And put it in his pocket—

QUEEN No more.

HAMLET A king of shreds and patches—

---

11 Deceived you at blind-man's bluff.
12 Without.
13 Be in a daze.
14 Not just sin rising up against virtue; 'hell' could also mean the female genitals and 'rebel' to become
    aroused.
15 Mutiny.
16 Makes the attack.
17 Reason acts as a pimp for sexual desire.
18 Lose their colour by being washed away.
19 Greasy, with an echo of 'semen'.
20 Soaked in, but a 'stew' was also a brothel.
21 Both these two terms mean 'love-talk', not sex.
22 Tenth.
23 With a play on 'the Vice, often called Iniquity, of the Morality plays, whose language and actions
    were both villainous and farcical' (*Hamlet*, ed. G. R. Hibbard (Oxford: Oxford University Press,
    1987), p. 282); see note 4 on p 101.
24 Common thief.

Enter GHOST.[25]

Save me, and hover o'er me with your wings,
You heavenly guards! What would your gracious
figure?

QUEEN Alas, he's mad.   105

HAMLET Do you not come your tardy son to chide,
That, laps'd in time and passion,[26] lets go by
Th'important acting of your dread command?
O say.[27]

GHOST   Do not forget. This visitation   110
Is but to whet thy almost blunted purpose.
But look, amazement on thy mother sits.
O step between her and her fighting soul.
Conceit[28] in weakest bodies strongest works.
Speak to her, Hamlet.   115

HAMLET How is it with you, lady?

QUEEN   Alas, how is't with you,[29]
That you do bend your eye on vacancy,
And with th'incorporal air do hold discourse?[30]
Forth at your eyes your spirits wildly peep,[31]
And, as the sleeping soldiers in th'alarm,   120
Your bedded hair, like life in excrements,
Starts up and stands on end.[32] O gentle son,
Upon the heat and flame of thy distemper
Sprinkle cool patience. Whereon do you look?

HAMLET On him, on him. Look you how pale he glares.   125
His form and cause conjoin'd, preaching to stones,
Would make them capable.[33]—Do not look upon me,
Lest with this piteous action you convert

---

25 The additional stage direction 'in his nightgown' is found in the First Quarto text. 'It is the only indication we have of how the Ghost appeared in this scene in Shakespeare's day' (Hibbard (see note 23), p. 282).
26 Having let both time and passion pass away.
27 The ghost never appeared at all for Jonathan Pryce's Hamlet (1980), but was an effect of Hamlet's psychological state; when the ghost spoke here and in Act 1 it was Hamlet talking to himself, 'an inner torment speaking in a strange, distorted voice, which was wrenched out of Hamlet in the midst of extreme pain and violent retching' (Dawson (see note 2), p. 163).
28 Imagination.
29 In Branagh's 1992 stage *Hamlet* the pathos of the ruined family is shown by Gertrude embracing the passionate Hamlet, who reaches out to his father while the ghost appears unseen. A similar moment was depicted by the Hamlets of both Barrymore (1922) and Finney (1976) (Hapgood (see note 4), pp. 214–15).
30 Talk to the insubstantial air.
31 It was thought that at moments of excitement the 'vital forces' of the body ('spirits') rushed to the surface.
32 'Excrements' meant any outgrowth of the body, hair or nails; so 'your hair is standing on end, not bedded down, as if it had life of its own'.
33 Receptive.

My stern effects.[34] Then what I have to do
Will want true colour—tears perchance for blood.[35]   130
QUEEN To whom do you speak this?
HAMLET Do you see nothing there?
QUEEN Nothing at all; yet all that is I see.[36]
HAMLET Nor did you nothing hear?
QUEEN No, nothing but ourselves.   135
HAMLET Why, look you there, look how it steals away.
    My father, in his habit as he liv'd![37]
    Look where he goes even now out at the portal.   *Exit Ghost.*
QUEEN This the very coinage of your brain.
    This bodiless creation ecstasy   140
    Is very cunning in.[38]
HAMLET My pulse as yours doth temperately keep time,
    And makes as healthful music. It is not madness
    That I have utter'd. Bring me to the test,
    And I the matter will re-word, which madness   145
    Would gambol from. Mother, for love of grace,[39]
    Lay not that flattering unction[40] to your soul,
    That not your trespass, but my madness speaks.
    It will but skin and film the ulcerous place,[41]
    Whiles rank corruption, mining[42] all within,   150
    Infects unseen. Confess yourself to heaven,
    Repent what's past; avoid what is to come;
    And do not spread the compost on the weeds
    To make them ranker. Forgive me this my virtue;
    For in the fatness of these pursy times[43]   155
    Virtue itself of vice must pardon beg,
    Yea, curb[44] and woo for leave to do him good.
QUEEN O Hamlet, thou hast cleft my heart in twain.
HAMLET O throw away the worser part of it
    And live the purer with the other half.   160

---

34 Intended deeds.
35 'The Ghost's reappearance seems to be weakening Hamlet's resolve instead of strengthening it'
    (*Hamlet*, ed. Philip Edwards (Cambridge: Cambridge University Press, 1985), p. 180).
36 In John Barton's 1980 Stratford production Barbara Leigh Hunt's Gertrude seemed really to have
    seen the ghost, and 'lay face down in terror, refusing to look again after a brief glance' (Dawson (see
    note 2), p. 156); her guilt was then all the more palpable and powerful.
37 The clothes he wore when alive.
38 Tendency to hallucinate which madness is skilful in producing.
39 Henry Irving's 1874–85 Hamlet famously laid his head in his mother's lap here in a moment of
    'sentimental domesticity' (Dawson (see note 2), p. 65).
40 Ointment which treats the symptom not the cause.
41 Provide a thin covering over a festering sore.
42 Sapping.
43 The grossness of these bloated and flatulent (but also money-driven?) times.
44 Bow.

Act 4, Scene 5, lines 16–168: Ophelia's madness and Laertes's rebellion

Hamlet is arrested for the murder of Polonius and immediately despatched to England under the guard of Rosencrantz and Guildenstern. They have sealed instructions for the King of England – who owes homage to Denmark after recent Danish raids – to execute the prince on his arrival there. On his way to the coast Hamlet sees the Norwegian Fortinbras and his army (now at peace with Claudius) passing through Denmark with Claudius's permission, apparently on their way to fight in Poland. In the meantime, the king and Gertrude have just heard that Ophelia has grown mad with grief at her father's death.

Ophelia's genuine and obvious madness stands in contrast to Hamlet's much more puzzling 'antic disposition'. Having had her life and emotions so ruthlessly controlled and policed by her father, in her madness she reveals the cost of the blatant suppression both of her feelings for her father and of the expression of her own sexuality seen elsewhere in the play. The idea that the mad often speak the truth unknowingly was commonplace in early modern thought (see Contextual Overview, **p. 14**), and Ophelia remarks cryptically that 'we know what we are, but know not what we may be' (lines 43–4). Perhaps she means that she can see the predicament of women in the patriarchal and occasionally misogynistic world of the play (see Modern Criticism, **pp. 66–70**), but can also see what lives they might lead if such oppression could be escaped.

A crowd of Danish people make a sudden appearance from the margins of the play as we discover that their dissatisfaction with events at court has led them not only to come to the side of Laertes, but even to demand a right to choose their government, ignoring all tradition, 'as the world were now but to begin' (line 103). Laertes's challenge is less 'political' in a sense: he is prepared to be damned for breaking his allegiance to the king (lines 131–3) so long as he can enact personal revenge for his father. Claudius for his part invokes, perhaps with conscious irony as a regicide, the belief that God's Providence will protect His anointed deputy on earth from all treason (lines 122–5). Thus the play dramatizes a number of important contemporary political ideas: humanist and puritan beliefs that monarchy should be limited by some form of popular consent, especially when the monarch lacks virtue (see Contextual Overview, **pp. 9–10**); the still existing threat to centralized royal power from an aristocratic code which put personal honour before any ultimate duty to the state; and the divine right theory which denied the legitimacy of any rebellion, even against a wicked monarch (see Contextual Overview, **p. 9**, and Contemporary Documents, **pp. 21–3**), here surely held up to a certain amount of scrutiny as it issues from the mouth of Claudius. In fact, Claudius's performance as the confident monarch, sure that he has God on his side, even, as in many productions, with a rebel's sword at his throat, demonstrates that power in the play can be secured by a confident playing of a role. The play's concern with the nature of acting and with the public exercise of power overlap here.

Laertes now takes on an important function as one of the play's pair of parallel avengers to Hamlet (the other being Fortinbras). His vengeance is passionate, sudden and heedless of the consequences. Fortinbras takes his revenge by following an indirect and perhaps cunningly plotted route to the throne once occupied by the man who slew his father (Old Hamlet). Both are set up as avengers in opposition to Hamlet, who seems to lack Laertes's precipitate rush to action and high sense of honour (a quality Hamlet admires in a soliloquy only printed in the Second Quarto, 4.4.53–6). Neither is he a commander of men, active in public life, like the suggestively machiavellian Fortinbras. But are we to condemn him for not being like either of these two opposing examples? The contrast also calls on the audience to reflect on the righteousness of revenge. Not all Shakespeare's contemporaries, by any means, regarded revenge as a simple moral duty (see Bacon in Contemporary Documents, **pp. 25–6**).

QUEEN Let her come in.   [*Exit Gentleman.*]
    [*Aside*] To my sick soul, as sin's true nature is,
    Each toy¹ seems prologue to some great amiss.
    So full of artless jealousy is guilt,
    It spills itself in fearing to be spilt.²   20

Enter OPHELIA³

OPHELIA Where is the beauteous majesty of Denmark?
QUEEN How now, Ophelia?
OPHELIA (*sings*) *How should I your true love know*
            From another one?
            By his cockle hat and staff   25
            *And his sandal shoon.*⁴
QUEEN Alas, sweet lady, what imports this song?
OPHELIA Say you? Nay, pray you, mark.
    (*sings*)   *He is dead and gone, lady,*
            He is dead and gone;   30
            At his head a grass-green turf,
            At his heels a stone.
    O ho!
QUEEN Nay, but, Ophelia—
OPHELIA Pray you, mark.   35
    [*sings*]   *White his shroud as the mountain snow—*

1 Trivial event.
2 A guilty conscience gives itself away in its clumsy eagerness not to appear guilty. In Michael Almereyda's 2000 film, Gertrude's speech is spoken as a voice-over as Gertrude laughs and drinks at a reception.
3 The First Quarto stage direction adds '*playing on a lute, and her hair down, singing*'. Joanne Pearce in Adrian Noble's 1992 production wore her father's blood-stained evening dress. In Branagh's 1996 film Kate Winslet's Ophelia appears in a strait-jacket which a solicitous Gertrude unfastens; in Almereyda's film a screeching Ophelia is a public embarrassment who is manhandled out of sight as soon as possible. Kozintsev's 1964 film stressed Ophelia's repression by showing her strapped into constraining mourning clothes after her father's death and then in this scene dancing a stiff parody of the formal dance which she was shown learning earlier in the film.
4 'Shoon' is an archaic form of 'shoes'. The 'cockle' hat and sandals are the clothes of the pilgrim.

Enter KING.

QUEEN Alas, look here, my lord.
OPHELIA (*sings*)   *Larded with sweet flowers*
          Which bewept to the grave did not go
          With true-love showers.   40
KING How do you, pretty lady?
OPHELIA Well, good dild[5] you. They say the owl was a baker's
    daughter. Lord, we know what we are, but know
    not what we may be. God be at your table.
KING Conceit[6] upon her father.   45
OPHELIA Pray let's have no words of this, but when they ask
    you what it means, say you this:
    (*sings*)   *Tomorrow is Saint Valentine's day,*
              All in the morning betime,
              And I a maid at your window,   50
              To be your Valentine.
              Then up he rose, and donned his clo'es,
              And dupp'd[7] *the chamber door,*
              Let in the maid that out a maid
              Never departed more.   55
KING Pretty Ophelia—
OPHELIA Indeed, without an oath, I'll make an end on't.
          By Gis[8] *and by Saint Charity,*
              Alack, and fie for shame,
          Young men will do't, if they come to't—   60
          By Cock,[9] *they are to blame.*
          Quoth she, 'Before you tumbled[10] *me,*
              You promis'd me to wed.'
    He answers,
              'So would I a done, by yonder sun,   65
              An thou hadst not come to my bed.'
KING How long hath she been thus?
OPHELIA I hope all will be well. We must be patient: but I
    cannot choose but weep, to think they should lay
    him i'th' cold ground. My brother shall know of it.   70
    And so I thank you for your good counsel. Come,
    my coach. Good night, ladies; good night. Sweet
    ladies; good night, good night.   *Exit.*

---

5 Reward.
6 Fanciful thoughts.
7 Undid.
8 Jesus.
9 God, but with an obvious double meaning.
10 Have sex with. In Branagh's 1996 film a flashback at this point shows Hamlet and Ophelia in bed.
    'A number of critics . . . have supposed that Hamlet and Ophelia have had sexual relations . . . For
    most of us, Ophelia's words are intensely moving because they show her deranged mind wandering
    over the sexual relations which she has *not* had' (*Hamlet*, ed. Philip Edwards (Cambridge:
    Cambridge University Press, 1985), p. 195).

KING Follow her close; give her good watch, I pray you.

[*Exit Horatio.*]

Oh, this is the poison of deep grief: it springs   75
All from her father's death. And now behold—
O Gertrude, Gertrude,
When sorrows come, they come not single spies,[11]
But in battalions. First, her father slain;
Next, your son gone, and he most violent author   80
Of his own just remove; the people muddied,[12]
Thick and unwholesome in their thoughts and whispers
For good Polonius' death–and we have done but
     greenly
In hugger-mugger[13] to inter him; poor Ophelia
Divided from herself and her fair judgment,   85
Without the which we are pictures, or mere beasts;
Last, and as much containing as all these,
Her brother is in secret come from France,
Feeds on this wonder, keeps himself in clouds,[14]
And wants not buzzers[15] to infect his ear   90
With pestilent speeches of his father's death,
Wherein necessity, of matter beggar'd,
Will nothing stick our person to arraign
In ear and ear.[16] O my dear Gertrude, this,
Like to a murd'ring-piece,[17] in many places   95
Gives me superfluous death.   *A noise within.*
                           Attend!
Where are my Switzers?[18] Let them guard the door.

Enter a Messenger.

What is the matter?
MESSENGER   Save yourself, my lord.
The ocean, overpeering of his list,[19]
Eats not the flats with more impetuous haste   100
Than young Laertes, in a riotous head,[20]
O'erbears your officers. The rabble call him lord,
And, as the world were now but to begin,

---

11 As lone scouts.
12 Confused, anxious.
13 Secretly.
14 Conceals his motives.
15 Does not lack scandal-spreaders.
16 Since they have no facts it seems that they must, without hesitation, make accusations about me to
     many people.
17 A cannon which shot out many small balls at once. At this point 'in the Olivier film Eileen Herlie
     [Gertrude] signalled her withdrawal from the King by turning her back on his bid for sympathy and
     resisting his attempted embrace' (*Shakespeare in Production: 'Hamlet'*, ed. Robert Hapgood
     (Cambridge: Cambridge University Press, 1999), p. 235).
18 Swiss mercenaries were often bodyguards to early modern monarchs.
19 Limits.
20 Insurrection, rebellion.

Antiquity forgot, custom not known—
The ratifiers and props of every word—²¹   105
They cry 'Choose we! Laertes shall be king.'
Caps, hands, and tongues applaud it to the clouds,
'Laertes shall be king, Laertes king.'
QUEEN How cheerfully on the false trail they cry!   109
Oh, this is counter,²² you false Danish dogs.   *A noise within.*
KING The doors are broke.

Enter LAERTES *with* Followers.

LAERTES Where is this king?—Sirs, stand you all without.
FOLLOWERS No, let's come in.
LAERTES   I pray you, give me leave.
FOLLOWERS We will, we will.
LAERTES I thank you. Keep the door.   [*Exeunt Followers.*] 115
                              O thou vile king,
Give me my father.
QUEEN [*holding him*] Calmly, good Laertes.
LAERTES That drop of blood that's calm proclaims me bastard,
Cries cuckold to my father, brands the harlot
Even here between the chaste unsmirched brow
Of my true mother.²³
KING   What is the cause, Laertes,   120
That thy rebellion looks so giant-like?—
Let him go, Gertrude; do not fear our person.
There's such divinity doth hedge a king²⁴
That treason can but peep to what it would,
Acts little of his will.—Tell me, Laertes,   125
Why thou art thus incens'd.—Let him go, Gertrude.—
Speak, man.
LAERTES Where is my father?
KING   Dead.
QUEEN   But not by him.
KING Let him demand his fill.
LAERTES How came he dead? I'll not be juggled with.   130
To hell, allegiance! Vows, to the blackest devil!
Conscience and grace, to the profoundest pit!
I dare damnation. To this point I stand,
That both the worlds I give to negligence,

---

21 They are behaving as if custom and precedent, which give all words meaning, had been abolished.
22 Laertes's followers are compared to hunting dogs which are following the trail backwards, away
     from their quarry. In Kozintsev's 1964 film Laertes was seen to be wielding his father's consecrated
     sword and accompanied by a large crowd of well-armed and well-organized followers.
23 Prostitutes were sometimes branded on the forehead; if Laertes were acting calm it would suggest
     that Polonius wasn't really his father. In Tony Richardson's 1969 film Laertes spits on Gertrude at
     this point.
24 God puts a barrier around kings which prevents treason carrying out its wishes. Derek Jacobi's
     Claudius in Branagh's 1996 film ironically raises both eyebrows on the word 'divinity'.

Let come what comes, only I'll be reveng'd   135
Most throughly for my father.
KING   Who shall stay you?
LAERTES My will, not all the world's.
And for my means, I'll husband[25] them so well,
They shall go far with little.
KING   Good Laertes,
If you desire to know the certainty   140
Of your dear father's death, is't writ in your revenge
That, swoopstake,[26] you will draw both friend and foe,
Winner and loser?
LAERTES None but his enemies.
KING   Will you know them then?
LAERTES To his good friends thus wide I'll ope my arms,   145
And, like the kind life-rend'ring pelican,
Repast them with my blood.[27]
KING   Why, now you speak
Like a good child and a true gentleman.
That I am guiltless of your father's death
And am most sensible in grief for it,   150
It shall as level to your judgment 'pear
As day does to your eye.
                              A noise within. [*Ophelia is heard singing.*]
                              Let her come in.
LAERTES How now, what noise is that?

                              Enter OPHELIA.

O heat, dry up my brains! Tears seven times salt
Burn out the sense and virtue of mine eye.   155
By heaven, thy madness shall be paid by weight
Till our scale turn the beam.[28] O rose of May!
Dear maid—kind sister—sweet Ophelia—
O heavens, is't possible a young maid's wits
Should be as mortal as an old man's life?   160
Nature is fine in love, and where 'tis fine
It sends some precious instance of itself
After the thing it loves.
OPHELIA (*sings*) *They bore him bare-fac'd on the bier,*
                    And in his grave rained many a tear—   165
Fare you well, my dove.
LAERTES Hadst thou thy wits, and didst persuade revenge,
It could not move thus.

25 Look after.
26 'Sweepstake': a gambler playing for all the stakes in one go.
27 The pelican was supposed to feed its young with its own blood.
28 'The balance (of the scales of Justice) tilts in our favour' (*Hamlet*, ed. G. R. Hibbard (Oxford: Oxford University Press, 1987), p. 306).

Act 5, Scene 1, lines 1–118: the gravediggers

Claudius pacifies Laertes. He explains how it was Hamlet who killed Polonius, and that he could not punish his nephew publicly because of his feelings for Gertrude, who 'lives almost by his looks' (4.7.12). Furthermore, Hamlet was too popular with the Danish people to be swept aside easily. A letter arrives for Horatio from Hamlet explaining that the prince is not in England. The ship taking him there was attacked by pirates. He boarded their ship and became their prisoner; Rozencrantz and Guildenstern, on his original ship, escaped and carried on towards England. A further letter to Claudius announces that Hamlet is now back in Denmark. Claudius conspires to help Laertes take a fatal revenge upon Hamlet by setting up a fencing match where Laertes will use a secretly poisoned sword.

The traditional reading of this scene has portrayed the gravediggers as ignorant busybodies in the manner of Shakespeare's Dogberry in *Much Ado About Nothing* or Elbow in *Measure for Measure*. In order to make their opening exchange funny, a great deal of stage business has had to be added, or alternatively this opening section of the scene down to line 60 has been cut altogether (as in the films of Olivier, Richardson and Almereyda); yet it appears in full in the First Quarto. The first part of the scene makes a great deal more sense if the men are not played as the foolish butts of a more educated audience's humour, but, taking the hint of their allusion to the radical anti-aristocratic slogan about the lack of 'gentlemen' in God's original creation (line 30), played as intelligent, sarcastic critics of a society where there is one law for the rich and another for the poor (lines 23–5). Rather than parrots of legal jargon they do not understand, they can be convincingly played as satirizing the law's pompous verbiage and chopped logic (lines 4–20). Such a reading is consonant with what we hear (4.5.81–3; 90–6; 4.7.18–21) and see (4.5.99–115) of the volatile and insurrectionary mood of the Danish people elsewhere in the play. It is also interesting that the Gravedigger engages in a battle over the right to give meaning to words with Hamlet (lines 115–132); just as Hamlet does with Claudius (see Key Passages, **pp. 124–5**). In this case, however, it is Hamlet – who thinks labourers lack refinement of feeling (lines 68–9) – who is defeated by the Gravedigger's subversive 'equivocation'. Indeed, actors playing Hamlet seem to have felt upstaged by this character after their absence since 4.4.[1] Some critics from the Marxist tradition have noticed how a play which depicts a country where the peasants are treading on the aristocrats' heels (lines 136–8) harbours utopian longings for a fairer society in the future (see Ryan, *Modern Criticism*, **pp. 85–7**).

In visual and thematic terms, however, the scene underlines how the protagonists are in effect engaged in digging graves for one another; death for them is not now far distant. The apparent futility of political ambition and personal

---

1   *Shakespeare in Production: 'Hamlet'*, ed. Robert Hapgood (Cambridge: Cambridge University Press, 1999), pp. 252–4.

vengeance in the face of common human mortality can also be seen to be foregrounded in this exchange.

Steven Pimlott, who directed the 2001 RSC *Hamlet*, regards the gravedigger as a man who is happy with his lot, happy just enjoying company and relating to people; he is a reminder to Hamlet that 'life is possible; probing it need not be agonising'.

Enter two Clowns [—the Grave-digger *and* Another].[2]

GRAVEDIGGER Is she to be buried in Christian burial, when she wilfully seeks her own salvation?[3]

OTHER[4] I tell thee she is, and therefore make her grave straight. The crowner hath sat on her,[5] and finds it Christian burial.   5

GRAVEDIGGER How can that be, unless she drowned herself in her own defence?

OTHER Why, 'tis found so.

GRAVEDIGGER It must be *se offendendo*,[6] it cannot be else. For here lies the point: if I drown myself wittingly, it argues   10 an act; and an act hath three branches—: it is, to act, to do, to perform; argal,[7] she drowned herself wittingly.

OTHER Nay, but hear you, Goodman[8] Delver—

GRAVEDIGGER Give me leave. Here lies the water—good. Here   15 stands the man—good. If the man go to this water and drown himself, it is, will he, nill he,[9] he goes, mark you that. But if the water come to him and drown him, he drowns not himself. Argal, he that is not guilty of his own death shortens not his own life.   20

OTHER But is this law?

GRAVEDIGGER Ay, marry, is't, crowner's quest law.[10]

OTHER Will you ha' the truth an't? If this had not been a

2 Two lower-class men, without necessarily the idea that they are comedians.
3 'Could he mean that she is trying to get to heaven before his time, or does he simply confuse salvation and damnation?' (*Hamlet*, ed. Philip Edwards (Cambridge: Cambridge Univesity Press, 1985), p. 213). Or is there a sarcastic tone to the Clown's speeches all the way through his dialogue with his friend, reflecting a shared disgust with the way that there is one law for the rich and one for the poor? Suicides were not usually buried with full Christian ritual in consecrated ground.
4 'There is nothing in what follows to indicate that the Second Clown is also a grave-digger. He seems simply to be a crony of the First Clown who has dropped by for a chat' (*Hamlet*, ed. G. R. Hibbard (Oxford: Oxford University Press, 1987), p. 320).
5 The coroner has considered her case (with a disrespectful *double entendre?*).
6 Usually read as the foolish gravedigger's mistake for *se defendendo*, legal Latin for a killing justified in self-defence.
7 'A vulgar perversion of the Latin *ergo* [therefore]' (Hibbard (see note 4), p. 321). But what if this is a coarse parody of legal language and reasoning?
8 Like the modern 'Mr' before an occupation.
9 Whether he wants to or not.
10 Coroner's inquest law.

gentlewoman,[11] she should have been buried out o'
Christian burial.   25
GRAVEDIGGER Why, there thou say'st. And the more pity that
great folk should have countenance[12] in this world to
drown or hang themselves, more than their even-Christen.[13]
Come, my spade. There is no ancient
gentleman but gardeners, ditchers, and grave-makers—they   30
hold up Adam's profession.[14]   [*He digs.*]
OTHER Was he a gentleman?
GRAVEDIGGER A was the first that ever bore arms.[15]
OTHER Why, he had none.
GRAVEDIGGER What, art a heathen? How dost thou understand   35
the Scripture? The Scripture says Adam digged.[16]
Could he dig without arms? I'll put another
question to thee. If thou answerest me not to the
purpose, confess thyself—
OTHER Go to.   40
GRAVEDIGGER What is he that builds stronger than either the
mason, the shipwright, or the carpenter?
OTHER The gallows-maker; for that frame outlives a
thousand tenants.
GRAVEDIGGER I like thy wit well, in good faith. The gallows does   45
well. But how does it well? It does well to those that
do ill. Now, thou dost ill to say the gallows is built
stronger than the church; argal, the gallows may do
well to thee. To't again, come.
OTHER Who builds stronger than a mason, a shipwright,   50
or a carpenter?
GRAVEDIGGER Ay, tell me that, and unyoke.[17]
OTHER Marry, now I can tell.
GRAVEDIGGER To't.
OTHER Mass, I cannot tell.   55
GRAVEDIGGER Cudgel thy brains no more about it, for your dull
ass will not mend his pace with beating. And when
you are asked this question next, say 'A grave-maker'.
The houses that he makes last till doomsday.
Go, get thee to Yaughan;[18] fetch me a stoup of liquor.   60

---

11 Lady.
12 Authority, privilege.
13 Fellow Christians.
14 A clear reference here to one of the well-known texts preached in the 1381 Peasants' Revolt. 'When
    Adam Delved / And Eva Span / Who was then the gentleman?' (There was no social hierarchy in the
    Garden of Eden; it is of man's construction, not God's intention.) The Gravedigger is saying that
    workers are the true, original gentlemen.
15 Have a heraldic coat of arms, with an obvious but telling pun.
16 In the Book of Genesis (3.23).
17 'Have done with the effort of thinking' (Hibbard (see note 4), p. 323).
18 Thought to be an ale-house keeper near the theatre.

[*Exit the Other Clown. The Grave-digger carries on digging.*]

(*Sings*)   In youth, when I did love, did love,
                   Methought it was very sweet:
                   To contract—O—the time for—a—my behove,[19]
                   Oh, methought, there—a—was nothing—a—meet.

[*While he is singing,*] *enter* HAMLET *and* HORATIO.

HAMLET Has this fellow no feeling of his business, that he sings in   65
grave-making?
HORATIO Custom hath made it in him a property of easiness.[20]
HAMLET 'Tis e'en so: the hand of little employment hath the
daintier sense.[21]
GRAVEDIGGER (*sings*) But age, with his stealing steps   70
                      Hath claw'd me in his clutch,
                      And hath shipped me intil[22] the land,
                      As if I had never been such.
                                    He throws up a skull.
HAMLET That skull had a tongue in it, and could sing once.
How the knave jowls it to the ground, as if t'were   75
Cain's jawbone, that did the first murder![23] This
might be the pate of a politician, which this ass now
o'er-offices,[24] one that would circumvent God, might
it not?
HORATIO It might, my lord.   80
HAMLET Or of a courtier; which could say 'Good morrow,
sweet lord. How dost thou, good lord?' This might
be my Lord Such-a-one, that praised my Lord
Such-a-one's horse, when he meant to beg it, might it
not?   85
HORATIO Ay, my lord.
HAMLET Why, e'en so, and now my Lady Worm's, chopless,
and knocked about the mazard[25] with a sexton's spade.
Here's fine revolution and we had the trick to see't.
Did these bones cost no more the breeding, but to play   90
at loggets[26] with 'em? Mine ache to think on't.
GRAVEDIGGER (*sings*) A pickaxe and a spade, a spade,
                      For and a shrouding-sheet,
                      O, a pit of clay for to be made

---

19 'To pass away the time to my own advantage' (Edwards (see note 3), p. 215).
20 He is so used to his job that he is indifferent to human remains.
21 Those who don't do manual work have the more sensitive feelings.
22 Into.
23 Cain committed the first murder; like Claudius, he killed his brother (see 3.3.37–8).
24 Lords it over.
25 Jawless, and knocked about the bowl.
26 'A country game in which wooden truncheons . . . were thrown at a fixed stake' (Edwards (see note
    3), p. 216).

For such a guest is meet.   95
[Throws up another skull.]
HAMLET There's another. Why, might not that be the skull of
a lawyer? Where be his quiddities²⁷ now, his quillities,
his cases, his tenures, and his tricks? Why does he
suffer this rude knave now to knock him about the
sconce with a dirty shovel, and will not tell him of his   100
action of battery? Hum! This fellow might be in's
time a great buyer of land, with his statutes, his
recognizances, his fines, his double vouchers, his
recoveries. Is this the fine of his fines, and the
recovery of his recoveries, to have his fine pate full of   105
fine dirt? Will his vouchers vouch him no more of
his purchases, and double ones too, than the length
and breadth of a pair of indentures? The very conveyances
of his lands will hardly lie in this box, and
must th'inheritor himself have no more, ha?   110
HORATIO Not a jot more, my lord.
HAMLET Is not parchment²⁸ made of sheepskins?
HORATIO Ay, my lord, and of calveskins too.
HAMLET They are sheep and calves which seek out assurance
in that. I will speak to this fellow.—Whose grave's   115
this, sirrah?
GRAVEDIGGER Mine, sir.

[Sings]   *Oh a pit of clay for to be made—*

HAMLET I think it be thine indeed, for thou liest in't.
GRAVEDIGGER You lie out on't, sir, and therefore 'tis not yours.   120
For my part, I do not lie in't, yet it is mine.
HAMLET Thou dost lie in't, to be in't and say 'tis thine. 'Tis
for the dead, not for the quick:²⁹ therefore thou liest.
GRAVEDIGGER 'Tis a quick lie, sir; 'twill away again, from me to
you.   125
HAMLET What man dost thou dig it for?
GRAVEDIGGER For no man, sir.
HAMLET What woman then?
GRAVEDIGGER For none neither.
HAMLET Who is to be buried in't?   130
GRAVEDIGGER One that was a woman, sir; but, rest her soul, she's
dead.
HAMLET How absolute the knave is. We must speak by the
card, or equivocation will undo us.³⁰ By the Lord,
Horatio, these three years I have taken a note of it, the   135

---

27 The first of a series of legal terms which Hamlet puns with to stress the insignificance of human
    affairs in the face of death.
28 On which legal documents were written.
29 Living.
30 Speak precisely, or cunning ambiguity will deceive us.

age is grown so picked[31] that the toe of the peasant
comes so near the heel of the courtier he galls his
kibe.[32]—How long hast thou been a grave-maker?

GRAVEDIGGER Of all the days i'th' year, I came to't that day that
our last King Hamlet overcame Fortinbras.   140

HAMLET How long is that since?

GRAVEDIGGER Cannot you tell that? Every fool can tell that. It
was the very day that young Hamlet was born—he
that is mad, and sent into England.

HAMLET Ay, marry. Why was he sent into England?   145

GRAVEDIGGER Why, because a was mad. He shall recover his wits
there. Or if a do not, 'tis no great matter there.

HAMLET Why?

GRAVEDIGGER 'Twill not be seen in him there. There the men are
as mad as he.   150

HAMLET How came he mad?

GRAVEDIGGER Very strangely, they say.

HAMLET How 'strangely'?

GRAVEDIGGER Faith, e'en with losing his wits.

HAMLET Upon what ground?   155

GRAVEDIGGER Why, here in Denmark.[33] I have been sexton here,
man and boy, thirty years.

Act 5, Scene 2, lines 213–408: the final duel; the deaths of Gertrude, Claudius, Laertes and Hamlet and the entry of Fortinbras

Hamlet's conversation with the gravedigger is interrupted by the arrival of Ophelia's funeral, attended by the king and Gertrude. The prince sees Laertes embracing his sister's body before it is interred, and leaps into the grave to struggle over the corpse, vowing that he loved Ophelia far more than Laertes ever did. Having been parted from his adversary, Hamlet is led offstage by Horatio. In the first part of this scene Hamlet tells Horatio without regret how he rewrote Claudius's sealed command to the King of England so that Rosencrantz and Guildenstern have been executed in his place. He realizes he does not have long before the news arrives from England of what has happened. A pretentious courtier, Osric, comes with Claudius's challenge to the fencing match with Laertes. Hamlet mocks his manner of talking, but agrees to the contest.

---

31 Fastidious.
32 Rubs against his chilblain.
33 At this point in the 1996 Branagh film, the Gravedigger and Hamlet exchange a mutual smile, and the low-key sardonic wit which has been the mood of the scene so far comes to an end. In the 2001 RSC production, Sam West's Hamlet settled down with Horatio here to share the Gravedigger's offered sandwiches and a quiet moment before an impromptu game of rugby with the skull.

Conventionally, a revenge tragedy ends in a court ritual or performance which acts as a cover for an act of vengeance which leaves the main characters all dead (see, for example, Kyd's *The Spanish Tragedy*, 1587, or Middleton's *Women Beware Women*, 1623). Here, Hamlet's new-found confidence in divine providence (lines 215–20) is tested. There is an obvious 'poetic justice' in Laertes being killed by his own poisoned sword, and in Claudius being made to drink the poisoned cup which he prepared for the prince (see Drake in Early Critical Reception, **pp. 41–2**). To what extent Gertrude deserves to die remains disputable, however. Her death seems to be a total accident, and can be seen to undermine any neat pattern of justice being done. Audiences may consider how sinful her behaviour has been reckoned to be (there is no evidence of her adultery while her husband was alive, but she has transgressed the biblical injunction not to marry her husband's brother – Leviticus 18.16). Some directors have sought to give her death a pattern and meaning (see note 23).

This is the moment, however, when Hamlet's indecision ends and he finally takes action. Inevitably, it is when he is himself mortally wounded. For psychoanalytic critics it is notable that it is only when his mother is dead that the Oedipal puzzle is solved and he can finally act (see Freud in Modern Criticism, **pp. 48–9**).

For twentieth-century critics like Bradley and Wilson Knight (see Modern Criticism, **pp. 49–53** and Critical History, **p. 34**), for whom the play's tragic stature depended on new hope arising from the destruction of a flawed hero whose sacrificial death removed an evil force, Fortinbras has to be an unequivocally good character. Often cut in production in the past in order to emphasize the tragedy of the individual prince at the expense of the play's politics, Fortinbras does not appear in any of Shakespeare's source material. His name means 'strong in arms' in French, and there is little to suggest that he is more than a cunning military adventurer. It was against him that Demark was rearming at the beginning of the play (1.1.73–82). Claudius secured his apparent disarmament through the diplomacy of Voltemand and Cornelius, but he then granted Fortinbras permission to march through Denmark, with his same forces, on the way to Poland (2.2.60–80). Exactly what he is doing in Elsinore at the head of an army at the end of the play is not made clear. He had earlier stated ambiguously that if Claudius 'would aught with us / We shall express our duty in his eye' (4.4.5–6) and he tells his army to 'go softly on' (4.4.8, according to the Second Quarto text). This may mean he is showing respect for Denmark and its king; or it could sound defiant. 'Softly' might also mean quietly, surreptitiously. One way of reading the play's ending is that while the court has been dealing with Hamlet, a foreign chancer has taken his opportunity to stage a coup. Certainly, there is something unsettling about the arrival of Fortinbras which recent directors have sought to underline.

HORATIO If your mind dislike any thing, obey it. I will forestall
their repair[1] hither, and say you are not fit.
HAMLET Not a whit, we defy augury.[2] There's a special providence   215
in the fall of a sparrow.[3] If it[4] be now, 'tis not to
come; if it be not to come, it will be now; if it be not
now, yet it will come. The readiness is all. Since no
man, of aught he leaves, knows aught, what is't to
leave betimes?[5] Let be.   220

A table prepared. Trumpets, Drums, *and* Officers *with cushions.*

Enter KING, QUEEN, LAERTES, [OSRIC,] *and all the* State,
and Attendants *with foils and daggers.*

KING Come, Hamlet, come, and take this hand from me.
                              [*Puts Laertes's hand into Hamlet's.*]
HAMLET Give me your pardon, sir, I have done you wrong;
But pardon it, as you are a gentleman.
This presence[6] knows, and you must needs have heard,
How I am punish'd with sore distraction.[7]   225
What I have done
That might your nature, honour, and exception
Roughly awake, I here proclaim was madness.
Was't Hamlet wrong'd Laertes? Never Hamlet.
If Hamlet from himself be ta'en away,   230
And when he's not himself does wrong Laertes,
Then Hamlet does it not, Hamlet denies it.
Who does it, then? His madness. If 't be so,
Hamlet is of the faction that is wrong'd;
His madness is poor Hamlet's enemy.[8]   235
Sir, in this audience,
Let my disclaiming from a purpos'd evil
Free me so far in your most generous thoughts
That I have shot mine arrow o'er the house
And hurt my brother.

---

1 The arrival of Laertes, Claudius and the others.
2 Here, a superstitious sense that something bad is about to happen.
3 God's purpose is at work even when a sparrow dies (Matthew 10:29).
4 Death.
5 'Since no one can tell from anything on earth what is the right moment to die, why trouble about
it?' (*Hamlet*, ed. John Dover Wilson (Cambridge: Cambridge University Press, 1934), p. 250).
'Twentieth century Hamlets', writes Hapgood (p. 268), 'have often focused on this passage as a
philosophical epiphany'. For Branagh's 1994 stage Hamlet, according to one reviewer whom
Hapgood quotes, 'a weary fatalism gives way to a spiritual illumination that seems to light up his
whole being'. David Warner's 1965 Hamlet, on the other hand, spoke it with a 'sad and hopeless
smile . . . a man without comfort and without hope, going to execution'.
6 (Royal) assembly.
7 Madness.
8 As Philip Edwards (*Hamlet* (Cambridge: Cambridge University Press, 1985)) points out (p. 235),
Hamlet was *not* mad when he killed Polonius, and he knows that Claudius knows what he was
doing when he stabbed Polonius through the hanging. This is not straight dealing with Laertes, no
matter what his current regrets may be, as perhaps Laertes realizes (lines 243–7).

LAERTES   I am satisfied in nature,[9]   240
Whose motive in this case should stir me most
To my revenge; but in my terms of honour[10]
I stand aloof, and will no reconcilement
Till by some elder masters of known honour
I have a voice and precedent of peace   245
To keep my name ungor'd.[11] But till that time
I do receive your offer'd love like love
And will not wrong it.
HAMLET   I embrace it freely,
And will this brother's wager frankly play.—
Give us the foils.   250
LAERTES Come, one for me.
HAMLET I'll be your foil,[12] Laertes. In mine ignorance
Your skill shall, like a star i'th' darkest night
Stick fiery off[13] indeed.
LAERTES   You mock me, sir.
HAMLET No, by this hand.   255
KING Give them the foils, young Osric. Cousin Hamlet,
You know the wager?
HAMLET   Very well, my lord.
Your Grace hath laid the odds o'th'[14] weaker side.
KING I do not fear it. I have seen you both,
But since he is better'd, we have therefore odds.[15]   260
LAERTES This is too heavy. Let me see another.
HAMLET This likes me well. These foils have all a length?
OSRIC Ay, my good lord.   *They prepare to play.*
        [*Enter* Servants *with*] *flagons of wine.*
KING Set me the stoups of wine upon that table.
If Hamlet give the first or second hit,   265
Or quit in answer of the third exchange,[16]
Let all the battlements their ordnance[17] fire:
The King shall drink to Hamlet's better breath,
And in the cup an union[18] shall he throw

---

 9 In my natural feelings.
10 As far as my personal honour is concerned.
11 A firm opinion that we can be at peace, which is based on precedent, and which leaves my honour
    undamaged. The formality of Laertes's language reveals his feelings and nervousness at this point.
12 The setting of a jewel, against which the jewel stood out in contrast, with an obvious play on
    words.
13 Stand out with its blaze.
14 Put your money on.
15 In my favour. 'Claudius is doing his best to cover up the fact that the *odds* are designed to give
    Laertes as many opportunities as possible to kill Hamlet' (*Hamlet*, ed. G. R. Hibbard (Oxford:
    Oxford University Press, 1987), p. 347).
16 Eventually hit Laertes in the third bout.
17 Cannons.
18 A valuable pearl, which on sumptuous occasions might be drunk dissolved in wine.

Richer than that which four successive kings   270
In Denmark's crown have worn—give me the cups—
And let the kettle[19] to the trumpet speak,
The trumpet to the cannoneer without,
The cannons to the heavens, the heavens to earth,
'Now the King drinks to Hamlet!' Come, begin.   275
And you, the judges, bear a wary eye.

HAMLET Come on, sir.

LAERTES Come, my lord.   *They play.*

HAMLET One.

LAERTES No.   280

HAMLET Judgment.

OSRIC A hit, a very palpable hit.

LAERTES Well, again.

KING Stay, give me drink. Hamlet this pearl is thine.[20]
    Here's to thy health.   *Drums; trumpets; and shot goes off.*
              Give him the cup.   285

HAMLET I'll play this bout first. Set it by awhile.
    Come.   *They play again.*
    Another hit. What say you?

LAERTES I do confess't.

KING Our son shall win.

QUEEN   He's fat[21] and scant of breath.   290
    Here, Hamlet, take my napkin, rub thy brows.
    The Queen carouses[22] to thy fortune, Hamlet.

HAMLET Good madam.

KING Gertrude, do not drink.

QUEEN I will, my lord, I pray you, pardon me.   295
         She drinks [and offers the cup to Hamlet].[23]

KING [*aside*] It is the poisoned cup. It is too late.

HAMLET I dare not drink yet, madam—by and by.

QUEEN Come, let me wipe thy face.

LAERTES My lord, I'll hit him now.

KING   I do not think't.

LAERTES [*aside*] And yet it is almost against my conscience. 300

---

19 Kettledrum.
20 Claudius puts the pearl in the cup. In some productions (and in the 1948 Olivier and 1996 Branagh films) the pearl is in fact the poison; in others it marks which goblet is not poisoned – he surreptitiously puts the poison in the other goblet.
21 Out of condition (?)
22 Drinks.
23 In some productions (though there is no textual evidence for this) Gertrude drinks even though she suspects the wine may be poisoned. In Michael Almereyda's 2000 film she seems deliberately to attempt to save her son's life by doing so. The screenplay to Branagh's 1996 film says that Gertrude 'delivers this line as a declaration of independence from the King: "she is her own woman now. And for a moment, all too brief, she and her son are happy" ' (*Shakespeare in Production: 'Hamlet'*, ed. Robert Hapgood (Cambridge: Cambridge University Press, 1999), p. 271).

HAMLET Come, for the third, Laertes. You do but dally.
I pray you, pass with your best violence.
I am afeard you make a wanton of me.[24]
LAERTES Say you so? Come on.They play.
OSRIC Nothing neither way.   305
LAERTES Have at you now.   [*Laertes wounds Hamlet; then, in
                                  scuffling, they change rapiers.*]
KING Part them; they are incensed.
HAMLET Nay, come again.   [*He wounds Laertes.*] *The Queen falls.*
OSRIC Look to the Queen there, ho!
HORATIO They bleed on both sides. How is it, my lord?   310
OSRIC How is't, Laertes?
LAERTES Why, as a woodcock to mine own springe,[25] Osric.
I am justly kill'd with mine own treachery.
HAMLET How does the Queen?
KING   She swoons to see them bleed.
QUEEN No, no, the drink, the drink! O my dear Hamlet!   315
The drink, the drink! I am poison'd.   *Dies.*
HAMLET O villainy! Ho! Let the door be lock'd!
Treachery! Seek it out.   [*Exit Osric.*]
LAERTES It is here, Hamlet: Hamlet, thou art slain.
No medicine in the world can do thee good;   320
In thee there is not half an hour's life.
The treacherous instrument is in thy hand,
Unbated and envenom'd.[26] The foul practice
Hath turn'd itself on me. Lo, here I lie,
Never to rise again. Thy mother's poison'd.   325
I can no more. The King—the King's to blame.
HAMLET The point envenom'd too! Then, venom, to thy work.
                                            Wounds the King.
ALL Treason! treason!
KING O yet defend me, friends, I am but hurt.
HAMLET Here, thou incestuous, murd'rous, damned Dane,   330
Drink off this potion. Is thy union here?[27]
Follow my mother.[28]   *King dies.*
LAERTES   He is justly serv'd.

---

24 Treat me like a spoiled child. In Branagh's 1996 film this remark gets laugh from the onlookers and
    enrages Laertes.
25 Like the proverbially stupid bird caught in my own trap.
26 Unprotected and poisoned.
27 The pearl, but also 'the potion effects the union of the king and queen' (Wilson Knight, p. 257).
    Hamlet keeps the puns going to the bitter end.
28 In Steven Pimlott's 2001 RSC production the wounded Claudius tried to crawl across to die next to
    Gertrude; Sam West's Hamlet produced a gun and brutally shot him to prevent this. In Olivier's
    1948 film the prince leaps fourteen feet from a gallery, sword in hand, onto the cowering Claudius
    to despatch him; 'the resolved Oedipal tangle leads to many self-assertion, but also to the possibil-
    ity of self-destruction' (Anthony B. Dawson, *Shakespeare in Performance*: '*Hamlet*' (Mancheser:
    Manchester University Press, 1995), p. 183). Olivier did the stunt himself and knocked the stand-in
    for Claudius unconscious. David Warner's 1965 prince ironically finished off Claudius by pouring
    the poisoned wine in his ear (Dawson, p. 143). In the eighteenth century Garrick made his Claudius
    fight back with his own sword before falling so that Hamlet did not appear to kill an unarmed man.

It is a poison temper'd[29] by himself.
Exchange forgiveness with me, noble Hamlet.
Mine and my father's death come not upon thee,   335
Nor thine on me.   *Dies.*
HAMLET Heaven make thee free of it. I follow thee.
I am dead, Horatio. Wretched Queen, adieu.
You that look pale and tremble at this chance,
That are but mutes or audience to this act,   340
Had I but time—as this fell sergeant, Death,
Is strict in his arrest—O, I could tell you—
But let it be. Horatio, I am dead,
Thou livest. Report me and my cause aright
To the unsatisfied.
HORATIO   Never believe it.   345
I am more an antique Roman[30] than a Dane.
Here's yet some liquor left.
HAMLET   As th'art a man,
Give me the cup. Let go, by Heaven, I'll ha't.
O God, Horatio, what a wounded name,
Things standing thus unknown, shall I leave behind me.   350
If thou didst ever hold me in thy heart,
Absent thee from felicity[31] awhile,
And in this harsh world draw thy breath in pain
To tell my story.   *A march afar off and shot within.*
What warlike noise is this?
            Enter OSRIC.
OSRIC Young Fortinbras, with conquest come from Poland,
To the ambassadors of England gives   356
This warlike volley.
HAMLET   Oh I die, Horatio.
The potent poison quite o'ercrows[32] my spirit.
I cannot live to hear the news from England,
But I do prophesy th'election lights   360
On Fortinbras. He has my dying voice.[33]
So tell him, with th'occurrents more and less
Which have solicited—[34] the rest is silence.   *Dies.*[35]

---

29 Mixed.
30 For the ancient Roman Stoics, suicide was an honourable and heroic end to a troubled life (though
   it does seem melodramatic in Horatio's case).
31 Happiness (in heaven).
32 Triumphs over, like a fighting cock.
33 Danish monarchs were elected by the nobility. Claudius had nominated Hamlet as the next king
   (1.2.109); now he does the same for Fortinbras.
34 The events which have produced . . . (Hamlet cannot complete the sentence).
35 In Olivier's 1948 film Hamlet dies sitting in Claudius's chair, having picked up the crown his uncle
   had dropped: he gains the throne at last.

HORATIO Now cracks a noble heart. Good night, sweet prince,
And flights of angels sing thee to thy rest.   365
                                                                    [*March within.*]
Why does the drum come hither?

Enter FORTINBRAS *and the English* Ambassadors, *and* Soldiers
with drum and colours.[36]

FORTINBRAS Where is this sight?
HORATIO   What is it you would see?
If aught of woe or wonder, cease your search.
FORTINBRAS This quarry cries on havoc.[37] O proud Death,
What feast is toward in thine eternal cell,   370
That thou so many princes at a shot
So bloodily hast struck?
1ST AMBASSADOR   The sight is dismal;
And our affairs from England come too late.
The ears are senseless that should give us hearing
To tell him his commandment is fulfill'd,   375
That Rosencrantz and Guildenstern are dead.
Where should we have our thanks?
HORATIO   Not from his mouth,
Had it th'ability of life to thank you.
He never gave commandment for their death.
But since, so jump[38] upon this bloody question,   380
You from the Polack wars, and you from England
Are here arriv'd, give order that these bodies
High on a stage[39] be placed to the view,
And let me speak to th'yet unknowing world
How these things came about. So shall you hear   385
Of carnal, bloody, and unnatural acts,[40]
Of accidental judgments, casual slaughters,
Of deaths put on[41] by cunning and forc'd[42] cause,
And, in this upshot, purposes mistook
Fall'n on th' inventors' heads. All this can I   390
Truly deliver.

---

36 Fortinbras has often been cut from productions; almost invariably in the eighteenth and nineteenth
   centuries the play ended on line 371. In Branagh's 1996 film the audience have seen his army
   staging a surprise attack on Elsinore, unknown to the protagonists and intercut with the duelling
   action, from line 230. They burst into the main palace hall, some crashing through the windows.
37 An appropriately aristocratic and violent hunting metaphor from Fortinbras: 'this heap of dead
   proclaims an indiscriminate and immoderate slaughter (of game)' (Dover Wilson (see note 5),
   p. 258).
38 Straight away.
39 A public platform, but not the first reference to the catastrophe as a piece of theatre (e.g. line 344
   above).
40 This line can be taken to refer to Claudius's deeds.
41 Caused by.
42 Contrived.

FORTINBRAS   Let us haste to hear it,
And call the noblest to the audience.
For me, with sorrow I embrace my fortune.
I have some rights of memory[43] in this kingdom,
Which now to claim my vantage[44] doth invite me.   395
HORATIO Of that I shall have also cause to speak,
And from his mouth whose voice will draw on more.
But let this same be presently perform'd[45]
Even while men's minds are wild, lest more mischance
On plots and errors happen.
FORTINBRAS   Let four captains   400
Bear Hamlet like a soldier to the stage,
For he was likely, had he been put on,[46]
To have prov'd most royal; and for his passage,
The soldier's music and the rites of war
Speak loudly for him.   405
Take up the bodies.[47] Such a sight as this
Becomes the field,[48] but here shows much amiss.
Go, bid the soldiers shoot.[49]
                          Exeunt marching, [bearing off the bodies,] after
                             which a peal of ordnance is shot off.

---

43 Traditional rights to the throne. 'We do not know what these are. What we do know is that the
    throne of Denmark now goes to a foreigner who at the beginning of the play was preparing to gain
    that throne by force of arms' (Edwards (see note 8), p. 242). In Branagh's 1996 film Fortinbras is
    crowned by one of his men at the end of this speech. In the 1965 Peter Hall/David Warner produc-
    tion 'the whole court, the troop of councillors and hangers on who have been there from the
    beginning, went to its knees when Fortinbras announced his "Vantage", with the menacing Osric
    taking the lead' (Dawson (see note 28), p. 143).
44 Favourable opportunity.
45 The story immediately be told.
46 Made king; perhaps a questionable judgement from one who did not know him. Rufus Sewell's
    Fortinbras in Branagh's 1996 film delivers the words 'most royally' with palpable insincerity.
47 In Olivier's 1948 film there was no Fortinbras; Hamlet's body was carried to the high rocky
    outcrop where he had earlier 'thought' his soliloquies. Kozintsev's 1964 film sees Hamlet's body
    carried out of the castle by Fortinbras's troops in front of a crowd of concerned Danish people,
    stressing the political rather than purely personal importance of the play's 'catastrophe'.
48 Battlefield.
49 In some productions, including the 1990 *Cheek by Jowl* touring production, this was the cue for
    the soldiers of a fascistic, leather-clad Fortinbras to round up for execution the remaining members
    of Claudius's court who may have been loyal to him. Wilson Knight, on the other hand, thought
    that Fortinbras 'should be young, fair, and have a rich voice, wearing a Viking helmet, Mercurially
    winged, and fine armour . . . strong-armed, with the material strength of Claudius and the spiritual
    strength of Hamlet, a white light upon him, the new hope of Denmark' (quoted in Hapgood (see
    note 23), p. 275).

4

Further Reading

Further Reading

Collections of Essays

David Farley-Hills (ed.), *Critical Responses to 'Hamlet'*, 4 vols (New York: AMS Press, 1997) is an extensive compilation of notable criticism until, currently, 1838. John D. Jump (ed.), *'Hamlet': A Selection of Critical Essays* (London: Macmillan, 1968) represents *Hamlet* criticism before the impact of theory; Martin Coyle (ed.), *'Hamlet': Contemporary Critical Essays* (London: Macmillan, 1992) contains important criticism from the 1980s. See also Arthur F. Kinney (ed.), *'Hamlet': New Critical Essays* (New York and London: Routledge, 2002); Mark Burnett and John Manning (eds), *New Essays on 'Hamlet'* (New York: AMS Press, 1994); and Kenneth Muir and Stanley Wells (eds), *Aspects of Hamlet* (Cambridge: Cambridge University Press, 1979).

Critical Interpretations

There are at least two useful overviews of *Hamlet* criticism: Michael Hattaway, *'Hamlet': An Introduction to the Variety of Criticism* (London: Macmillan, 1987) is a brief but incisive survey; and Paul Gottschalk, *The Meanings of Hamlet: Modes of Literary Interpretation since Bradley* (Albuquerque, NM: University of Mexico Press, 1993) is a sophisticated analysis of the development of criticism in the twentieth century. Stanley Wells (ed.), *Shakespeare Survey 45; 'Hamlet' and its Afterlife* (Cambridge: Cambridge University Press, 1993) contains much fascinating material on the play's critical and stage history. Ann Thompson and Neil Taylor, *Writers and their Work: 'Hamlet'* (Plymouth: Northcote House, 1996) is an excellent brief introduction to critical approaches to the play.

From the vast range of criticism not already in this book, I make the following and selective recommendations. Extracts from these texts do not appear in this book, but I have referred to some of them in the Critical History section.

From the psychoanalytical tradition

Janet Adelman, *Suffocating Mothers: Fantasies of Maternal Origin in Shake-speare's Plays, 'Hamlet' to 'The Tempest'* (London: Routledge, 1992), chapter 2, deploys a feminist psychoanalytical reading to maternal sexuality in the play to analyse the basis of tragedy itself.

Ernest Jones, *Hamlet and Oedipus* (London: Victor Gollancz, 1949) is the famous interpretation of the play which influenced Olivier.

Jacqueline Rose, '*Hamlet*: The Mona Lisa of Literature', in *Shakespeare and Gender: A History*, ed. Deborah E. Barker and Ivo Kamps (London and New York: Verso, 1995) takes up Freud's and Eliot's readings to show how in the readings femininity itself is regarded as problematic and troubling.

Important feminist readings of the play

Patricia Parker, *Literary Fat Ladies: Rhetoric, Gender, Property* (London: Meth-uen, 1987) analyses the connections between rhetoric and gender in the play.

Elaine Showalter, 'Representing Ophelia: Woman, Madness and the Responsi-bilities of Feminist Criticism', in *Shakespeare and the Question of Theory*, ed. Patricia Parker and Geoffrey Hartman (New York and London: Methuen, 1985) is an examination of how the role on stage has been used to construct certain kinds of 'female' 'madness'.

Rebecca Smith, 'A Heart Cleft in Twain: The Dilemma of Shakespeare's Gertrude', in *The Woman's Part: Feminist Criticism of Shakespeare*, ed. Carolyn Ruth Swift Lenz, Gayle Greene and Carol Thomas Neely (Urbana, Chicago and London: University of Illinois Press, 1980) is a defence of the character of Gertrude as a loving mother, in defiance of the critical tradition.

(Both Showalter and Smith's articles are also in the collection edited by Martin Coyle.)

Recommended criticism which is, broadly speaking, historicist (see Critical History, pp. 55–7)

Graham Holderness, *Hamlet* (Milton Keynes and Philadelphia: Open University Press, 1988) is a close reading of the play from a broadly cultural materialist perspective.

Annabel Paterson, *Shakespeare and the Popular Voice* (Oxford: Basil Blackwell, 1995), chapters 3 and 5, provocatively puts the play in the context of the radical politics of the era.

Leonard Tennenhouse, *Power on Display: The Politics of Shakespeare's Genres* (New York and London: Methuen, 1988) is a New Historicist account of how power depends not only on force, but also on the ability to stage oneself effectively.

Three fascinating recent critical responses which focus, in different ways, on the power of the play to give pleasure to its audience

Catherine Belsey, *Shakespeare and the Loss of Eden* (London: Macmillan, 1999), chapter 5, puts the play in the context of the mythical resonances of Cain's murder of Abel and of the mediaeval 'dance of death', and considers how *Hamlet* plays on our own cultural experience of death and kinship.

Ewan Fernie, *Shame in Shakespeare* (London: Routledge, 2002), chapter 5, argues how Hamlet's journey through shame away from self-concern parallels the experience of the tragic audience.

Frank Kermode, *Shakespeare's Language* (London: Allen Lane, 2000), pp. 96–125, explains how the play's use of a single figure of speech explores a central idea in its drama.

An examination of how the play itself represents theatrical representation

Robert Weimann, 'Mimesis in *Hamlet*', in *Shakespeare and the Question of Theory*, ed. Patricia Parker and Geoffrey Hartman (New York and London: Methuen, 1985).

Stage and Film History

Few play texts in history have had their realization in performance as well documented. In this book I have extensively used the most recent commentaries: Anthony B. Dawson, *Shakespeare in Performance: 'Hamlet'* (Manchester: Manchester University Press, 1995) and Robert Hapgood (ed.), *Shakespeare in Production: 'Hamlet'* (Cambridge: Cambridge University Press, 1999), and also drawn on Mary Z. Maher, *Modern Hamlets and their Soliloquies* (Iowa City: University of Iowa Press, 2003). Other very useful recent collections include John A. Mills, *'Hamlet' on Stage: The Great Tradition* (Westport CT: Greenwood Press, 1985) and J. C. Trewin, *Five and Eighty Hamlets* (London: Hutchinson, 1987). Two modern Hamlets have written detailed accounts of their experience in the role: Steven Berkoff's *I Am Hamlet* (London: Faber, 1989) and Michael Pennington's *Hamlet: A User's Guide* (London: Nick Hern, 1985).

Bernice Kliman's *'Hamlet': Film, Television and Audio Performance* (London and Toronto: Toronto University Press, 1988) is a very useful overview of its topic. See also Neil Taylor (as above, p. 140), 'The Films of *Hamlet*' in *Shakespeare and the Moving Image: The Plays on Film and Television*, ed. Anthony Davies and Stanley Wells (Cambridge: Cambridge University Press, 1994), Harry Keyishian, 'Shakespeare and Movie Genre: the Case of Hamlet', in *The Cambridge Companion to Shakespeare on Film*, ed. Russell Jackson (Cambridge: Cambridge University Press, 2000) and Deborah Cartmell, *Interpreting Shakespeare on Screen* (London: Macmillan, 2000), chapter 2.

There are specific contemporary accounts of the Olivier film in Brenda Cross, *The Film 'Hamlet': A Record of its Production* (London: Saturn Press, 1948) and Alan Dent (ed.), *'Hamlet', the Film and the Play* (London: World Film Publications, 1948); see also Peter Donaldson, 'Olivier, Hamlet and Freud', in *Shakespeare on Film: Contemporary Critical Essays*, ed. Robert Shaughnessy (London: Macmillan, 1998). On the Branagh film, see also Bernice W. Kliman, 'The Unkindest Cuts: Flashcut Excess in Kenneth Branagh's *Hamlet*', in Deborah Cartmell and Michael Scott (eds), *Talking Shakespeare* (Basingstoke: Palgrave, 2001), and Lisa Starks, 'The Displaced Body of Desire: Sexuality in Kenneth Branagh's *Hamlet*', in *Shakespeare and Appropriation*, ed. Christy Desmet and Robert Sawyer (London: Routledge, 1999).

Online Resources

Basic editions of the three texts are available on the Internet as follows.

Q1: http://web.uvic.ca/shakespeare/Annex/DraftTxt/Ham/Ham_Q1

Q2: http://web.uvic.ca/shakespeare/Annex/DraftTxt/Ham/Ham_Q2

F: http://web.uvic.ca/shakespeare/Annex/DraftTxt/Ham/Ham_F

The two Quartos are also available in an excellent British Library resource, which includes links to live recordings of certain speeches in historic productions. Start from: www.bl.uk/treasures/shakespeare/homepage.html

An 'enfolded' text, making Q2 and F available on the same screen, is at http://www.global-language.com/enfolded.html

A very wide-ranging bibliography on the character of Ophelia in and beyond the play can be found at http://members.cox.net/academia/ophelia/html

There is an image database of more than forty different productions of the play as part of Christie Carson's 'Designing Shakespeare' site. It can be found at http://www.pads.ahds.ac.uk

A detailed record of all Royal Shakespeare Company performances, including cast lists and reviews up to 1990, is at www.shakespeare.org.uk/main/3/339

Images of American productions of Shakespeare can be found at http://www.ulib.csuohio.edu/Shakespeare/ where there are pictures of *Hamlet* on the US stage from 1913 to 1980. The script of Robert Lepage's adaptation of the play, *Elsinore*, is available online at http://www.canadianshakespeares.ca/a_elsinore.cfm

Hamlet on the Ramparts (http://shea.mit.edu/ramparts/) is a site maintained by Massachusetts Institute of Technology and the Folger Shakespeare Library, which contains a collection of texts, images and film – in particular, early silent footage –

relevant to Act 4, Scenes 4 and 5. There is a website gateway devoted to the 1989 Branagh film at www.geocities.com/Athens/Parthenon/6261/hamlet.html

Selected Videos and DVDs

Hamlet, dir. Laurence Olivier (GB, 1948), Two Cities Films; Rank Classic Collection.

Hamlet, dir. Grigori Kozintsev (USSR, 1964), Lenfilm [video only].

Hamlet, dir. Tony Richardson (GB, 1969), Woodfall; RCA/Columbia Pictures International Video [video only].

Hamlet, dir. Rodney Bennett (GB/USA, 1980) BBC/Time-Life TV.

Hamlet, dir. Franco Zeffirelli (USA, 1990), Warner Brothers.

Hamlet, dir. Kenneth Branagh (GB, 1996), Castle Rock; Columbia Tristar.

Hamlet, dir. Michael Almereyda (USA, 2000), Film Four.

Hamlet, dir. Kevin Kline (USA, 2004), Metrodome.

Index

Related titles from Routledge

Macbeth
A Sourcebook
Alexander Leggatt

William Shakespeare's **Macbeth** (c.1606) is a timeless tale of murder, love
and power, which has given rise to heated debates around such issues as
the representation of gender roles, political violence and the dramatisation
of evil.

Taking the form of a sourcebook, this guide to Shakespeare's play offers:

- extensive introductory comment on the contexts, critical history and
  performance of the text, from publication to the present

- annotated extracts from key contextual documents, reviews, critical works
  and the text itself

- cross-references between documents and sections of the guide, in order
  to suggest links between texts, contexts and criticism

- suggestions for further reading.

Part of the *Routledge Guides to Literature* series, this volume is essential
reading for all those beginning detailed study of **Macbeth** and seeking not
only a guide to the play, but a way through the wealth of contextual and
critical material that surrounds Shakespeare's text.

0–415–23824–2 (hbk)
0–415–23825–0 (pbk)

978–0–415–23824–3 (hbk)
978–0–415–23825–0 (pbk)

Available at all good bookshops
For further information on our literature series,
please visit www.routledge.com/literature/series.asp

For ordering and further information please visit:
www.routledge.com

Related titles from Routledge

Shakespeare
The Basics
Sean McEvoy

The way in which Shakespeare's plays are studied has undergone considerable change in recent years. The new edition of this bestselling guide, aimed squarely at students new to Shakespeare, is based on the exciting new approaches shaping Shakespeare studies. This volume provides a thorough general introduction to the plays and a refreshingly clear guide to:

• Shakespeare's language

• The plays as performance texts

• The cultural and political contexts of the plays

• Early modern theatre practice

• New understandings of the major genres.

Sean McEvoy illustrates how interpretations of Shakespeare are linked to cultural and political contexts and provides readings of the most frequently studied plays in the light of contemporary critical thought.

Now fully updated to include discussion of criticism and performance in the last five years, a new chapter on Shakespeare on film, and a broader critical approach, this book is the essential resource for all students of Shakespeare.

0–415–36245–8 (hbk)
0–415–36246–6 (pbk)

978–0–415–36245–0 (hbk)
978–0–415–36246–7 (pbk)

Available at all good bookshops
For further information on our literature series,
please visit www.routledge.com/literature/series.asp

For ordering and further information please visit:
www.routledge.com